CHOICES

PRE-INTERMEDIATE STUDENTS' BOOK

T0385818

MICHAEL HARRIS • ANNA SIKORZYŃSKA

CONTENTS

	Language	**Skills**

CONTENTS

	Language	Skills

1 TIME

Objectives: Listen, read and **talk about** lifestyles and sport; **describe** and **discuss** photos; **write** a description of an ideal day; **learn more about** present tenses.

TOPIC TALK

1 Look at the photos (a–c). Think about the questions (1–3) then tell the class your answers.

1 How are the people feeling? (relaxed, tired, stressed)
2 When do *you* get stressed about time? (e.g. in exams,)
3 Are you a 'morning person' or a 'night person'?

2 `1.2` `1.3` ➔ SKILLS BUILDER 1 **Use the strategies in the Skills Builder to listen to three people and match them with the photos (a–c).**

3 `1.4` `1.5` Listen again to the first person. Complete the information in the network.

Routines

I'm ¹ *very*/*I'm not very* organised.
I sleep ² *eight/nine* hours a night.
I go to bed at about ³ *10.30/11.30.*
I get up at ⁴ *7.30/7.40.*
I feel tired ⁵ *in the morning/at night.*
On Thursday, I ⁶_____ .
At the weekend, I ⁷_____ .

have breakfast, lunch, dinner, a shower **at ... o'clock**
do my homework, jobs in the house, sport
play football, basketball, computer games
go swimming, jogging, cycling **go on** Messenger
go to school, extra classes, the cinema, the park, parties
spend time with my friends/family, at home

4 `1.6` Pronunciation **Listen and repeat the sentences. Notice the unstressed words.**

➔ LANGUAGE CHOICE 1 AND 2: VOCABULARY PRACTICE

5 Work in groups. Use the network to talk about *your* routine.

5

DAILY LIFE

Warm Up

1 **Work in pairs. Ask and answer the questions.**

1 What do you use to plan your time, e.g. calendars, planners, a diary … ?
2 What things do you do at the same time every day?
3 Which of these things do you *choose* to do and which are obligations?

Reading

2 → SKILLS BUILDER 11 **Read the book review. Use the strategies in the Skills Builder to decide if it is about:**

a people with problems
b people with unusual lives
c people with daily routines

3 → SKILLS BUILDER 12 **Use the strategies in the Skills Builder to match the paragraphs (1-6) with the headings (a-g). There is one extra heading.**

a A definition of eccentrics *2*
b A twenty-first century king
c Eccentric men and women
d A solitary life
e Talking to eccentrics
f An interesting book
g A book about eccentrics

4 **Read the text again. Answer the questions.**

1 Why does Tom Leppard look unusual?

   Ninety-two percent of his body has tattoos.

2 Why doesn't he need a clock or watch?
3 How often does he see other people?
4 Where does 'King Arthur' live?
5 What does he do on 21 June?
6 Does the reviewer think it is a good book?

SEARCH

Saturday reading

English Eccentrics 1.7

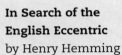
In Search of the English Eccentric
by Henry Hemming

'A funny, timely, moving encounter with a dying breed'
JON RONSON
'The new Michael Palin' TATLER

1 Most of us have very ordinary daily lives. We get up at the usual time, spend hours at school or work and come home at the same time every evening. In his book on English eccentrics, Henry Hemming looks at unusual people with very different lives from ours.

2 According to Hemming, eccentrics are not mad; they see the world differently from us, have their own personal timetables and are not worried about people's opinions of them.

3 In his book, Hemming looks at our national tradition of eccentrics and meets lots of different eccentric people. He interviews a professional boxer in aristocratic clothes, an adventurous inventor, a successful fashion designer and a famous rock musician.

4 Hemming finds people like Tom Leppard, the Leopard Man. Ninety-two percent of his body has tattoos. Tom lives alone on a beautiful, windy Scottish island in a cabin. He does not need a watch or a clock because he has no obligations. He gets up and goes to bed when he wants to. 'I can do what I like and when I like,' he says. 'And that is paradise.' On a typical day, Tom feeds the birds or goes for a swim in the sea. Every two weeks he goes to town in his kayak. He goes to the bank, gets food and then goes back home. Tom is a hermit 'but I never get lonely here,' he says.

5 Hemming's favourite eccentric is the friendly John Rothwell, now called King Arthur after the sixth century British king. 'King Arthur' does not work and has no routine or typical day. He rides around Britain on his motorbike and campaigns to save historic monuments and trees. 'I don't have a home,' says Arthur. 'I never sleep two nights in the same bed.' He does not need a diary to plan his life and his only important date is 21 June, the summer solstice. Then, Arthur goes to Stonehenge to see his 'people', the hippies and pagans at the festival.

6 Hemming's book is full of wonderful characters and is often very funny. It is definitely worth reading.

5 Vocabulary **Look at the Word Builder. Complete it with the adjectives in** blue **from the text.**

> **Word Builder** Making adjectives
>
> | Noun | Adjective |
> |---|---|
> | 1 beauty/success/wonder | *beautiful* |
> | 2 fame/adventure | |
> | 3 aristocrat/history | |
> | 4 day/wind/friend/fun | |
> | 5 nation/person/profession | |

➜ LANGUAGE CHOICE 3: VOCABULARY PRACTICE

6 **Complete the sentences with words from Exercise 5.**

1 It is often cold and __windy__ in Scotland.
2 Roger Federer was very _____ last year and won lots of competitions.
3 My _____ routine is always the same.
4 My sister is very _____ and loves extreme sports. She is also very _____ and loves people.
5 I'd like to be a _____ footballer and play for the England _____ team.

Writing

7 **Look at the Sentence Builder. How do you say the words in bold in your language?**

> **Sentence Builder** Linkers
>
> 1 They have their own personal timetables **and** are not worried about our opinions.
> 2 Tom feeds the birds **or** goes for a swim.
> 3 King Arthur does not work **but** rides around Britain.
> 4 He goes to the bank, gets food **and then** goes back home.
>
> ➜ SKILLS BUILDER 22

8 **Use the linkers in brackets to join the sentences. Leave out words where possible.**

1 In the morning, I have a shower. I have breakfast with my family. (*and*)

   In the morning, I have a shower and have breakfast with my family.

2 On Thursday afternoons, we play basketball. We sometimes go swimming. (*or*)
3 I meet my friends on Friday nights. I come home before ten o'clock. (*but*)
4 On Saturdays, I go cycling with my dad. I have lunch at my grandma's. (*and then*)
5 On Sunday evenings, I do my homework. I listen to music at the same time. (*and*)

9 **Work in pairs. Choose one of the options (a–c) and write notes.**

get up at ten o'clock / have breakfast next to the pool / phone friends

a your ideal day on holiday
b your ideal school day
c your ideal Saturday

10 **Tell the class about your ideal day.**

I get up at ten o'clock and then I have breakfast next to the pool or I phone friends …

Your Choice

No Comment

'I am not eccentric but I am more alive than most people. I am an electric eel in a pond of goldfish.'

Edith Sitwell, English poet

GRAMMAR
GO SLOW

Warm Up

1 Look at the photos (a–c). Who is happy and relaxed? Why?

2 Read the text. Which of these things does the Slow Movement promote?

- fast food restaurants
- eating with your family
- yoga and tai chi
- difficult exams

3 Do you think the Slow Movement is a good idea? Why/Why not?

⊙ Lifestyle

Slow is *Beautiful* ⟨1.8⟩

In the modern world, we do everything fast. We do not have time to relax or spend time with our family and friends. For people in the Slow Movement, this is crazy. They think we need to slow down and enjoy life.

Slow Food people cook meals at home and eat at the table, with their families and not in front of the TV. The movement started in Italy in 1986, to protest against the first McDonald's restaurant in Rome.

Slow Cities promote quiet lifestyles. Martin, a 19-year-old student, is living in London now but he comes from Ludlow, Britain's first Slow City. He says, 'Life in London is too fast and noisy. I prefer Ludlow, my hometown – it's quiet, the air is clean and everybody is relaxed'.

Many people are taking up 'Slow Exercise': yoga or tai chi. Sophie, a teenager from Birmingham, is talking about her yoga practice: 'I practise every morning before school and I go to classes twice a week. Teenagers' lives are crazy nowadays – after school, we run from extra language classes to music lessons and feel tired a lot of the time. Yoga relaxes me and gives me lots of energy.'

In Slow Schools students have time to think and discuss ideas. Tests and grades are less important. And luckily, the number of these schools is growing fast.

Present Simple and Continuous

4 Read the Present Simple sentences (1-4) from the text. Match them with the uses (a-b).

1 We **do** everything fast.
2 They **think** we need to slow down and enjoy life.
3 I **prefer** Ludlow.
4 I **go** to classes twice a week.

a a habit, a regular activity
b a present state, feeling or opinion

5 Read the Present Continuous sentences (1-2) from the text. Match them with the uses (a-b).

1 Martin **is living** in London.
2 Sophie **is talking** about her yoga practice.

a It's happening right now, at the time of speaking.
b It's happening around now, not just at this moment.

Practice

 LANGUAGE CHOICE 4

6 Match the sentences (1-6) with the contexts (a-b).

1 I'm doing homework.
2 I do homework.

a I am a hard-working student.
b I am busy now.

3 I'm not drinking coffee.
4 I don't drink coffee.

a I don't like the taste.
b It's part of my new, healthy lifestyle.

5 I'm walking the dog.
6 I walk the dog.

a I'm in the park with my dog.
b It's my dog so it's my job to walk him.

 LANGUAGE CHOICE 5

7 Complete the dialogue in a bookshop with the Present Simple or the Present Continuous.

Alex: Hi, Sonia! What [1] _are you doing_ (you / do) here?
Sonia: I [2] _____ (look) for a vegetarian cookbook.
Alex: [3] _____ (you / often / cook)? At my home, we [4] _____ (not cook). Usually, my mum [5] _____ (buy) ready-made meals in the supermarket or we [6] _____ (order) pizza.
Sonia: Cooking is fun! My gran [7] _____ (teach) me to cook. She [8] _____ (never eat) fast food or ready-made meals. This week we [9] _____ (try) some vegetarian recipes.
Alex: I [10] _____ (not eat) vegetables. I [11] _____ (think) they're horrible!
Sonia: They are not! Why don't you have lunch with us? Gran [12] _____ (make) roast vegetables!

Grammar Alive
Talking on your mobile

8 **1.9** Listen to three telephone conversations. Where are Robbie, Tina and Jack? What are they doing?

9 Work in pairs. Use the cues to make your own mobile conversations. Use the Present Continuous.

A: Hi, Ewa! Where are you? Can you talk now?
B: I'm on the train. I'm going to Oxford. Can I ring you back?
A: Okay, speak to you later.

• train / go to Oxford • street / wait for the bus
• café / have tea with a friend • park / jog
• shopping centre / buy shoes
• hospital / visit sister

Talking about habits

10 **1.10** Listen to the dialogue. What is unhealthy about the boy's lifestyle?

11 Work in pairs. Use the cues to ask and answer questions. Use the Present Simple.

A: Do you eat meat?
B: No, I don't. I eat fruit and vegetables.

A starts
1 eat meat?
2 cook?
3 watch TV?
4 listen to classical music?

B answers
1 eat fruit and vegetables
2 buy ready-made meals
3 listen to the radio
4 listen to jazz and soul

B starts
5 go for walks?
6 eat fast food?
7 go to bed late?
8 play computer games?

A answers
5 go cycling
6 prepare food at home
7 go to bed at 10 p.m.
8 watch DVDs

12 Work in pairs. Use some of the expressions below to tell your partner about your family's lifestyle.

I watch TV for about two hours every day and four or five at the weekend. My mother cooks …

• watch TV • cook at home • eat fast food
• go for walks • eat in front of the TV • sleep eight hours or more • talk to family • spend time with friends • go to bed early

13 How 'slow' is your partner's life? Tell the class.

3 SKILLS
RACES

Warm Up

1 **Vocabulary** Look at the network and the photos (a-c). Answer the questions.

1 What activities are part of a triathlon?
2 What equipment do you need for:
   a swimming b running c cycling?
3 What kinds of races do you like taking part in or watching? Has your school or area got an athletics club/swimming club/cycling club?

Races
Athletics: running races - 100m sprint, 1500m, marathon
Cycling: road races, track races, mountain bike events
Swimming: freestyle, breaststroke, crawl, backstroke
Triathlon: cycling, running, swimming

Equipment
ball, bike (mountain/road/triathlon), boots, cap, goggles, helmet, running shoes, shorts, skis, sunglasses, swimsuit, water bottle, wetsuit

➥ LANGUAGE CHOICE 6: VOCABULARY PRACTICE

Listening

2 **1.11 1.12** Listen to a conversation between a student and his PE teacher about triathlon. Check your guesses from Exercise 1.

3 **1.13 1.14** Listen again. Choose the best answer to the questions.

1 Why is triathlon very good exercise?
   a because of the long distances b because you do more than one sport c because you use all your muscles
2 What is Stephen good at?
   a swimming and running b cycling and swimming
   c running and cycling
3 What are the distances for cycling in Olympic triathlon?
   a 14 kilometres b 40 kilometres c 44 kilometres
4 What equipment do students at the school need to buy for the cycling part of triathlon?
   a goggles b a water bottle c a helmet
5 How often is training for triathlon at the school?
   a twice a week b three times a week
   c four times a week
6 What does Stephen decide to do?
   a wait and think about it b start doing triathlon
   c do the triathlon next year

DVD Choice

4 Look at the photos (a-c) again. Guess the answers to the questions.

1 Which of the two men (1-2) in photo a is the athlete (Simon Lessing) and which is the journalist (Simon Thomas)?
2 In what order do they do the three sports?
3 How does the journalist feel afterwards?

5 **DVD 1** Watch the DVD and check your guesses from Exercise 4.

6 **DVD 1** Watch the DVD again. Answer the questions.

1 How many times has Simon Lessing been world champion?
2 How long is the run (in miles) in the Olympic triathlon?
3 How much of the triathlon (e.g. ¼, ½, ⅓) are they doing today?
4 Why are the transition stages between parts of triathlon important?

7 Would you like to try triathlon? Why/Why not?

Watching and Speaking

8 `1.15` `DVD 2` **Listen to or watch the dialogue. What do Judy and Adam think about the Tour de France? Find three factual mistakes in the description of the photo below about:**
1 the man with the camera (x 2)
2 the cyclists

9 `1.16` `DVD 2` **Listen to or watch the dialogue again. Complete the sentences in the Talk Builder with the words below.**

probably   ~~maybe~~   in the middle of   on the right
in the foreground   in the background   because
definitely   perhaps   on the left   behind

Talk Builder Describing photos

1 The three cyclists _____ the photo are very hot.
2 Look, that guy _____ with the camera is wearing shorts.
3 _____ it's Spain _____ it's hot and sunny there.
4 Yes, but it's _____ in France.
5 Yes, it's _____ the Tour de France.
6 Look at those guys _____ .
7 The guy _____ is winning.
8 Look at those people _____ _____ the cyclists.
9 _____ we're near the finish.

➔ SKILLS BUILDER 38

---

10 `1.17` Pronunciation **Listen and repeat the sentences. Notice the contractions.**

11 **Choose the correct option to complete the description of photo a from Exercise 1.**

In the [1]*foreground/background* of the photo you can see two people. They are [2]*definitely/maybe* athletes because they are running and wearing special clothes. In the [3]*background/foreground* you can see lots of trees and it is sunny so it is probably in the summer. The runner on the [4]*right/left* is wearing sunglasses and is very tall. The other man is [5]*probably/definitely* more tired because he is smaller and [6]*maybe/because* they are running quite fast.

12 **Choose one of the photos (a–b) on page 128. Write notes to answer the questions (1–4) about the photo.**

1 What is the picture about? Where is it from? Why do you think that?
2 What is happening? Who is in the photo? What are they doing? What are they feeling?
3 What time of day/year is it? What is the weather like?
4 What else you can see in the photo? (e.g. in the background)

13 **Work in pairs. Ask and answer the questions in Exercise 12 about the photos.**

Your Choice

Language Review Module 1

1 Routines **Complete the gaps with the correct words.**

My sister is a university student and she is not
¹_____ organised. She goes to bed ²_____ about
2 a.m. and sleeps only five or six hours ³_____ night.
She doesn't ⁴_____ breakfast because she is always
tired ⁵_____ the morning. And it takes her an hour
to ⁶_____ a shower and get ready for her classes.
⁷ _____ the weekend, she ⁸ _____ a lot of time
with her friends – they ⁹_____ to clubs and parties.
She usually studies ¹⁰_____ night. I don't think her
lifestyle is healthy!   **/10**

2 Making adjectives **Use the words in brackets to complete the sentences with the correct adjectives.**

The film is great. It is a ¹¹_____ (beauty) story and it
is ¹²_____ (fun) at the same time.

Leonardo DiCaprio is a ¹³_____ (fame) actor and all his
films are ¹⁴_____ (success).

Rome is a ¹⁵_____ (wonder) city – it has lots of
¹⁶_____ (history) buildings.

The ¹⁷_____ (day) life of ¹⁸_____ (profession)
footballers is often quite ordinary.

It is often cold and ¹⁹_____ (wind) in Scotland but the
people are very ²⁰_____ (friend).   **/10**

3 Linkers **Use the linkers in brackets to rewrite the sentences. Leave out unnecessary words.**

21 The dress was cheap. It was really nice. (*but*)
22 Teenagers often wear black clothes. They often
    have original hairstyles. (*and*)
23 We have breakfast. We leave home. (*and then*)
24 My brother likes sport. I prefer reading. (*but*)
25 My friends don't like theatre. They don't like
    opera, either. (*or*)   **/5**

4 Present Simple or Present Continuous **Complete the dialogue with the correct forms of the verbs in brackets.**

A: Hi, Adam. What ²⁶_____ (you / do) here?
B: Hi. I ²⁷_____ (look for) a book for my sister. She
       ²⁸_____ (like) fantasy. And you?
A: I ²⁹_____ (buy) some DVDs for my dad. He ³⁰_____
       (learn) Spanish and he ³¹_____ (want) to watch
       some Spanish films. What ³²_____ (you / think)
       about this film? It's by Pedro Almódovar.
B: I ³³_____ (not know) much about Spanish cinema.
       I only ³⁴_____ (watch) action films. My sister
       ³⁵_____ (have) a lot of Spanish DVDs. I'm sure she
       can lend you some.
A: Thanks! So I can spend this money on some games.
                                                         /10

5 Describing photos **Look at the photo and complete the description with the words below. There are two extra words.**

background   because   behind   probably
definitely   foreground   left

The photo shows a group of people having a meal in
the garden. They are ³⁶_____ a family because
they are different ages and look a bit similar. In the
³⁷_____ , we can see a big table with a lot of
food – it looks really delicious. The people around the
table are ³⁸_____ enjoying the meal because they
are all smiling. In the ³⁹_____ , there is a man in a
yellow shirt. ⁴⁰_____ him, we can see a house and
a big grill with some food on it.   **/5**

Self Assessment

1.18 Listen and check your answers. Write down your
scores. Use the table to find practice exercises.

Exercise	If you need practice, go to
1	Language Choice 1 and 2
2	Language Choice 3
3	Students' Book (SB) p.7 ex 8
4	Language Choice 4 and 5
5	SB p.11 ex.11

12

LEARNING LINKS: 1 **Check Your Progress 1** → MyLab / Workbook page 9. Complete the **Module Diary**.
2 **Sound Choice 1** → MyLab / Workbook page 10. Choose three pronunciation activities to do.

2 FUN

Objectives: **Listen, read** and **talk about** free time activities; **read** an advert; **write** an invitation to a party; **discuss** and **describe** photos; **learn about** the Present Perfect and *some/any/no/a lot of/a few/a little*.

TOPIC TALK

1 Look at the photos (a–c). What do you think of the hobbies? Classify them:

cool crazy silly boring exciting dangerous creative relaxing challenging

2 1.19 1.20 Listen to three people. What two hobbies do they each do? <u>Underline</u> their hobbies in the network.

Free time

I'm really into _____ .
I do it every *weekend/month*.
I also like _____ .
I don't enjoy _____ .
I'd like to try _____ .
I like it because it's *creative/fun*.

Hobbies
acting, art, cycling, dancing, singing, freerunning, sport
collecting coins, stamps, music DVDs
making model aeroplanes, jewellery
doing gymnastics, photography, yoga
playing air guitar, the piano, the saxophone, board games (e.g. chess), computer games

3 1.21 1.22 Listen again. Why do they like their favourite hobby? How often do they do it?

4 1.23 Pronunciation Listen and repeat the sentences. Notice the contractions.

LANGUAGE CHOICE 7: VOCABULARY PRACTICE

5 Work in groups. Use the network to talk about *your* free time activities.

a making model aeroplanes

b freerunning

c playing air guitar

4

GRAMMAR
CHARLIE CHAPLIN

Warm Up

1 Look at the photos (a–d) and read the information about Charlie Chaplin. What kind of characters do you think he played – funny, successful, romantic?

The British comedian, Charlie Chaplin (1889–1977) was one of the most creative people of the silent-film era in Hollywood. His character, The Tramp, in his big trousers, small jacket, big shoes and funny hat is famous all over the world. His best films are *The Gold Rush*, *City Lights* and *The Great Dictator*.

2 **1.24** Alex is watching a Charlie Chaplin film. Read and listen to the conversations (1–3). Match them with the photos (a–d). There is one extra photo.

1
Tony: Why are you laughing, Alex? Oh, you're watching Chaplin …
Alex: Yes, it's *The Gold Rush*, one of my favourite films.
Tony: What's going on? Is the big man trying to kill the Tramp? Has he done something wrong?
Alex: Yeah, he has. He's eaten their last bit of food and they have nothing to eat.

2
Tony: Why is he looking at her like that? Who is she?
Alex: It's Gloria. I think he has fallen in love with her. Just look at his face.
Tony: True, he looks a bit funny.

3
Tony: He's so elegant and the table looks great. What's happening?
Alex: He's made New Year's Eve dinner for Gloria and her friends. He's cooked a turkey!
Tony: So why's he sad ?
Alex: The girls haven't arrived. Poor man! He's alone on New Year's Eve.

3 Do you think Chaplin's Tramp is funny? What modern comedians do you like? Why?

Present Perfect (1)

4 Read the sentences in the Present Perfect. Which 3rd forms of the verbs in **bold** are regular (*-ed*) and which are irregular?

Affirmative	
He **has fallen** in love.	
They **have made** dinner.	

Negative	
He **hasn't cooked** chicken.	
They **haven't arrived**.	

Questions	Short answers
Has he **done** anything wrong?	Yes, he has.
	No, he hasn't.
Have you **had** lunch?	Yes, I have.
	No, I haven't.
What **has** he **done** wrong?	

14

Grammar Alive Explaining causes

8 **1.25** Listen to three dialogues. Why are Amy, Jane and Sylvia unhappy?

9 Work in pairs. Use the cues to make dialogues.

A: *You look tired.*
B: *I'm fine. I've just run all the way to school!*

A starts
1 look tired
2 look fantastic
3 be okay?
4 look excited

B answers
1 fine / run all the way to school
2 thanks / lose 5 kilograms
3 I am not / eat too much
4 I am / meet a gorgeous boy / girl

B starts
5 look very happy
6 look worried
7 love your dress
8 look sad

A answers
5 I am / win a competition
6 yes / lose my mobile
7 thanks / make it myself
8 I am / fail my driving test

10 **Game** Work in pairs. Student A say what you are feeling. Student B guess the reason. Use the cues below and your own ideas.

A: *I'm angry.*
B: *Have you had an argument with someone?*
A: *No, I haven't.*
B: *Have you failed a test?*
A: *Yes, I have.*

Feelings:
angry, happy, excited, sad, worried

Reasons:
buy a new dress/CD/computer/bike
break my computer/DVD player
fail/pass a test/exam
learn to drive/make pizza/repair a bike
lose your MP3 player/mobile phone/a game
make a date with someone
win a competition

No Comment

'A day without a laugh is a wasted day.'

Charlie Chaplin

5 Read the rule. Match the past actions (1-3) with their present consequences (a-c).

• We use the Present Perfect when something happened in the past but we can see its consequences now.

1 *The Tramp **has eaten** the last bit of food.*
2 *The Tramp **has fallen** in love.*
3 *Gloria and her friends **haven't arrived**.*

a *The Tramp is sad.*
b *The Tramp is looking at the girl romantically.*
c *The man is angry.*

Practice

6 Are the verbs below regular (R) or irregular (I)? Write the 3rd forms.

clean – cleaned

be *I*	break	bring	buy	clean *R*	close
come	cook	discover	do	drink	eat
fall	find	forget	get	go	have
learn	lose	make	meet	open	pass
put	read	see	take	win	write

➡ IRREGULAR VERBS LIST, PAGE 115

➡ LANGUAGE CHOICE 8

7 Complete the dialogues with the verbs in the Present Perfect.

1 A: Why is everybody laughing? *Have you done* (you / do) something funny?
  B: Mike _____ (fall) into the swimming pool, in his best suit.

2 A: I'm so happy! I _____ (pass) my final exams!
  B: Lucky you! I _____ (not pass) mine. My holidays are ruined.

3 A: Be careful! I _____ (break) a bottle and there's a lot of glass on the floor.
  B: And of course you _____ (not clean) it up!

4 A: Look, he _____ (bring) her flowers!
  B: Yes, I think he _____ (fall) in love with her.

➡ LANGUAGE CHOICE 9

LESSON **5** SKILLS

GAMING

Warm Up

1 Do you play computer games? What are your favourites? How often do you play?

Reading

2 Work in pairs. One person reads about *Final Fantasy VII* and one person about *The Sims*. Write notes to answer the questions (1-5).

1 How old is the game?
2 How much does it cost?
3 What is the game about?
4 What equipment do you need to play it?
5 Why is it good fun to play?

3 Work in pairs. Ask and answer the questions from Exercise 2.

4 Vocabulary ➲ SKILLS BUILDER 13 Now read both adverts. Use the strategies in the Skills Builder to match the words in blue with the meanings (1-6).

1 pictures in a computer game
   graphics
2 extra computer programs with new characters, places or stories
3 a place in a game (e.g. a planet)
4 the experience of the computer game player
5 games with situations from the real world
6 games where you become one of the characters

5 Would you like to play the two computer games? Why/Why not? Tell the class.

Classic Computer Games

FINAL FANTASY VII

Description
This historic role-playing game came out a very long time ago, in 1997. You are Cloud, a young soldier and you travel around the planet and fight against the evil empire of Shinra. The game is for PlayStations 1 and 2. Price: $40.

Special features
• an absolutely amazing story about friends, love and fighting evil
• fifty hours of fantastic 3D game-play
• some really brilliant music by the composer Nobuo Uematsu
• twenty beautiful locations
• lots of very exciting battles and nine characters you can play

Reviews   Add to basket $40

'This is possibly the greatest computer game ever made.'
Game Fan Magazine
'I was really into this when I was a kid and I think it's my all-time favourite game.' **Don Murphy**

Description
The first version of *The Sims* (2000) is the most successful personal computer game ever! In this great simulation game you can make and control people. You can make friends, look for love and get a job. You can make a perfect family or one with lots of problems. This collection has the game and seven extra expansion packs. *The Sims* works on most PCs. Price: €20.

Special features
• some really wonderful graphics and cool game-play
• very good lessons to help you start playing the game
• with the expansion packs you can have parties, go on holiday and become a star

Reviews   Add to basket €20

'We've got the new versions of *The Sims* but I don't think they are better than the old *Sims*. I still really love that first version!'
Alison Unwin
'I didn't enjoy playing computer games when I was a teenager and then *The Sims* came along. It was absolutely brilliant!'
Karen Thompson

6 Look at the Sentence Builder. How do you say the sentences in your language?

> **Sentence Builder** Opinions
>
> **I think (that)** *The Sims* is very good.
> **I don't think (that)** *The Sims* is very good.

↘ LANGUAGE CHOICE 10

7 Work in pairs. Use the cues below to give your opinions. Add your opinions about other kinds of games.

1 old games (good fun/very exciting/interesting)

   I don't think that old games are very exciting.

2 simulation games (too long/very good/too easy)
3 sports games (exciting/very interesting/fantastic)
4 car games (difficult/very relaxing/very good)
5 puzzle games (relaxing/too difficult/boring)
6 role-playing games (exciting/too difficult/very interesting)

Listening

8 1.26 1.27 → SKILLS BUILDER 2 Use the strategies in the Skills Builder to answer the questions about a radio interview.

1 What is the survey about?
   a European computer games ⓑ European gamers
   c popular games in Europe

2 In which country do a lot of people play computer games?
   a the UK b Finland c Spain

3 How many young gamers regularly do sports?
   a ¼ (a quarter) b ⅓ (a third) c ½ (half)

4 What is the proportion of male to female gamers in the UK?
   a 38/62 b 51/49 c 71/29

5 On average, how many hours a week do teens play?
   a 16 b 5 c 19

6 Most teens play games
   a with their family b with friends c on their own

7 Why do people play computer games?
   a because it's good fun b because they are bored
   c because it's exciting

8 Why do people like gaming more than TV?
   a it's more relaxing b you need to think
   c you learn a lot

9 Your Culture Do many people play computer games in your country? Who are the most active gamers? What games are most popular now?

10 Vocabulary Look at the Word Builder. Classify the adjectives below as general, negative or strong.

> slow fantastic relaxing amazing silly
> wonderful good bad new

> **Word Builder** Modifiers
>
> General adjectives
> **quite/really/very** + *interesting, creative, ...*
> Negative adjectives
> **quite/really/very/a bit** + *boring, long, difficult, ...*
> Strong adjectives
> **really/absolutely** + *great, perfect, terrible, ...*

↘ LANGUAGE CHOICE 11: VOCABULARY PRACTICE

11 Work in pairs. Use the Word Builder to say sentences about the things below.

A: *Computer games are really great.*
B: *Yes, they're very exciting.*

> computer games board games chess
> Charlie Chaplin films dancing
> making model aeroplanes photography
> collecting stamps singing cycling acting

12 Choose a or b. Write notes about why you like it. Use modifiers and adjectives from the Word Builder.

a your favourite computer game
b your favourite board/card game (e.g chess)

13 Work in pairs. Ask and answer questions about your games.

A: *What's your favourite game?*
B: *I'm really into chess.*
A: *Why do you like it?*
B: *Because it's challenging. You need to think ...*

Your Choice

No Comment

'Video games are bad for you? They said that about rock 'n' roll.'

Shigeru Miyamoto, Japanese game designer

LESSON 6 A FIESTA

Crowds fly into Pamplona (1.28)

Up to two million **tourists** have come to **Pamplona** this **weekend** for the **San Fermín festival**. **They will spend a lot of money in Pamplona's restaurants over the next week.**

The famous bull runs are the highlight of the festival. Runners wear white shirts and trousers and red scarves. They run 840 metres with six dangerous, 500-kilogram bulls. They cannot carry any objects except newspapers. They have to run really fast and often have no time to escape the bull.

I spoke to Tom Barnes, who has come to Pamplona with a few friends. 'We just want to have some fun', he says. 'Do we have any experience of bull runs? No, but we're quite fit, so, with a little luck, there won't be any trouble. I know some bulls can be dangerous but I'm sure we'll be okay.'

Every year, between 200 and 300 people get injured, some of them seriously, and thirteen people have died over the last 100 years. There are also a lot of protests from animal rights activists but there are no signs that the fiesta will end.

Warm Up

1 Read the newspaper article about the festival in Pamplona. What do these numbers refer to?

1 *thirteen people have died*

1 13   2 840   3 500
4 2,000,000   5 200-300

some, any, no, a lot of, a few, a little

2 Complete the lists with more nouns in blue from the text.

uncountable nouns: *money, ...*
countable nouns (singular): *weekend, ...*
countable nouns (plural): *tourists, ...*

3 Find an example in the text for each rule (1–6).

1 **some** + uncountable noun: _____
 some + countable noun (plural):
 some bulls

2 **any** + uncountable noun: *any experience*
 any + countable noun (plural): _____

3 **no** + uncountable noun: _____
 no + countable noun (plural): *no signs*

4 **a lot of** + uncountable noun: _____
 a lot of + countable noun (plural): *a lot of protests*

5 **a few** + plural noun: _____

6 **a little** + uncountable noun: *a little luck*

4 Read the sentences (1–3) from the text. <u>Underline</u> the correct words in the rules below.

1 *We just want to have **some** fun.*
2 *Do we have **any** experience in bull runs?*
3 *They can**not** carry **any** objects.*

- We usually use *some/any* in affirmative sentences.
- We usually use *some/any* in questions and negative sentences.

5 (1.29) Choose the correct words to complete the dialogue. Then listen and check your answers.

Tom: Okay, are you ready for tomorrow morning?
Bill: I have ¹*a lot of/a little* questions. Is it dangerous?
Tom: Yes, it is. There are ²*some/a few* injuries every year. You can stay at home.
Bill: Oh no, I want to run. But I haven't got ³*some/any* white clothes.
Tom: Okay, we still have ⁴*any/a lot of* time so let's go and buy ⁵*a little/some* cheap shirts and trousers now. And we need ⁶*no/a few* red scarves.
Bill: And then let's have ⁷*any/some* fun. I'm sure we can meet ⁸*a little/some* nice local people.
Tom: Come on, Bill! We need to get ⁹*a little/a few* sleep. We don't want ¹⁰*any/no* bulls to run faster than we do.

→ LANGUAGE CHOICE 12

6 Use the words below and Exercise 3 to make sentences about the photo.

There are a lot of people in the photo but I can't see any children.

people   bulls   men   shops   houses   rain
injured people   children   police officers   balconies

18

Writing Workshop 1

1 **Work in pairs. Ask and answer the questions.**

1 Do you enjoy parties? Are you a party person?
2 What makes a good party? Put the things (a–e) in order of importance.
a the music b the people c the food and drink
d the place e the time

2 **Read the party invitation. Would you like to go to the party? Why/Why not?**

Tickets ONLY £5!

SPRING PARTY!

We're organising a party to celebrate spring.
We're raising money for musical instruments.
The party is at the College Sports Hall at 8 p.m.
on 23 March.
Don't miss our live rock group, the Xtreme Dodos,
or our DJ, Dana, with some really cool dance
music. You can also take part in our fancy-dress
competition (theme – 'Rock Stars').
Snacks and soft drinks provided.
Interested? Contact Nicky Buckley (09876538) or
Stu Harvey (01873045).

Text Builder

3 **Read the invitation again. In what order can you find this information?**

a Where and when is it?
b What is there to eat and drink?
c How much are the tickets? *1*
d What is the party for?
e Who do you have to contact?
f Why is it going to be a good party?

4 **Now answer the questions in Exercise 3.**

a *the College Sports Hall at 8 p.m. on 23 March*

5 **Look at the Sentence Builder. Which of the linkers (*for* or *to*) comes before a verb? Do the linkers show *when*, *where* or *why* you do something?**

> **Sentence Builder** Purpose linkers
>
> 1 We're raising money **for** musical instruments.
> 2 We're raising money **to** buy musical instruments.
>
> → SKILLS BUILDER 23

6 **Use the words in brackets to answer the questions. Use *to* or *for*.**

1 Why do you listen to music? (relax)

   I listen to music to relax.

2 Why do you play computer games? (fun)
3 Why are you doing this exercise? (learn English)
4 Why is he learning English? (get a good job)
5 Why do you revise your English? (pass my exams)

7 **Write an invitation for a party.**

→ SKILLS BUILDER 24

1 **What sort of party do you want to organise? Think about question 2 in Exercise 1 again.**

2 **Write notes to answer the questions in Exercise 3 about your party.**

3 **Use your notes to write your invitation.**

4 **Check your invitation for grammar and spelling mistakes.**

8 **Work in pairs. Read your partner's party invitation. Would you like to go to his/her party? Tell the class and give reasons.**

I think that Susana's party is really cool. It's in a great place and it's got fantastic music.

19

Speaking Workshop 1

1 Look at the two messages about the St. Patrick's day parade. What kind of information (e.g. day, time) is missing?

Alison
Pierre called. He wants to go to the St Patrick's Day celebrations this ¹ Saturday.
It starts at ² _____ o'clock. Phone him at Paul's ³ _____ before ⁴ _____ o'clock. His number is ⁵ _____

Pierre
⁶ _____ phoned. Okay, but she's got a ⁷ _____ lesson at ⁸ _____ o'clock. Meet her at ⁹ _____ at ¹⁰ _____ o'clock.

2 1.30 1.31 Listen and complete the phone messages.

3 1.32 Pronunciation Listen and write the five questions you hear. Then <u>underline</u> the stressed words. Listen again and repeat the questions.

Can I speak to Alison, please?

4 Match the words (a–c) with the sentences (1–3) in the Talk Builder. How do you say the words in **bold** in your language?

a kilt   b celebration   c parade

Talk Builder Vague language

1 It's **like** a big party.
2 There's **a sort of** walk with music.
3 The musicians wear **a kind of** skirt for men.

→ SKILLS BUILDER 39

---

5 1.33 Pronunciation Listen and repeat the expressions.

6 What are these words from the first two modules? Tell the class.

1 It's a kind of male animal. It's big and dangerous and it can run very fast! *bull*
2 It's a kind of film without sound.
3 It's a sort of game where you make and control people.
4 It's a kind of person with a very strange life.
5 It's a sort of exercise for relaxation.

7 → SKILLS BUILDER 40 Work in pairs. Use vague language to describe three things from the photo in Exercise 1.

---

8 Describe and discuss a photo.

→ SKILLS BUILDER 38

1 Look at the photo below. Think about the answers to the questions. Write notes. Use vague language to help you.
  1 Where is the celebration?
  2 Why do you think the people are celebrating?

2 Work in pairs. Talk about the photo and ask and answer the questions above.

9 What is your favourite celebration in your country? Why? Tell your partner.

LEARNING LINKS: 1 Read and listen to the poem in **Culture Choice 1** on page 102. Then do a project about a celebration in your country.
2 Check Your Progress 2 → MyLab / Workbook page 17. Complete the **Module Diary**.
3 Exam Choice 1 → MyLab / Workbook pages 18–20.

MODULE 3 MONEY

Objectives: **Listen**, **read** and **talk about** money, shops and markets; **write** a short advert; **act out** shopping situations; **learn more about** the Present Perfect.

TOPIC TALK

1 In which of the photos (a–c) are people earning, spending or saving money?

2 1.34 1.35 **Listen to four people (1–4). Match them with their 'money personality' (a–d).**

a spends a lot   c worries a lot about money
b saves a lot   d is good at making money

3 1.36 1.37 **Listen again to the first person. Complete the information in the network.**

Money

I'm ¹ *quite good*/*not very good* with money.
I get ² *£6*/*£16* a week pocket money.
I earn ³ *£13*/*£30* from a part-time job.
I save ⁴ *£15*/*£50* a month and put it in my bank account.
I spend money on ⁵ _____ .
I enjoy shopping ⁶ _____ .

CDs/music downloads, clothes, computer games, cosmetics (e.g. shampoo, make-up), DVDs, food and drink (e.g. sweets, crisps, soft drinks), going out (e.g. to the cinema), mobile phone calls, presents, second-hand things (e.g. clothes, books)

online (e.g. on eBay)
at charity, discount, book, clothes, computer **shops**
- -
at shopping centres, street markets, supermarkets

4 1.38 Pronunciation **Listen and repeat the sentences. Notice the numbers.**

➡ LANGUAGE CHOICE 13:
VOCABULARY PRACTICE

5 Work in groups. Use the network to talk about *your* life. What is your 'money personality'?

a

b

28

c

21

SAVING MONEY

Warm Up

1 **Work in pairs. Look at the money-saving tips (1-6). Choose the three best tips. Can you add any others? Tell the class.**

1 When you get money for a present, put it in the bank.
2 Before you buy something, check out prices online.
3 Sell your old stuff online with your parents' help.
4 Go shopping for cheap clothes at charity shops.
5 Buy clothes in discount shops or shop in the sales.
6 Celebrate Valentine's Day on 15 February.

Reading

2 **Read the magazine article quickly. Which of the tips from Exercise 1 are _not_ mentioned?**

3 **Vocabulary Read the article again. Match the words in blue from the text with the definitions (a-j).**

a a large group of people _crowd_
b to spend (money)
c the first night of a film
d not generous
e something old but valuable
f careful with money
g to find out about
h a blouse or T-shirt
i some flowers
j things with a good price

4 **⊙ SKILLS BUILDER 14 Use the strategies to decide if the sentences are true (T) or false (F).**

1 Most young people are frugal. _F_
2 Frugal people like spending lots of money.
3 Some Hollywood actresses like saving money.
4 Some things cost sixty percent less the day after Valentine's Day.
5 Helen advises buying things like jeans online.

5 **Vocabulary Look at the Word Builder. Complete the gaps with the words below. Check your answers in paragraphs 4 and 5 of the text.**

packet bouquet pair ~~bit~~ bottle can box

> **Word Builder** Quantities
>
> 1 a _bit_ * of advice/information/fun/luck/water/money
> 2 a ___ of perfume/water/orange juice
> 3 a ___ of chocolates/matches
> 4 a ___ of roses/flowers
> 5 a ___ of cola/lemonade/beans
> 6 a ___ of crisps/biscuits/sweets
> 7 a ___ of jeans/socks/sunglasses
>
> * _a bit of_ can go with all uncountable nouns

↘ LANGUAGE CHOICE 14: VOCABULARY PRACTICE

Be Frugal, it's cool! (1.39)

It's cool to wear second-hand clothes and sell your old things online.

1 It's Saturday afternoon in Birmingham city centre and young people are buying the latest fashions. But one young woman is not with the crowd. She is looking for bargains in a small charity shop.

2 'I hate paying a lot for clothes,' says Helen Howard, a student at Birmingham University. 'In the past, people thought I was mean but now it's cool to be frugal. People have less money these days and they're worried about the environment. You can get great bargains in charity shops or at the sales. I bought this Versace top for £4.50 and these Diesel jeans for £5.'

3 Helen is typical of the new attitude to money and even Hollywood stars are doing it. 'I love going to markets and second-hand clothes shops to look for things,' says Kiera Knightley. Angelina Jolie wore a $26 vintage dress at a recent film premiere and does not use expensive face creams. 'The main thing is to get enough sleep and drink lots of water,' she says.

4 According to Helen, there are lots of fun ways to save money. 'For example, have a party and swap clothes, CDs, computer games and books with your friends or sell your old things online. Walk or cycle to school and go to the library to get books and DVDs. One bit of advice is to celebrate Valentine's Day on 15 February. A bouquet of roses, a box of chocolates or a bottle of perfume is up to half price the day after!'

5 Before you buy anything expensive, like jeans, check out prices online. You can find some great bargains. 'Always think before you fork out money,' says Helen. 'Also think about small items. Before you get that packet of crisps or can of cola, wait. Do you really need it? And as for that pair of jeans – maybe it isn't so important after all.'

6 Replace the words in *italics* with words from Exercise 5.

1 *a bit of*

I am good at saving money and finding bargains. I had ¹*some* money from my parents for my birthday and I bought ²*some* shoes in a charity shop for £5! When I go out, I sometimes buy ³*some* cola or ⁴*some* crisps - but not very often. I always carry ⁵*some* water and ⁶*some* peanuts with me. When I want ⁷*some* flowers to give to my girlfriend I always pick them from our garden. And I always buy Christmas presents after Christmas in the sales. You can get ⁸*some* chocolates for half the price!

Writing

7 Look at the adverts. Do you think the items are good value? Why/Why not?

FOR SALE €2 Rock T-shirt
This small, black cotton T-shirt is in good condition. It's not new but it still rocks!

Contact Mark: 098654223
Please phone after 7 p.m.

For Sale Only €14

Nearly-new Casio watch with silver metal bracelet (Classic A168W-1) This cool men's watch has got an alarm clock, stopwatch and lithium battery.
Contact Simon: 06514321

8 Look at the Sentence Builder. Find more adjectives in the adverts for each category.

Sentence Builder Adjective order

	Opinion	Size/Age	Colour	Material	Make/Type	Noun
a	nice	small	green	leather	woman's	jacket

➜ SKILLS BUILDER 25

9 Order the adjectives.

1 (metal / green) sunglasses
   green, metal sunglasses
2 (school / new) bag
3 (brown / small) wallet
4 (fantastic / mini) skirt
5 (new / cool) MP3 player
6 (role-playing / exciting) computer game

10 What have *you* got to sell? Choose an object and write an advert for it. Think about age, size, colour, price, etc.

11 Bring your object into class. Try to sell it to your classmates!

No Comment

'Saving money is a fine thing – especially if your parents have done it for you.'

Winston Churchill, former British Prime Minister

GRAMMAR
MY FAVOURITE SHOP

Warm Up

1 Look at the photo of the shop. Which of the things below do you think it sells?

costumes DVDs comics food games computers magazines masks

2 Read the reviews and check. Would you like to visit the shop? Why/Why not?

3 Read the reviews again. Which reviewer:

1 is into reading comics?
2 has a family who like fantasy?
3 has met someone famous in the shop?

FAVOURITE THINGS

Forbidden Planet [1.40]

1 Have you ever visited Forbidden Planet? It's great for sci-fi, horror and fantasy fans. I've visited the shop hundreds of times and I've never left without a bargain. It's got everything – magazines, comics, books and DVDs. You ask for the latest role-playing game and they have already ordered it! I've found old comics there that you can't find in any other shop. Occasionally, writers or comic book artists come and sign their books (but the shop can't get you Tolkien's signature on your copy of *The Lord of the Rings*!). I've often bought signed books there (they are worth a fortune now!). **Gandalf**

2 Discover geek wonderland! I can spend hours there. They've got lots of DVDs and gadgets. I've always found great presents there: a DVD of *Spirited Away* for my sister, a toy figure of Frodo for my cousin, a replica of Indiana Jones' hat for my dad, a Darth Vader costume for my little brother. The shop is great for *Star Wars* fans, too: I've bought three light sabres there. Oh and I've seen famous people in there a couple of times. Have you been there yet? Go now and 'may the force be with you!' **Leia**

Present Perfect (2)

4 Read the Present Perfect sentences (1-3) from the text. <u>Underline</u> the correct words in the rule below.

1 *I **have** always **found** great presents here.*
2 *I **have bought** three light sabres here.*
3 *I **have seen** famous people in here a couple of times.*

• We use the Present Perfect when *we know/we do not know or care* exactly when the past action happened.

5 Find six examples of the Present Perfect in the first review.

Practice

6 Use the cues to make sentences in the Present Perfect.

1 Gandalf / find / old comics / at Forbidden Planet

Gandalf has found old comics at Forbidden Planet.

2 Leia / buy / some great presents there
3 Leia / see / famous people / a couple of times / in the shop
4 Gandalf / not buy / a book with Tolkien's signature
5 Leia / be / to the shop / many times
6 Leia / spend / a lot of money there

→ LANGUAGE CHOICE 15

7 Look at the Sentence Builder and complete sentences (1-6) with the correct form of the Present Perfect and *ever* or *never*.

> **Sentence Builder** *ever/never*
> Have you **ever** visited Forbidden Planet?
> I have **never** left without a bargain.

1 My dad _has never bought_ (buy) clothes in a second-hand shop.
2 _____ (you / sell) anything?
3 I _____ (visit) an open-air market.
4 _____ (you and your friends / spend) all day in a shopping mall?
5 My parents _____ (give) me expensive presents.
6 _____ (you / be) to a designer shop?

8 Look at the Sentence Builder below. Which word, *already* or *yet*, is used with a affirmative sentences? b questions and negative sentences? Translate the two words into your language.

> **Sentence Builder** *already/yet*
> They have **already** ordered it.
> Have you been to Forbidden Planet **yet**?
> I haven't been there **yet**.

➤ LANGUAGE CHOICE 16

9 Work in pairs. Use the cues to make dialogues with *already* or *yet*.

1 **A:** earn money? → **B:** find a job
  A: *Have you earned any money yet?*
  B: *No, I haven't. But I have already found a job.*

2 **A:** buy Christmas presents →
  B: buy a Christmas tree
3 **A:** buy a laptop? →
  B: save some money for one
4 **A:** do your homework? →
  B: write the essay for Monday
5 **A:** wash the dishes? →
  B: clean my room

Grammar Alive Experiences

10 **1.41** Listen to two dialogues. Match the people (1-4) with the experiences (a-d) and write sentences about them in the Present Perfect.

Jake has been to the Alps.

1 Jake   a see Hugh Grant
2 Colin   b be to the Alps
3 Sara   c climb Ben Nevis
4 Amy   d see Brad Pitt and George Clooney on the telly

11 Work in pairs. Use the cues to make dialogues.

A: *Have you (ever) found money in the street?*
B: *No, I haven't. But I've won money in the lottery.*

A starts
1 find money in the street?
2 do shopping online?
3 buy clothes in a charity shop?

B answers
1 win money in the lottery
2 check out prices online
3 buy books in second-hand bookshop

B starts
4 earn money?
5 find bargain in a shop?
6 buy a computer?

A answers
4 receive pocket money
5 find bargain in a market
6 buy a computer game

12 Use the cues below to write true sentences about your life. Use the Present Perfect and *already* or *yet*.

I haven't finished school yet.

finish school   pass my driving test   be abroad
choose a future job   read *Hamlet*
have a girlfriend/boyfriend   see ... (a new film)
listen to the news today   drive a car

13 Use the cues to write the quiz questions. Ask and answer the questions in pairs and check your answers on page 114.

1 *Have you ever bought second-hand clothes?*

Are you extravagant or frugal?

1 buy second-hand clothes
2 save all your birthday money
3 buy an expensive mobile/MP3 player
4 stay in a tent
5 spend all your money in one day
6 try an expensive sport (e.g. golf, sailing, tennis)
7 visit a fashionable club
8 have a holiday in a four-star hotel

Warm Up

1 **Vocabulary** Put the words (a–g) into the correct category in the network.

a = Accessories (footwear)
a a pair of shoes
b a clock made in 1854
c a 1971 John Lennon record
d batteries
e a pair of earrings
f a Persian carpet
g a kilo of bananas

Antiques:
furniture, silver and gold, old books, old records

Electronic goods:
computer games, CDs, DVDs, videos

Market products

Arts and crafts:
leather goods, ceramics, textiles

Food and drink:
fruit and vegetables, meat and poultry, fish and seafood, herbs and spices

Clothes:
men's/women's, designer, second-hand, shoes
Accessories:
handbags, jewellery, scarves

→ LANGUAGE CHOICE 17: VOCABULARY PRACTICE

Listening

2 **2.1** **2.2** Listen to an interview about the markets in the photos (a–c). Which of the markets:

1 has up to 400,000 visitors a day? *b*
2 has sixty different kinds of fruit?
3 has good clothes for young people?
4 is a good place to buy old records?
5 has 4000 different shops?
6 has fantastic wild mushrooms?

3 **2.3** **2.4** Listen again. What bargains can you get in each market?

4 **Your Culture** Work in pairs. Ask and answer the questions.

1 What famous markets are there in your country?
2 What markets are there in your area? What can you buy there? Are things cheaper than in normal shops?

DVD Choice

5 **DVD 3** Watch the documentary about Camden market. Which of the products from the network in Exercise 1 can you see?

6 **DVD 3** Watch again. Are the sentences true (T) or false (F)?

1 There are three different markets at Camden. *F*
2 The market is over fifty years old.
3 The Roundhouse was a famous shop.
4 10,000 visitors come to the market every weekend.
5 Camden is a good place for alternative clothes.
6 There are no street performers at Camden.

7 Work in pairs. Ask and answer the questions.

1 Would you like to visit Camden? Why/Why not?
2 What would you like to buy or do there?

a La Boqueria

b Grand Bazaar

c Camden

Watching and Speaking

8 (2.5) DVD 4 **Listen to or watch the situation in Camden market. Answer the questions.**

1 Who is Sophie buying a present for?
2 What size T-shirt does she choose?
3 What's the problem with the T-shirt?
4 How much does the scarf cost?
5 How much change does she get?
6 Why can't the shopkeeper wrap the scarf?

9 (2.6) **Look at the Talk Builder. Listen to the expressions and complete them.**

Talk Builder Shopping

A: Can I ¹_____ you?
B: Yes, can I have a look at those ²_____ , please?
A: What ³_____ ?
B: Medium. ⁴ _____ I try it on, please?
A: Of course, the changing ⁵_____ is over there.
B: It's a bit too ⁶_____ . How much is this ⁷_____ ?
A: Seven pounds ⁸_____ .
B: Okay. Can I have this ⁹_____ , please?
A: Thanks. ¹⁰_____ pounds fifty change.
B: Could you wrap it up, ¹¹_____ ?
A: I'm ¹²_____ . I haven't got any paper.

➔ SKILLS BUILDER 41

---

10 (2.7) Pronunciation **Listen and repeat the questions from the Talk Builder. Notice the polite intonation.**

11 ➔ SKILLS BUILDER 41 **Work in pairs. Act out the dialogue in the Talk Builder.**

12 **Imagine that you are going to Camden Market. Choose two things to buy. Then work in pairs. Take turns to act out the dialogues at the market.**

13 **What did you buy from your partner? Tell the class.**

I bought a goth T-shirt and a pair of boots!

Your Choice

Language Review Modules 2 and 3

1 Free time/Money **Complete the text with the correct words.**

I'm not very ¹_____ with money. My parents give me £50 ²_____ money a month and I don't put any of it into my bank ³_____ . I ⁴_____ this money at music shops: I am really ⁵_____ heavy metal. I buy a lot of CDs ⁶_____ – internet auctions are great for CDs. I ⁷_____ listening to music because it relaxes me. I also like ⁸_____ computer games. I ⁹_____ a lot of money on clothes because I only buy ¹⁰second-_____ clothes at charity shops. **/10**

2 Modifiers/Quantities **Complete the text with the correct words.**

My family is ¹¹*really/quite* wonderful. So for my birthday, my brother gave me a ¹²_____ of roses — they were ¹³*very/absolutely* perfect. My mum bought me a ¹⁴_____ of designer jeans. They are ¹⁵*a bit/very* small but I wear them every day. I got a ¹⁶_____ of perfume and a ¹⁷_____ of chocolates from my father. He is usually ¹⁸*a bit/quite* creative but this time his presents were ¹⁹*a bit/absolutely* boring. Anyway, he is ²⁰*quite/really* fantastic. **/10**

3 Adjective order/Purpose linkers **Order the words in the sentences.**

21 leather / new / I've got / cool / trousers
22 chess / for / I play / fun
23 songs / to / I learn / my English / improve
24 green / some / I bought / nice / socks
25 bag / I put it in / plastic / a / blue   **/5**

4 Present Perfect **Complete the dialogue with the verbs in the Present Perfect.**

A: ²⁶_____ (you / see) the last Johnny Depp film?
B: No, I ²⁷_____ (not see) any of his films.
A: Why are you crying? What ²⁸_____ (happen)?
B: Someone ²⁹_____ (steal) my wallet.
A: I'm so happy. I ³⁰_____ (win) a trip to London!
B: Lucky you! I ³¹_____ (not be) to London. Can I come too?   **/6**

5 Present Perfect and adverbs **Choose the correct adverb in brackets. Put it in the correct place in the sentence.**

32 I've earned a lot of money. (*ever/never*)
33 Has your class been on a class trip? (*already/yet*)
34 Have you tried sushi? (*ever/already*)
35 I've passed my driving test. (*already/yet*)
36 My team has won a football game. (*never/yet*)   **/5**

6 *some, any, no, a lot of, a few, a little* **Choose the correct words to complete the sentences.**

A You need ³⁷*a few/a little* luck during the exam if you don't have ³⁸*any/no* knowledge.
B Have you got ³⁹*a few/some* time to help me find ⁴⁰*any/a few* Christmas presents?
C There is ⁴¹*a lot of/a few* blood in ⁴²*some/any* horror films.
D I've got ⁴³*any/no* experience but ⁴⁴*a lot of/a little* famous people started their careers like that.   **/8**

7 Shopping/Vague language **Complete the dialogue between the shop assistant (SA) and the customer (C).**

SA: Hello. Can I ⁴⁵_____ ?
C: Yes. Have you got any um … they're a ⁴⁶_____ of tight trousers with Lycra …
SA: Ah yes, leggings! What ⁴⁷_____ ?
C: Small, I think.
SA: Here you are.
C: Can I ⁴⁸_____ please?
SA: Of course. The changing rooms are over there …
C: ⁴⁹_____ ?
SA: They're £25.
C: Okay, I'll take them. ⁵⁰_____ for me?
SA: Sorry, we don't wrap things.   **/6**

Self Assessment

2.8 **Listen and check your answers. Write down the scores. Use the table to find practice exercises.**

Exercise	If you need practice, go to
1	Language Choice 7 and 13
2	Language Choice 11 and 14
3	SB p.23 ex. 8 p.19 ex. 6
4	Language Choice 8 and 15
5	SB p.25 ex. 7 and 9; Language Choice 16
6	Language Choice 12
7	SB p. 20 ex 4 and 6; p.27 ex. 9

LEARNING LINKS: 1 Check Your Progress 3 → MyLab / Workbook page 27. Complete the **Module Diary.**
2 Sound Choice 2 → MyLab / Workbook page 28. Choose three pronunciation activities to do.

Objectives: Read, listen to and tell stories; write an email and describe an experience; learn about the Past Simple, Past Continuous and Present Perfect.

TOPIC TALK

① Look at the pictures (a-c). Which of the stories looks the most interesting? Why?

② 2.9 2.10 Listen to three descriptions (1-3). Match them with pictures (a-c).

③ 2.11 2.12 Listen again to one of the descriptions. Complete the information in the network.

④ 2.13 Pronunciation Listen and repeat the sentences. Notice the expression with *it's*.

LANGUAGE CHOICE 18: VOCABULARY PRACTICE

⑤ Work in groups. Use the network to talk about *your* favourite book or film.

Stories

My favourite ¹(book)/film is *The Count of Monte Cristo* by Alexandre Dumas.
It's ²_____ .
It takes place in ³*France/Spain.*
It's about a young ⁴*soldier/sailor.* Some soldiers arrest him and then take him to a prison ⁵*on an island/in Ireland.*
It's really ⁶_____ .

Types
a/an adventure, cowboy, crime, detective, fantasy, folk, ghost, historical, horror, love, science fiction, short **story**
- -
a bestseller, classic, comedy, fairy tale, romantic comedy, romance, thriller

Opinions
boring, brilliant, depressing, exciting, funny, imaginative, interesting, romantic, sad, scary, violent

29

LESSON 10 A GHOST STORY

Warm Up

1 Read the information about the Glencoe Massacre. What is the link between the Massacre and the photo below?

The Glencoe Massacre

In the winter of 1692, British soldiers and members of the Campbell clan killed almost forty of the MacDonalds of Glencoe, in Scotland, in their homes. Another forty people, mainly women and children, died of cold when they were trying to escape.

2 Read the text. Who was the old man? What was strange about him?

Some years ago, I was in Scotland with a group of **(2.14)** friends. We all loved Scottish mountains so we went hiking there almost every year.

We were walking through a beautiful valley called Glencoe, when we saw a tall man standing beside the road. He had long white hair and was wearing a kilt. He was carrying a stick. He looked like a character out of a history book. We asked him to join us for a group photo. He agreed but he never said a word. So I took the photo and we walked on. When I turned round a moment later to wave goodbye, he was not there.

That evening, when we were having dinner at the local inn, we asked the owner about the old man. 'Ahh! You've met the ghost of Glencoe!' he said. 'He was killed during the massacre 400 years ago. His spirit still walks along the River Coe.'

Later that night, when I was looking through the photos, I discovered something odd about the group photo that we took. The old Scotsman wasn't there. There was just an empty space between my friends.

3 Your Culture **Do you know any ghost stories from your country? Tell the class.**

Past Simple and Continuous

4 Complete the lists with regular and irregular verbs in the Past Simple from the text.

regular verbs: *loved, ...*
irregular verbs: *went, ...*

5 Find the verbs in red and in blue in the text. Match the two groups with the uses of the Past Simple.

a events in the past
b states, situations and habits in the past

6 Read the sentences in the table. Find more examples of the Past Continuous in the text.

Affirmative	
He **was wearing** a kilt.	
We **were wearing** kilts.	
Negative	
He **wasn't wearing** a kilt.	
We **weren't wearing** kilts.	
Questions	**Short answers**
Was he **wearing** a kilt?	Yes, he was.
	No, he wasn't.
Were they **wearing** kilts?	Yes, they were.
	No, they weren't.
What **was** he **wearing**?	

7 Read the sentence from the text. Complete a and b with the names of the tenses.

We were walking through Glencoe when **we saw** a tall man.

a a background activity/situation (Past _____ tense)

b an event or a point in time (Past _____ tense)

Practice

8 Use the Past Continuous or the Past Simple to answer the questions about the text.

1 What were the tourists doing when they saw the strange man?

They were walking in Glencoe.

2 What did the tourists do when they saw the strange man?
3 What did the man do when they invited him to join them for the photo?
4 What were the tourists doing when they spoke to the owner of the inn?

➤ LANGUAGE CHOICE 19

9 Use the cues, the Past Simple and the Past Continuous to write sentences about ghost sightings.

1 stay in an old hotel – see a man in sixteenth-century clothes

I was staying in an old hotel when I saw a man in sixteenth-century clothes.

2 camp with friends – hear a strange noise near our tent
3 walk my dog – see a ghostly figure in the distance
4 visit a castle – see a lady in white with no head
5 climb a tower – a man on a black horse fly past me
6 visit a church – hear a horrible scream

10 Work in pairs. Find out what your partner was doing at the times below. Ask and answer questions in the Past Continuous.

A: *What were you doing on Sunday at 5 p.m.?*
B: *I was watching a DVD.*

• on Sunday at 5 p.m.
• at 9 p.m. last night
• at 7 a.m. this morning
• yesterday at 4 p.m.

Grammar Alive Telling an anecdote

11 **2.15** Listen to Anna, Peter and James talking about their last holiday. Which of them:

a didn't go on holiday? b had a very wet experience?
c did something nice for a stranger?

12 Work in pairs. Use the pictures and the cues to talk about the situations.

I was eight years old. It was my birthday and I was very excited. I was running downstairs when …

1
eight years old – excited, run downstairs – fall – break arm

2
ride bike on holiday – big dog run towards me – fall off bike – into river

3
walk in mountains – talk to friends – see £20 on the ground – buy lunch for everyone

4
sit in class – form teacher explain the school rules – my mobile ring – get my first punishment

13 Choose a situation (a–c) or your own idea. Write notes for a short anecdote (real or invented). Describe the background and what happened.

a your first memory b a holiday adventure
c a dangerous/scary situation

14 Tell your anecdotes in groups. Ask and answer questions about your memories.

A: *What were you doing?*
B: *I was playing in the garden with my sister. My parents were reading.*
C: *What happened?*
B: *I fell out of a tree and broke my arm!*

Warm Up

1 Look at the photos (a–d) from *The Count of Monte Cristo*. Try to guess the order of the events.

Reading

2 Read part one of the story quickly and check your guesses from Exercise 1.

Part One   2.16

It was 1814. Louis XVIII was King of France and the ex-emperor Napoleon was in exile on the island of Elba in the Mediterranean. A young sailor on a French ship, Edmond Dantès, was in Elba and agreed to take a secret letter from Napoleon to his supporters in France. After Edmond returned to his home city of Marseilles, a royal judge found out about the letter. Then, on the day of Edmond's wedding to his beautiful girlfriend, Mercedes, the king's soldiers came to his house and arrested him.

From the boat, Edmond saw the Château d' If. 'No prisoners ever leave that terrible castle alive!' he thought.

The guards put Edmond into a small, dark underground cell. Days, weeks and months passed and Edmond was afraid of going mad. Then, one evening he heard a noise under the floor. Suddenly, a hole appeared and an old man climbed out of a tunnel.

'Hello, my name is Faria,' he said. The two men soon became very good friends. Faria was a wise priest and taught Edmond a lot about languages and science. When Faria became very ill, Edmond looked after him and saved his life. Later, Faria told Edmond about some fantastic treasure on the small island of Monte Cristo.

When Faria died a few years later, the guards put his body into a bag. This gave Edmond a good idea. 'Only dead people leave this prison!' He opened the bag with Faria's knife, took the body to his cell and put it in his bed. After that, he got into the bag and waited patiently.

Two guards carried Edmond outside and tied a heavy stone around his feet. It was cold and he could hear big waves around the prison. Luckily, Edmond was a sailor and was not afraid of the sea.

The guards picked up the bag and threw it into the sea. Edmond fell and fell and then hit the water. The stone pulled him down and down but in the end Edmond cut open the bag, cut off the stone and came to the surface.
He was free!

3 Read the story. Answer the questions.

1 Why did the soldiers arrest Edmond?

because he took Napoleon's letter to France

2 Where did the judge send him?
3 Where did they keep him?
4 Who was Faria and how did he help Edmond?
5 Why did Faria tell Edmond about the treasure?
6 How did Edmond plan to escape?
7 What did the guards do with the bag?
8 How did Edmond get out of the bag?

4 Your Culture What classic stories do you know in your language? Which is your favourite?

5 Look at the Sentence Builder. How do you say the sentences in your language?

Sentence Builder
Adjectives and prepositions
Edmond was not **afraid of the sea**.
He was **afraid of going mad**.

LANGUAGE CHOICE 20

6 Work in pairs. Use the cues and your ideas to ask and answer questions.

A: *What are you good at?*
B: *I'm good at playing tennis. And you?*

bad at/good at tennis/dancing/playing football
(not) interested in reading classics/
collecting things/playing video games/computers/art
(not) afraid of flying/the dark/heights
worried about/relaxed about exams/
marks at school/being late/losing things

Listening

7 2.17 2.18 → SKILLS BUILDER 3 Listen to part two of the story. Use the strategies in the Skills Builder to decide if the sentences are true (T) or false (F).

1 A big ship rescued Edmond from the sea. *F*
2 The ship took him to the island of Monte Cristo.
3 Edmond stayed on the island for a few days to look for the treasure.
4 He found the treasure in a cave and took some of the silver.
5 He bought a big boat and returned to collect more of the treasure.
6 He changed his name to the Count of Monte Cristo.

8 2.19 Vocabulary Listen to the sentences from the story. Match the verbs (1-7) in the Word Builder with the meanings (a-e).

a go directly   d arrive
b collect someone   e leave
c return (x 3)

Word Builder Multi-part verbs (1)
1 pick (someone) up   5 go back to (a place)
2 get to (a place)   6 sail back to (a place)
3 come back to (a place) 7 go straight to (a place)
4 go away

LANGUAGE CHOICE 21: VOCABULARY PRACTICE

9 Correct these sentences about your life.

1 My dad always picks me up from school at four o'clock.

My mum sometimes picks me up from school at three o'clock.

2 I usually get to school at ten o'clock.
3 When I get to school in the morning I go straight to the cafeteria.
4 In September, I go back to school after the holidays.
5 I feel sad when my sister goes away to university.
6 I went back to my old primary school last week.

10 Memory Game. Work in groups of three. Choose two of the things (a-c) to remember from the story. Close your books and write notes.

Edmond – in underground prison cell/E met a priest – Faria/F knew a lot

a what happened (the events in the story)
b information about the characters
c information about the places/objects

11 How much can you remember? Each person gives a piece of information. The last person to stop is the winner!

A: *Edmond met a priest in the prison.*
B: *The priest knew a lot.*
C: *Edmond's prison cell was underground.*

No Comment
'I took a speed-reading course and read *War and Peace* in twenty minutes. It's about Russia.'

Woody Allen, American film director

Your Choice

12 GRAMMAR
A LOVE STORY

Warm Up

1 Look at the phrases below. Order the events in a 'typical' romance.

1 – *meet somebody*

go out with somebody   fall in love with somebody
~~meet somebody~~   get married   go on a date   get on
well with somebody   ask somebody out   get engaged

2 Read the text. How did Michael and Juliet meet and get engaged?

Love is in the air (2.20)

A man fell in love with a passenger on a flight from Belfast to Newcastle and the airline helped him find her.
Juliet in seat 2B and Michael in 2C got on brilliantly – but Michael was shy and he didn't ask Juliet for her phone number. Later he contacted the airline with a message for Juliet: 'Please get in touch!'. Juliet phoned him and agreed to go on a date with him. They told us about their romance.

Michael said, 'I've never met a woman like Juliet. I fell in love at first sight.'

Juliet said, 'I've fallen in love a few times but not like this. This is a fairytale romance.'

A spokeswoman for the airline said, 'We have had all kinds of problems: people have lost their luggage, men have asked for our flight attendants' phone numbers. There have been some strange requests but not like this one.'

Michael and Juliet have just got married and are now on their honeymoon in Spain.

Present Perfect and Past Simple

3 Read the sentences (1-4) from the text and match them with the explanations (a-b).

1 Juliet **has fallen** in love a few times.
2 Michael **fell** in love at first sight.
3 Michael didn't **ask** Juliet for her number.
4 Men **have asked** for our flight attendants' phone numbers.

a We know exactly when it happened in the past e.g. (*during the flight to Newcastle*).
b We don't know or it doesn't matter when it happened in the past.

4 Match the pictures (a-b) with the sentences (1-2). Which activity happened recently and has visible consequences in the present?

1 They have fallen in love.
2 They fell in love in the 1950s.

5 Match the questions (1-4) with the responses (a-b).

1 Why are you so happy?   a I fell in love.
2 Why did you get married?   b Oh, I've fallen in love.
3 Is George Clooney   a Yes, he's had a lot of
  popular with women?   girlfriends.
4 Was Charlie Chaplin   b Yes, he had a lot of
  popular with women?   girlfriends.

➤ LANGUAGE CHOICE 22

6 Complete the interview with the verbs in the Present Perfect or the Past Simple.

1 A: ¹ *Have you ever been* (you / ever be) married?
  B: No, I ² _____ (not be) married but I ³ _____ (be) engaged a few times. I ⁴ _____ (meet) my girlfriend in 2009, when I ⁵ _____ (go) skiing in Italy.

2 A: How ¹ _____ (your parents / meet)?
  B: On a train. My dad ² _____ (help) my mum to carry her backpack.
  A: Are they happy?
  B: Oh yes, I ³ _____ (never / see) a happier couple.

7 Work in pairs. Use the cues below to start conversations about past experiences. Then ask two questions about details.

A: *Have you been abroad?*
B: *Yes, I have.*
A: *Where did you go?*
B: *To Italy.*

Have you (ever)

be abroad?   travel by plane?   read a book in English?
earn some money?   break your leg or arm?

Writing Workshop 2

1 **Look at the pictures and read Jack's email.
Who is Andy?**

a his friend **b** his cousin **c** his brother

Subject: The weekend
To: Andy   andrevans@bt.internet.com
From: Jack's   jackokemp@talk39.com

Hi Andy,
1 How are things? Everything's fine here – school is
the same – but I had a real adventure at the weekend.
2 On Saturday, I was at my mate Sam's farm. We
were having a great time on quad bikes when Sam
suddenly shouted: 'A bee's stung me!' At first, I didn't
think it was serious but then Sam's hand became
red and swollen and he couldn't breathe properly. I
phoned Sam's mum immediately. After that, I took
Sam back to the farmhouse on his quad. It took ten
minutes but felt like hours. Luckily, the ambulance
was there and they quickly took him into hospital. In
the end, Sam was fine. Later, Sam's parents gave me
one of their quad bikes as a reward and I was really
happy!
3 Write soon. Love to Auntie Sue, Uncle Dave
and grandma.
Jack

---

2 **Read the email again. Imagine you are Jack.
Answer the questions.**

1 Where were you?
  I was at Sam's farm.
2 Who was with you?
3 What were you
  doing?
4 What happened?

5 Why was it scary?
6 What did you do?
7 What happened in
  the end?
8 How did you feel?

Text Builder

3 **Analyse the email.**

1 Match the parts of the email (1–3) with:
   a his experience **b** introduction **c** ending
2 Find words and expressions that mean:
   a *Please, write.* **b** *I'm okay.*
   c *Give my love to …* **d** *How are you?*
   e *Hello …*
3 Find linkers in blue that:
   a describe the order of events (x 4) *at first*
   b describe how things happen (x 2)
   c give opinions (x 1)

4 ➔ SKILLS BUILDER 26 **Look at the story linkers
in the Skills Builder. Choose the correct linkers to
complete the story below.**

I was playing tennis when I ¹*suddenly/immediately/
quickly* heard the ambulances. ²*After that/At first/In
the end*, I thought it was a car accident but then I saw
smoke in the town centre. I ³*suddenly/immediately/
luckily* rang my mum because her office is there but
there was no reply. ⁴*At first/After that/In the end*, I
rang my sister but she didn't know anything. So I got
on my bike and rode ⁵*suddenly/quickly/later* into town.
I was going over the bridge when my mum rang. She
was all right. She ⁶*after that/in the end/immediately*
came over and picked me up in the car. She told me
about the fire. It was in her building but ⁷*in the end/
luckily/suddenly* nobody was hurt.

5 **Write an email to a friend about a frightening
experience.**

➔ SKILLS BUILDER 27

1 **Think of a scary experience. Use the
   ideas below or invent your own story.**
   • a fire   • an accident
   • a medical emergency   • a robbery

2 **Write notes to answer the questions
   in Exercise 2 about your own experience.**

3 **Use your notes to write your email.**

4 **Check your email for these things:**

   • parts of the story that are not clear
   • mistakes with vocabulary and grammar
   • organisation and layout

SKILLS
Speaking Workshop 2

1 2.21 2.22 Look at the picture and find two differences from the email in Writing Workshop 2. Then listen and find five more differences.

2 2.23 Pronunciation Listen to Kelly's reactions (1–4). Match them with their meanings (a–d).

1 Mm.	a very surprised (about
2 Oh no!	something good)
3 Wow!	b interested
4 Really?	c not interested
	d very surprised (about
	something bad)

3 2.24 Listen again to her reactions and repeat them. Notice the intonation.

4 Look at the Talk Builder. Which of the oral linkers in **bold** do we use to:

a link two events? b go back to the story?
c hesitate?

Talk Builder Telling stories

1 **Err ... Well**, I was at my mate Sam's farm.
2 **Anyway**, we stopped in a field.
3 **Umm ... You know**, I didn't think it was serious.
4 **But then** it started to go red and swollen.
5 **And then** he couldn't breathe properly.

→ SKILLS BUILDER 42

---

5 Work in pairs. Complete the sentences to tell a story. You can add your own ideas.

A: What did you do *yesterday/last week/ at the weekend*?
B: Well, I went to *the cinema/a concert/ a football match*.
A: *Mm./Really?*
B: Anyway, I met *my ex-boyfriend/girlfriend/an old friend/my favourite film star*.
A: Wow!/Really?
B: You know, we talked a lot. And then we went to a *café/club/luxury restaurant*.
A: *Mm./Really?*
B: Well, we were *talking/dancing/having dinner* but then *he/she* left because *he/she suddenly felt ill/his/her mum rang/journalists were taking photos of us*.
A: *Mm./Oh no!*

6 Tell a story about a frightening experience.

→ SKILLS BUILDER 42

1 Reread your story from Writing Workshop 2.

2 → SKILLS BUILDER 43 Use the strategies in the Skills Builder to prepare to tell your story. Use your notes from Writing Workshop 2.

3 Work in pairs. Take turns to tell your story to your partner. When you listen, use phrases from the Talk Builder to show surprise and interest.

7 Tell the class about your partner's story.

Monika's story is really scary. It's about an accident at a pond. It took place on a farm when she was only three. She was playing near the pond when she fell in ...

LEARNING LINKS: 1 Read and listen to a story by Charles Dickens in **Culture Choice 2** on page 104. Then do a project about a famous writer from your country.
2 **Check Your Progress 4** → MyLab / Workbook page 35. Complete the **Module Diary**.
3 **Exam Choice 2** → MyLab / Workbook pages 36–38.

GENERATIONS

Objectives: **Listen**, **read** and **talk about** family, generations and style; **express** opinions, **agree** and **disagree**; **write** opinions; **learn more** about the Present Perfect.

TOPIC TALK

1 **Look at the photo. Think about the questions (1-2). Then tell the class your answers.**

1 How many generations can you see in the photo?
2 How often does your family get together?

2 `2.25` `2.26` **Listen to three people (1-3) and find them in the photo.**

3 `2.27` `2.28` **Listen again to the first person. Complete the information in the network.**

➡ LANGUAGE CHOICE 23: VOCABULARY PRACTICE

4 `2.29` Pronunciation **Listen and repeat the plural nouns. Notice the endings.**

5 **Work in groups. Use the network to talk about *your* family.**

Families

I've got one sister and two ¹*cousins*.
I don't often see my ² _____ .
I get on well/okay with my ³ _____ .
I sometimes argue with my ⁴ _____ .
My parents and I have ⁵*different/the same* tastes in music and fashion. They can't stand ⁶ _____ .
My parents get angry when I ⁷ _____ .

Relatives
aunts, cousins, grandparents, half-brother/sisters, mother/father-in-law nephews/nieces, parents, stepfather/mother, uncles

Fashion
tight/baggy jeans, long/short skirts/dresses, T-shirts with slogans, tattoos, piercings, hairstyles (short/long/dyed hair), jackets with hoods, leggings

don't do my homework, tidy my room
----
come home late, wear 'different' clothes, spend hours on the computer

13 SKILLS GENERATION GAPS

Warm Up

1 Look at the photos (a-e). Which of them are from the 1980s and which are from now?

Reading

2 Read the blog. Why was there a generation gap in the 80s between parents and teens? Why is there one now?

3 ➡ SKILLS BUILDER 15 Use the strategies to match the author's intentions (1-6) with the blog entries (a-e). There is one extra intention.

1 To explain his/her generation to older people. *d*
2 To express opinions about 80s music and fashion.
3 To give advice to parents of digital teenagers.
4 To talk about his/her generation gap in the 1980s.
5 To describe the technology when he/she was a teenager.
6 To ask for help with his/her two teenagers.

4 Which of the bloggers (a-e) has these opinions?

1 'Teens now have better technology than we did.' *b*
2 'Teenagers use computers too much!'
3 'My parents were conservative when I was a teenager.'
4 'Life has changed a lot because of digital technology.'
5 'Our lives are very different from our parents'.'

5 Vocabulary Look at the Word Builder. Complete the words (1-10) from the blog. Then match them with the definitions (a-j) below.

Word Builder Compounds		
Nouns	**Adverbs/Adjectives**	**Verbs**
1 web*site*	5 on_____	8 to_____load
2 web_____	6 off_____	9 to up_____
3 home_____	7 real-_____	10 to multi_____
4 lap_____		

a connected to the Net b disconnected from the Net
c get something from the Net d put something on the Net
e to do different things at the same time
f the first page on a website g a group of web pages
h an online document i in the present j a portable computer

➥ LANGUAGE CHOICE 24: VOCABULARY PRACTICE

6 Work in pairs. Ask and answer the questions.

1 How long do you spend online every day?
2 What are your favourite websites and what do you download from the Net?
3 What do you upload to your homepage?

Home	1950s	1960s	197

The Generation Bl

 a MY GENERATION GAP
Posted by ZETA – Wednesday, 4 June

I was a teenager in the 80s and I still love the music. Rap was starting and rock bands like Metallica and U2 were big but my favourite singer was Madonna. I had wild hair and lots of jewellery and I wore miniskirts, leggings and denim jackets. I thought I was so cool! My mum and dad couldn't stand my music or my clothes and we had lots of arguments.
4 comments:

b Kevtech said: I remember the 1980s, too but I wasn't really into fashion. I got a Nintendo console for my thirteenth birthday and then my dad bought one of the first personal computers, an Apple Mac. He had a mobile phone, too – it was enormous! Kids these days are lucky with all the technology they've got.
Posted 04/06/12 at 19.15 p.m.

c Koolpapi said: Interesting topic! I agree about the 80s, it was a fantastic time to be a teenager. Now, I've got two teenage sons and I'm the parent. We get on well and they even like some of my music! However, they spend ALL their life on their laptops. They log on and spend hours online before logging off again. I use computers, too but I don't use them all the time. What can I do?
Posted 04/06/12 at 19.33 p.m.

Writing

7 Look at the Sentence Builder and rewrite sentences (1-3) using the words in bold.

Sentence Builder Contrast linkers

1 **Although** they don't look different, they certainly are.
2 They don't look different **but** they certainly are.
3 They don't look different. **However**, they certainly are.

➔ SKILLS BUILDER 28

---

1 My dad uses a computer a lot but he can't upload or download files.
   Although my dad _____ , _____ *files.*
2 I am interested in computers but we haven't got the internet at home.
   I am _____ , _____ , *we* _____ *at home.*
3 My mum likes some of my clothes. However, she hates my hairstyle!
   My mum _____ *she* _____ .

---

8 Choose one of the blog entries (a-e) from Exercise 2 and reply to it with your opinions.

Zeta, I think that your post is very interesting. I really like the music from the 1980s, too, but I can't stand the clothes! Although my mum and dad were teenagers in the 1980s …

9 Work in pairs. Read your partner's opinions from Exercise 8. Do you agree with him/her? Tell the class.

We think that young people today are different from our parents.

No Comment

'A teenager is someone who cannot get information from anything not plugged in.'

Bill Cosby, American comedian

| 1980s | 1990s | 2000s | 2010s |

)

d MegaMaxine said: So, you've noticed, Koolpapi! We're the first digital generation and we multitask all the time. We have real-time chats online with our friends or post messages on their homepages. We upload music, photos and jokes to our webpages. We download music to our MP3 players or mobiles so we can listen to it offline. We play interactive computer games with people around the world. We surf the Net for our studies and log on to websites to express our opinions.
Posted 04/06/12 at 21.33 p.m.

e DrPsycho said: Koolpapi, your sons are part of 'Generation Now'. Although they don't look very different from previous generations, they certainly are. Today's teens have grown up with the Net and, for them, the virtual world is as important as the real world. They are digital natives and you are a digital immigrant. Talk to your sons about what they do online and get online yourself! Go digital, too!
Posted 04/06/12 at 22.12 p.m.

Your Choice

14 ACROSS GENERATIONS

(2.31)

Barbara (born 1935)

I was born before World War II and politics has always been important in my life. My grandfather died in the war in 1943. My aunt spent years in a communist prison in the 1950s. In the 1970s and 1980s my family fought for democracy in my country.

My granddaughter, Maria, has always lived in a democratic country. She has grown up with shops full of nice things and has never seen a queue longer than ten people, except outside a club! We have been very close since she was born in 1989 – she is a great girl, she helps me a lot and she has taught me to use the internet.

Maria (born 1989)

My granny has had an amazing life. She's like living history: she's seen three political systems, a world war and a revolution. Since 1989, she has worked for the government.

She is not really into music or fashion – she's never had fashionable clothes. She has always been interested in technology – she has had a computer for years, she surfs the internet and emails her friends.

My granny has been my best friend for my whole life. I never argue with her. She tells me incredible stories from the past and I tell her things that I never tell my parents.

Warm Up

1 **How much do you know about your parents' and grandparents' youth? Think about the things below:**

home
job
hobbies
free time

My grandparents lived in the country. They had a very small piece of land and they were very poor. My parents ...

2 **Read the profiles and answer the questions.**

1 What is the relationship between Barbara and Maria?
2 Which part of the world are they from?
  a North America b Eastern Europe
  c South America
  How did you know?
3 What do Barbara and Maria like about each other?

3 **Is it easier for young people to have a good relationship with their grandparents than with their parents? Why/Why not?**

Present Perfect (3)

4 **Read the sentences (1–2) from the text. Underline the correct words in the rule below. Find three more examples of this use of the Present Perfect in the text.**

1 *She **has** always **been** interested in technology.*
2 *My granny **has had** a computer for years.*

• We use the Present Perfect to talk about situations that started in the past and *are still going on/are no longer true*, with verbs like *be, have, like, love, know* and adverbs like *always, never, all my life*.

Practice

5 Translate the sentences (1–2) from the text into your language. Then match them with the correct context (a–b).

1 *My granny **has** always **been** my best friend.*
a We became friends when I was a teenager.
b She was my friend when I was a child, a teenager and she's my friend now.

2 *She **has** never **had** fashionable clothes.*
a She didn't dress fashionably as a young woman but she does now.
b She didn't have fashionable clothes when she was young and she doesn't have any now.

➥ LANGUAGE CHOICE 25

6 Complete the sentences about Barbara and Maria with the verbs in the Present Perfect and *always* or *never*.

1 Barbara *has always been* interested in politics. (be)
2 Barbara _____ into fashion. (be)
3 Barbara _____ her own business. (have)
4 Barbara and Maria _____ friends. (be)
5 Maria _____ in a democratic country. (live)
6 Maria _____ her grandmother. (love)

7 Look at the Sentence Builder and complete the rules below with *for* and *since*.

> **Sentence Builder** *for/since*
>
> **Since 1989,** she has worked for the government.
> She has worked for the government **for over twenty years**.

- We use _____ to refer to a period of time, *e.g. two years, a week, my whole life.*
- We use _____ to refer to a starting point, *e.g. 2004, yesterday, I was born.*

➥ LANGUAGE CHOICE 26

8 Work in pairs. Use the cues, the Present Perfect and *for* or *since* to make dialogues.

A: *How long have Barbara and Maria been best friends?*
B: *They have been best friends since Maria was a child.*

1 Barbara and Maria are best friends / Maria was a child
2 Barbara has a computer / years
3 you have a computer / last week
4 your dad works abroad / two years
5 you live in the countryside / 2003
6 your sister has a dog / six months

Grammar Alive Looking back

9 **2.32** Listen to three dialogues between Maria and her family. How long:

a has Maria's mother had a black jacket?
b has Maria's grandmother had a gold necklace?
c has Maria known Adam?

10 Work in pairs. Use the cues and the Present Perfect to respond to the sentences.

1 I love your dress!
(Oh, I / have it / for years)

A: *I love your dress!*
B: *Oh, I've had it for years.*

2 So your grandfather lives in Croatia …
(Yes, he / live there / all his life)
3 Do you like spinach?
(No, I / hate it / always)
4 Oh, you have a dog!
(Yes, I / have him / since I was ten)
5 Is Mike your good friend?
(Yes, I / know him / for ages)
6 How was your physics test?
(Well, I / be a science genius / never)

11 Use the cues below to make true sentences about yourself. Use the Present Perfect and a time expression: *always, never, for* or *since.*

I've known my best friend since I was three.

know my best friend	be in this classroom
be interested in ….	love/hate rap
live in my flat/house	have a bike
have short/long hair	

12 Quiz Work in pairs. Student A look at page 114 and Student B look at page 128. Ask and answer questions.

B: *How long has Albert Einstein been dead?*
A: *Albert Einstein has been dead since 1955.*
B: *So he's been dead for over fifty years.*

DVD Choice

Warm Up

1 Vocabulary Work in pairs. Look at the network. Which things do you disagree or argue about with your parents?

We sometimes argue when I forget to tidy my room.

make
too much noise

forget to
lay the table, take the rubbish out, tidy my room, do my homework, do the shopping

spend too long
in the bathroom, on the computer, watching TV

Arguments

leave
my bedroom, the living room, the kitchen **in a mess**

get
bad marks at school, a punishment at school

want to
come back home late, go out with friends, have a party, have more pocket money

➡ LANGUAGE CHOICE 27: VOCABULARY PRACTICE

2 Which of the things below are useful/not useful when you are having a discussion or argument with your parents?

a speak quietly
b get angry
c give people time to speak
d leave the room
e think before talking
f interrupt people
g give reasons for your opinions/suggestions
h find a quiet place
i make positive suggestions/ offer to do things
j be patient
k speak loudly or shout

Listening

3 2.33 2.34 Listen to a psychologist. She is speaking about talking to parents. Check your answers from Exercise 2.

4 2.35 2.36 Listen again and answer the questions.

1 What is normal for parents and teenagers?
2 Why is it bad to get angry?
3 When is a bad time to talk?
4 Where is a good place to talk?
5 How can you prepare before you talk to your parents about something important?

5 How useful were the psychologist's suggestions in your opinion? What positive suggestions can you make?

6 Look at the photos (a–c) from a BBC comedy programme. Guess the answers to the questions.

1 Where are the people? What is the relationship between them?
2 What activities is the boy doing at the same time?
3 What are the boy and the man talking about? Are they having an argument?

7 DVD 5 Watch the DVD first without sound and then with sound. Check your guesses from Exercise 6.

8 DVD 5 Watch the DVD again. Are the sentences true (T) or false (F)?

1 Today was Jake's last day at school. *F*
2 Jake answers all his father's questions.
3 Jake is doing his homework about the holidays.
4 Jake's dad can multitask.

Watching and Speaking

9 (2.37) (DVD 6) **Look at the photos (1-2) above and listen to or watch the dialogues. Answer the questions.**

1 What do they argue about (dialogue 1)?
2 What do they agree on (dialogue 2)?

10 (2.38) (DVD 6) **Listen to or watch the second dialogue again. Which expressions in bold in the Talk Builder:**

a express opinions?   b agree?   *1*
c disagree?   d ask for opinions?

Talk Builder Giving opinions

1 **I agree with you** about that.
2 **Personally, I think** 11.30 is a better better time.
3 **What do you think?**
4 **I'm sorry, I don't agree with you.**
5 **In my opinion**, 11.30 is very late.
6 **I don't think** it's late.
7 **You're right**.
8 **Do you think** 11.15 would be okay?
9 **I really think** it's a bit unfair.
10 **I disagree** with that.

→ SKILLS BUILDER 44

---

11 (2.39) *Pronunciation* **Listen to the opinions and repeat them.**

12 **Work in pairs. Complete the sentences. Then take turns to say the sentences and agree or disagree. Use expressions from the Talk Builder.**

A: *I think twelve o'clock is a good time to come home.*
B: *I agree with you about that.*

1 I think _____ o'clock is a good time to come home.
2 In my opinion, _____ hour(s) of TV a day is enough.
3 Personally, I think _____ (pounds/euros etc.) pocket money a week is okay.
4 _____ hours a week on the internet is enough.
5 _____ in teenagers' bedrooms are okay. (computers/TVs/DVD players)

---

13 **Work in pairs. Choose three of the options (a-f) to talk about.**

a times to come home
b jobs to do at home
c time on the computer/internet/watching TV
d pocket money
e things in your bedroom
f money for mobile phone

A: *Do you think five euros pocket money a week is okay?*
B: *I don't think that's very good. In my opinion ...*

Your Choice

No Comment

'My daughter thinks I'm nosy – at least that's what she wrote in her diary.'

Jenny Abrams

Language Review Modules 4 and 5

1 Stories/Families **Complete the texts with the correct words.**

A Agatha Christie wrote lots of [1]*detective/cowboy* stories. There are murders in her books but also a lot of humour – I think they are really [2]*funny/sad*. Some of her stories [3]_____ place in exotic locations, like Egypt. Most of them are [4]_____ a Belgian detective Hercules Poirot. She has written lots of [5]best _____ .

B I get on really [6]_____ with my parents. We have the same [7]_____ in fashion. Just like me, my mother doesn't like dyed [8]_____ and tattoos. My dad can't [9]_____ piercings and [10]_____ with hoods.   /10

2 Adjectives and prepositions **Complete the sentences with the correct prepositions.**

I'm not afraid [11]____ teachers but I'm often worried [12]____ exams.
I'm interested [13]____ computers but I'm really bad [14]____ playing video games.
I'm quite relaxed [15]____ the test results because I'm good [16]____ writing essays.   /6

3 Multi-part verbs (1)/Compounds **Complete the dialogue with the correct words.**

A: I'd like to go on holiday.
B: Go to Dubrovnik. They have an excellent tourist [17]web____ . I've [18]____loaded some hotel addresses. I can email them to you.
A: My [19]lap___ is broken so I'm [20]____line at the moment. How do you get [21]____ Dubrovnik?
B: You can take a train and go straight [22]___ Dubrovnik. A friend of mine could pick you [23]____ at the station. When do you want to come [24]____ ?   /8

4 Past Simple and Continuous **Complete the text with the correct tenses.**

I [25]_____ (walk) in the forest when I [26]_____ (see) a little cottage. An old woman [27]_____ (sit) in front of it. She [28]_____ (ask) me to sit down and [29]_____ (go) inside to get something to drink. I [30]_____ (rest) under a tree when I [31]_____ (see) her again – she [32]_____ (run) towards me with a big knife in her hand. I [33]_____ (start) running away. She [34]_____ (touch) my back when … I woke up from this horrible dream!   /10

5 Present Perfect and Past Simple **Complete the dialogue with the correct tenses.**

A: You [35]_____ (do) a lot of interesting things in your life.
B: Oh, yes. I [36]_____ (be) to all continents. Two years ago I [37]_____ (sail) across the Atlantic.
A: Is there anything you [38]_____ (not do) yet?
B: I [39]_____ (never have) a family. But I [40]_____ (fall) in love last year and I hope to get married soon.   /6

6 *for/since* **Complete the sentences with the time expressions in brackets and *for* or *since*.**

41 My family has lived in the country _____ . (years)
42 There has been a sauna in our house _____ . (last year)
43 We've had a pet _____ . (I was ten)
44 My grandparents have been married _____ . (fifty years)
45 My sister has been in love _____ . (Saturday)   /5

7 Opinions **Complete the dialogue with the expressions below. There is one extra expression.**

In my opinion   Anyway   What do you think
Personally   I agree with you   I'm sorry, I don't agree

A: [46]_____ , teenagers get on much better with their grandparents than with their parents. [47]_____ ?
B: [48]_____ . I get on very well with my parents, too. [49]_____ , I think that if you are nice, your parents are nice to you, too.
C: [50]_____ . My parents are always angry with me, even if I'm nice.   /5

Self Assessment

2.40 **Listen and check your answers. Write down the scores. Use the table to find practice exercises.**

Exercise	If you need practice, go to
1	Language Choice 18, 23
2	Language Choice 20
3	Language Choice 21, 24
4	Language Choice 19
5	Language Choice 22
6	Language Choice 26
7	SB p.42

6 MUSIC

Objectives: **Listen**, **read** and **talk about** music; **write** a letter to a magazine;
learn more about have *to/not have to*, *can/can't*, *may*, *must* and *must not*.

TOPIC TALK

1 3.1 **Look at the photos (a–c) and listen to the music. Which music do you think the people in the photos are listening or dancing to?**

2 3.2 **Look at the network. Listen to the music again and classify the styles of music.**

1 punk

3 3.3 3.4 **Listen to someone talking about music. Complete the information in the network.**

Music

¹ *I'm really into*/*I'm not really into* music.
I just love listening to ² _____ .
I can't stand ³ _____ .
⁴ *I'm crazy about*/*I'm not crazy about*
Kaiser Chiefs.
⁵ *I've got*/*I haven't got* a good singing voice.
⁶ *I can play*/*I'd like to play* the ⁷ _____ .

Styles
blues, country and
western, heavy metal,
hip hop, rap, jazz, pop,
punk, reggae, rock,
soul, techno
- -
chill-out, classical,
dance, folk, indie,
new age, world **music**

Instruments
bagpipes, cello, clarinet, drums,
keyboard, flute, guitar, harp, piano,
saxophone, trumpet, violin

4 3.5 **Pronunciation Listen to words from the network and underline the main stress.**

instrument

LANGUAGE CHOICE 28:
VOCABULARY PRACTICE

5 **Work in groups. Use the network to talk about *your* interests in music.**

45

GRAMMAR
MY BAND

a The Spice Girls

b Metallica

c U2

Warm Up

1 Look at the photos (a-c). Do you know any of these bands? Do you know how they started?

2 Read the text below. Which tips (a-e) does the expert give for starting a band?

a Play many different styles of music.
b Don't worry if you can't play an instrument.
c Play songs of famous bands.
d Practise a lot.
e Enter a TV competition.

3 Would you or your friends like to form a band? Which of the expert's tips do you think are the most useful?

Teenagestuff.com

starting a band 3.6

How do you start a band?
First, you have to find some other people who want to play music. They don't have to know how to play instruments. You can learn together. Lots of famous bands have done it this way. Then choose your kind of music (e.g. rock or punk). You don't have to play one style only but it's helpful at the beginning.

Where do we get the music?
You can write the music yourself. And you have to find a good lyrics writer, too. Write a few songs and try them out. But think of other people's music, too. Most new bands play other people's music before they can write their own.

How much do we need to practise?
A lot! And you have to find a good place. You can use someone's garage or ask your parents – maybe they don't mind the noise? Practise as often as you can but remember – you have to go to school, too!

How can we start performing?
You can enter a TV competition but then you have to queue for auditions, you can't play your own music and you have to put on make-up … So I think it's better to play your songs at a school dance or at a friend's birthday party first.

have to/not have to, can/can't

4 Read the sentences (1-4) from the text. Write the modals in bold in the table next to their meanings (a-d).

1 You **have to** go to school.
2 You **don't have to** play only one style.
3 You **can** write the music yourself.
4 You **can't** play your own music.

1 ___can___ = a It's possible/allowed.
2 _____ = b It's not possible/not allowed.
3 _____ = c It's necessary.
4 _____ = d It's not necessary.

Practice

➤ LANGUAGE CHOICE 29

5 Complete the sentences with the correct form of *have to, not have to, can* or *can't*.

The life of a dancer is not easy. They ¹_have to_ practise a lot. My friend Ivan is a dancer and he often ²_____ perform every day. He ³_____ be really fit so he ⁴_____ do exercise, like yoga or swimming. Dancers ⁵_____ be quite slim so they ⁶_____ eat everything, they ⁷_____ be on a diet all the time. Also, they ⁸_____ eat just before the show – the last meal ⁹_____ be at least two hours earlier. But they ¹⁰_____ get up very early because training usually starts at twelve o'clock.

➤ LANGUAGE CHOICE 30

6 Use the cues to write sentences with *have to, not have to, can* or *can't*.

1 I can't go out now.
   I have to practise the new song.
   (practise the new song)
2 You don't have to play solo.
   (play with the band)
3 We can play our own music.
   (copy other bands' music)
4 You don't have to play an instrument.
   (learn with your band)
5 The concert is free.
   (buy a ticket)
6 Guitars are really expensive.
   (buy a new one every year)

7 Work in pairs. Use the cues and your own ideas to describe the life of rock musicians. Use *have to, not have to, can* or *can't*.

Rock musicians don't have to get up early.

go on tours   write music   play an instrument
sign autographs   wear smart clothes   get up early
study at a music academy   grow long hair
write their own lyrics

Grammar Alive Complaining

8 **3.7** Listen to two conversations. Match the people (1-4) with the things they have to do tonight (a-d).

1 Jane   a write an essay
2 Kevin   b practise playing an instrument
3 Tom   c work on a project
4 Martha   d revise for a test

9 Decide which of the things below a music student (M) and a sports student (S) have to do.

- [M] learn to read music
- [ ] run 5 kilometres every day
- [ ] give concerts for the family
- [ ] wear a suit at concerts
- [ ] carry heavy equipment
- [ ] practise outside in winter
- [ ] carry a guitar around
- [ ] play matches in the rain
- [ ] be on a special diet
- [ ] practise the guitar for three hours a day

10 Work in pairs. Student A is a music student and Student B is a sports student. Use the ideas from Exercise 9 and *have to* and *not have to* to make dialogues.

A: *I have to practise the guitar for three hours a day.*
B: *But you don't have to run 5 kilometres every day.*

11 Use the cues and *can, can't* and *have to* to make dialogues.

A: *I've got a headache.*
B: *Why don't you go for a walk?*
A: *I can't. I have to go to my guitar lesson.*

1 headache – go for a walk – go to guitar lesson
2 sleepy – get some sleep – listen to a concert on the radio
3 no money – find a weekend job – play concerts at weekends
4 hungry – have a sandwich – go to a dance class in half an hour
5 bored – go out – read a book about Bach
6 tired – get some rest – find some old songs on the internet

12 Work in groups. Who is the best at complaining? Take turns to talk about the things you *have to* and *can't* do in life. You can invent information.

A: *I have to wash up every day and I have to help make dinner. And I can't go out at the weekend because I have to study.*
B: *That's nothing. I have to get up at five o'clock because I have to practise the violin before I leave for school.*

Warm Up

1 Your Culture **Work in pairs. Answer the questions.**

1 What music festivals are there in your country? Have you ever been to one? Would you like to go to one?

2 What bands would you like to see live?

Reading

2 **Read the article. Which of the festivals:**

a is in a capital city? *Sziget*
b is not near a river?
c has a big dance tent?
d has fewer foreigners?
e is usually very hot?
f is quite similar to a British festival?

3 **Read the article again. Choose the best answers to the questions.**

1 What is the author of the article trying to do?
a review the music of the festivals
(b) recommend the three festivals
c give travel information about them
d describe his/her experiences

2 What is better about the festivals than those in the UK?
a the small number of big groups
b the variety of the music
c the organisation and facilities
d the weather and the price

3 Why is FIB a good place to go?
a the number of young Brits there
b the music, beach and weather
c the organisation and the beach parties
d You can party all day.

4 Why does the author recommend EXIT?
a the great party atmosphere
b the number of stages
c It is on the River Danube.
d There is a social theme.

5 What is special about Sziget?
a It has got a big variety of music.
b It is a very big festival.
c It is great for culture in general.
d It has a lot of foreigners.

4 **Which of the festivals would you like to go to? Tell the class and give reasons.**

ROCK on the Continent 3.8

Tired of the rain and mud, high prices and queues at the big British rock festivals like Reading or Glastonbury? Want to combine a festival with some sun and fun abroad? Tim Hughes checks out three of Europe's biggest and best festivals.

1 FIB: the hot, sandy one

Where: In Benicàssim on the Mediterranean Coast between Barcelona and Valencia.

When: 16-19 July

What music: A big variety of pop, indie rock and electronic music. You can find big names like Oasis, Franz Ferdinand and Leonard Cohen.

Who goes: More than half the audience are foreigners and most of these are Brits in their twenties.

FIB (Festival Internacional de Benicàssim) started in 1995 and has got larger every year. The music goes on until 8.00 in the morning so you can party all night and then chill out on the beach. It's VERY hot but is definitely worth going to. It's like a big UK festival on a beach with nice weather.

2 EXIT: the big party one

Where: In a historic fortress on the Danube in Novi Sad in northern Serbia.

When: 9-12 August

What music: Some big names like The Prodigy and Moby. Twenty-five stages with everything from rock to reggae and from blues to chill-out.

Who goes: Most people are local but more foreigners come every year.

EXIT was started by three university students in 2000. Every year there's a social theme (this year it's the environment). We recommend the fantastic atmosphere, the dance arena for 20,000 people and the parties on the banks of the Danube. Watch the sun come up in the morning - it looks amazing.

3 Sziget: the city one

Where: An island in the Danube in the beautiful city of Budapest in Hungary.

When: 12-17 August

What music: Forty different stages with lots of variety and some great world music. Big names include Lily Allen and Snow Patrol.

Who goes: Over 400,000 people (half of them from outside Hungary) but it never feels crowded.

Sziget (island in Hungarian) started in 1993 and is now one of Europe's biggest festivals. It is more than just a music festival – it's got art, film and street theatre. The organisation is great and Budapest, with its historic sights and nightlife, is a fifteen-minute bus ride from the island. We recommend the huge dance tent – the music there sounds great.

5 Look at the Sentence Builder. How do you say the sentences in your language?

> **Sentence Builder** Verbs + adjectives
> 1 The music there **sounds great**.
> 2 It **looks amazing**.
> 3 It never **feels crowded**.

➜ LANGUAGE CHOICE 31

6 Work in pairs. Ask and answer the questions.

1 What new albums do you think sound good?
2 What kind of music sounds good at parties?
3 How do you feel when you listen to music?
4 What singers do you think look cool?

Listening

7 **3.9** **3.10** ➜ SKILLS BUILDER 4 **Listen to Sarah's answers (1-5) and match them with the questions (a-f). There is one extra question.**

a Where do you get music from?
b What's your favourite song?
c When do you listen to music? *1*
d How often do you go to concerts?
e What sort of music do you like?
f Do you like dancing?

8 Vocabulary **Look at the Word Builder. When do you do these things?**

I turn the volume up when a song I like comes on the radio.

> **Word Builder** Multi-part verbs (2)
> 1 When I listen to rap, **I turn the volume up**.
> 2 **I turn down** the radio when my parents get angry.
> 3 **I turn on** my MP3 player when I'm studying.
> 4 **I turn off** my MP3 player when I'm at school.

➜ LANGUAGE CHOICE 32: VOCABULARY PRACTICE

9 Choose five of the options (a-h). Write questions.

How many hours a day do you listen to music?

a listening habits
b spending on music
c music sharing
d favourite bands/singers

e reasons for listening
f favourite styles
g favourite song
h concerts and festivals

10 Work in groups. Ask and answer your questions. Tell the class your results.

Your Choice

GRAMMAR

18 MUSIC RULES

KINGSTOWN 3.11
CLASSICAL MUSIC SCHOOL
– RULES AND REGULATIONS

🎼 Students must attend all classes. They may be late only twice during the term.

🎼 All students must take part in a choir or an orchestra. Rehearsals and concerts are compulsory and students must not come late or leave early. During concerts students must wear black trousers/long skirts and white shirts.

🎼 Students may wear their own clothes but they must be clean and tidy. Bright colours are not allowed. Short sleeves are allowed but students must not wear shorts.

🎼 Hair must be clean and tidy. Boys' hair must be above the collar. Girls may have long hair but they must tie it back. Students must not dye their hair. Girls may wear make-up during concerts.

Warm Up

1 Look at the photo. What type of school does it show? What are the people doing?

2 Read the rules for Kingston Classical Music School. Can the students:

a come late to classes?
b wear jeans at concerts?
c have long hair?

3 Which rules are the same and which are different in your school? Which do you find strange?

may, must and *must not*

4 Read the formal rules (1–3) from the text and match them with the meanings (a–c).

1 Students **must** attend all classes.
2 Students **may** wear their own clothes.
3 Students **must not** wear shorts.

a It's possible/allowed.
b It's necessary.
c It's not possible/allowed.

5 Find more rules in the text and finish each sentence with two examples of students' activities.

1 It is possible for girls to _____ .
2 It is not possible for boys to _____ .
3 It is necessary for all students to _____ .

↘ LANGUAGE CHOICE 33

6 Complete these language school rules with *may*, *must* and *must not*.

1 Course books are compulsory. Students _must_ bring course books to every lesson.
2 The school is noise-free. Students _____ play music during the breaks.
3 Students _____ use mobile phones during lessons. However, they _____ use mobile phones during breaks.
4 Students _____ come to school on their bikes but they _____ leave them in front of the school. Students _____ bring the bikes into the school building.
5 Eating and drinking is only allowed in the cafeteria. Students _____ eat or drink during lessons.

7 Make up the rules and regulations for your own music club. Use *may*, *must* and *must not*. Do not be too serious!

Visitors may wear anything but they must not wear black.

Writing Workshop 3

1 Read the album reviews (a-c). What adjectives are used to describe the things below?

album/record - disappointing/repetitive

album/record   song/track   singer   voice   singing   lyrics

a Some of the songs are exciting and the lyrics on a couple of the songs are interesting. However, I am afraid the singer is not very talented and does not have a very strong voice and the guitar playing is repetitive and boring.

b Some of the lyrics are quite imaginative and are about real life. However, the singing is poor and this album is very disappointing. The keyboard playing and the drums are terrible!

c There is one catchy track but most of the songs are boring because of the weak lyrics and singing. This album is repetitive and similar to their earlier records. The guitar playing is very disappointing, too.

2 Read the letter from a reader to a magazine. Which of the reviews (a-c) in Exercise 1 is she writing about?

Dear Editor,

1 I am writing about last Friday's review of the new Dead Canaries album. Although I am a regular reader of your magazine, I found this article very disappointing.

2 The reviewer thinks that the record is not very original and is just like their previous albums. According to the review, there is one good song but the rest are not very exciting and the singing, guitar and lyrics are poor.

3 I am sorry but I totally disagree with the reviewer. I think that Ricky is a talented singer and the lyrics are interesting because they are about real life for young people in Britain now. In my opinion, there are some great, catchy songs like *Hello Friday*.

4 In conclusion, I think the review is very unfair.

Yours faithfully,

Claire Ramsey

Text Builder

3 Read the letter again. Match the paragraphs (1-4) with the headings (a-d).

a conclusion *4*
b reasons for disagreeing
c reason for writing
d the reviewer's opinions

4 Find formal expressions in blue in the letter with these meanings (1-8).

1 All the best, *Yours faithfully*
2 For me, it was a really bad article.
3 Hi there.
4 I want to tell you about …
5 The review says …
6 Anyway, …
7 I think …
8 The reviewer's wrong!

5 Write a letter to a magazine in reply to a review about your favourite album.

→ SKILLS BUILDER 29

1 Choose one of the reviews (a-c) in Exercise 1. Imagine it is about your favourite album. Write notes with your opinions.

the singing is poor - NO! - Jack Johnson = fantastic singer

2 Use your notes to write a letter to a music magazine. Write four paragraphs.

3 Check your letter for spelling mistakes.

6 Work in pairs. Read your partner's letter. Do you agree with him/her about the album? Tell the class.

I agree with Tom about the singing but I don't agree with him about the lyrics. I don't think they are very interesting.

51

Speaking Workshop 3

The O2 Arena

Green Day in concert: ¹ 9 April at ² _____ p.m.

Tickets: from ³ £ _____ to £55.

Tickets available from:

Website: www.theO2.co.uk http://www.theO2.co.uk/

Box office: Tel: ⁴ _____ (twenty-four hours a day & ⁵ _____ days a week)

Transport: bus, underground (Jubilee Line) and boats (⁶ £ _____ return from central London).

Restaurants and cafés: ⁷ _____ food, hotdogs, pizzas, sandwiches and ⁸ _____ and chips.

1 🔊 **3.12** **3.13** Look at the photo and the advertisement from the O2 Arena in London. Listen and complete the information (1-8).

2 🔊 **3.14** Pronunciation Listen to the sentences (1-5) from the phone conversation. <u>Underline</u> the unstressed words that are difficult to hear.

1 It's on Saturday, <u>the</u> ninth <u>of</u> April <u>at</u> 7 p.m.
2 And how much are tickets?
3 And how can I get to the O2 Arena?
4 There are buses twenty-four hours a day.
5 There are lots of cafés and restaurants at the Arena.

3 🔊 **3.15** Listen again and repeat the sentences.

4 🔊 **3.16** **3.17** Listen to a conversation about a concert. Which short replies (a or b) do you hear?

Talk Builder Agreeing and disagreeing		
	Agree	Disagree
1 I'm into Slipknot.	a Me too.	b I'm not.
2 I really like Kaiser Chiefs.	a Me too.	b I don't.
3 I'm not a heavy metal person.	a Me neither.	b I am.
4 I don't like Kaiser Chiefs' latest record.	a Me neither.	b I do.

➡ SKILLS BUILDER 45

5 Write replies to these statements with *your* opinions. Use expressions from Exercise 4.

1 I'm not into punk.
2 I really like heavy metal.
3 I like loud music.
4 I'm really into rap.
5 I really hate folk music.
6 I don't think Beyoncé is very good.

6 Work in pairs. Say things about music and agree or disagree with them.

A: *I hate heavy metal.*
B: *I don't. I like it.*

7 Have a discussion about music.

➡ SKILLS BUILDER 44 AND 45

1 Write notes about these things.
 a your favourite music styles / why you like them
 b your favourite singers / why you like them

2 ➡ SKILLS BUILDER 46 Practise saying the expressions. Read the strategies for discussions.

3 Work in groups. One person says something and the others agree or disagree. Give reasons.

A: *I'm really into world music. It's different from ordinary pop music.*
B: *Me too. I think it's great.*
C: *I don't! I don't think it's very exciting. All those strange instruments.*

8 What did you agree about? Tell the class.

We agree that world music is interesting.

LEARNING LINKS: 1 Listen to a song in **Culture Choice 3** on page 106. Then do a project about a song from your country.
52   **2 Check Your Progress 6** → MyLab / Workbook page 53. Complete the **Module Diary**.
     3 Exam Choice 3 → MyLab / Workbook pages 54-56.

Objectives: **Listen**, **read** and **talk about** health; **have** a doctor's appointment; **write** instructions; **learn more about** future tenses.

TOPIC TALK

1 Look at the photos of Katy and Tom from age progression software. In which photos do they look older: b or c? Why do you think they look older?

2 3.18 3.19 Listen to three people (1-3). Match them with the descriptions (a-c).

a very healthy b quite healthy
c very unhealthy

3 3.20 3.21 Listen again to the first person. Complete the information in the network.

Katy (18)

Katy (50, non-smoker)

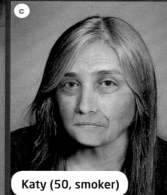
Katy (50, smoker)

Health

I've been to hospital ¹ (twice) / three times.
² I've had/I've never had a bad illness or accident.
I sometimes ³ ____ .
I occasionally ⁴ ____ .
I need to ⁵ ____ .
I really need to ⁶ ____ .

have a cold, cough, headache, sore throat, temperature
have diarrhoea, earache, flu, hayfever, stomachache, toothache
feel depressed, faint, sick, tired, weak

do **more** exercise, eat **more** fruit/vegetables, sleep **more**
eat **less** junk food/chocolate, stop smoking, sunbathe **less**, watch **less** TV

4 3.22 Pronunciation Listen and repeat the difficult words. Notice the differences between the spelling and the sounds.

→ LANGUAGE CHOICE 34: VOCABULARY PRACTICE

5 Work in groups. Use the network to talk about *your* health.

Tom (18)

Tom (50)

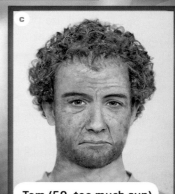
Tom (50, too much sun)

SKIN MATTERS

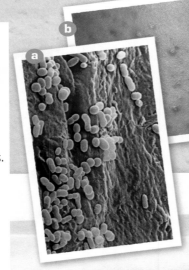

Warm Up

1 Match the statements (1-5) with the photos (a-e). Which one do you think is false?

1 People with fair skin have a greater risk of skin cancer. *e*
2 Our skin has billions of microbes.
3 We lose 4 kilograms of skin every year.
4 Bad food (like chocolate) causes spots.
5 Tattoos damage your skin.

Reading

2 Read the magazine page quickly and match the letters (1-4) with the replies (a-d). Check your guesses from Exercise 1.

1 b

DEAR DOC

This week, dermatologist Dr Jane Henderson answers readers' questions.

1 Dear Doc,
I'm worried because I'm pale and I've got dry skin. What can I do to look healthier?
Emily, 18

3 Dear Doc,
I've got fair skin but I like sunbathing. How can I protect my skin?
Daniel, 17

2 Dear Doc,
I've got oily skin and spots. I wash my face several times a day but it doesn't help. My mum says I have them because I eat junk food.
Al, 16

4 Dear Doc,
I've had a tattoo on my leg since I was seventeen. At first, I thought it was great but now I hate it. How can I get rid of it?
Jenny, 23

» a First, don't wash your face so often. Your skin has millions of microbes and washing destroys 'good bacteria'. Wash your face twice a day with warm water. Second, don't touch your face with your hands and wash them before and after meals. Finally, the best solution is to use special creams. Stress and a bad diet are not good for skin but the real reason for spots is hormones.

» b Maybe you are naturally pale like your parents or perhaps you aren't getting enough sunshine and Vitamin D. Spend more time outside. Exercise is good for healthy skin, too. For dry skin, use special soap. Showers actually dry out your skin so remove dry skin with a brush (we lose 4 kilograms a year!). Then, put on moisturising cream.

» c Our skin is our body's biggest organ but we often don't look after it. Tattooing permanently damages your skin. Removal creams don't really work and laser treatment hurts you a lot and leaves a mark. Next time, 'think before you ink!'

» d People with fair skin must be very careful with the sun because they have a bigger risk of skin cancer. There are lots of things you can do. First, always avoid burning. Second, stay in the shade in the middle of the day. Third, always use a high factor sun cream (50+) and put it on regularly throughout the day. Finally, always wear a sun hat and sunglasses.

3 ➡ SKILLS BUILDER 16 **Use the strategies to choose the best answer to the questions.**

1 What is bad for dry skin?
  (a) showers b exercise c soap d moisturising cream
2 What is bad advice for avoiding skin cancer?
  a cover your skin b put on sun cream once a day
  c stay out of the sun when it is strong
  d wear a hat in the sun
3 What is good advice for spots?
  a wash your face every hour b eat junk food
  c wash your hands every day d put special cream on them
4 What causes spots?
  a a bad diet b hormones c washing d stress
5 What is the doctor's advice about tattoos?
  a have laser treatment to eliminate them
  b use creams c be sure you really want one
  d never have a tattoo

4 **Work in pairs. Which of the advice is the most useful for you?**

5 Vocabulary **Look at the pairs of words in the Word Builder. How do you say the words in bold in your language? Are they confusing for you? Why?**

> **Word Builder** Confusing words
> 1 *use/wear*
>   **Use** a high factor sun cream. / **Wear** a sun hat.
> 2 *actually/now*
>   Showers **actually** dry out skin. / **Now** I hate it.
> 3 *food/meal*
>   I eat junk **food.** / Wash after **meals.**
> 4 *damage/hurt*
>   Tattooing **damages** your skin. / It **hurts** you a lot.
> 5 *great/big*
>   I thought it was **great.** / It leaves a **big** mark.

➤ LANGUAGE CHOICE 35: VOCABULARY PRACTICE

6 **Choose the correct word to complete the sentences.**

1 In the past, not many people had tattoos.
  Actually/Now, lots of people have them.
2 That's not Simon's pen. *Actually/Now* it's mine.
3 I have problems with my hair so I *use/wear* special shampoo and *use/wear* a hat in the summer.
4 That tattoo's really *big/great*! It's really artistic but it is a bit *big/great*.
5 I love Chinese *meals/food*. We had a great *meal/food* in that new restaurant last week.
6 The sun *damages/hurts* the skin and sunburn *damages/hurts* a lot.

Writing

7 ➡ SKILLS BUILDER 30 **Look at the linkers in blue in the text. Which of these (a, b or c) do they do?**

a give reasons for things b order or list things
c compare things

8 **Match the pictures (a–c) with the instructions (1–3). Then use linking words from the text to order the instructions.**

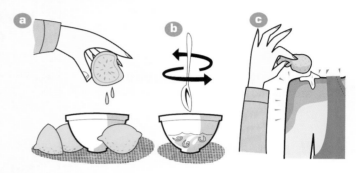

Lemon juice remedy for sunburn

1 Put it on the sunburn with a sponge.
2 Squeeze three lemons to get the juice.
3 Mix it with two cups of cold water.

First, squeeze three lemons …

9 **Work in pairs. Read two remedies for dandruff. Student A look at page 114. Student B look at page 128. Ask and answer questions.**

A: *What do you do first?*
B: *First, squeeze …*

10 **Choose one of the problems (a–f) and think of a remedy for it (real or invented). Use ideas and language from Exercises 8 and 9.**

a spots   d dry skin
b oily skin e dandruff
c sunburn   f a cold

11 **Work in pairs. Ask and answer questions about your remedies.**

Your Choice

20 GRAMMAR HEALTH THREATS

a antibiotics

Warm Up

1 Look at the photos (a-d). How do these things affect our health?

2 Read the interview with a health expert. What are the future health problems?

3 Which of the threats do you think are the most serious? Which can we avoid?

will, may and *be going to*

4 Read the predictions (1-3) from the text and <u>underline</u> the verb forms that refer to the future. Then match them to the uses (a-c).

1 *Bugs love high temperatures so they are going to spread faster than ever.*
2 *I'm sure more allergies will develop.*
3 *Tropical diseases may move into colder regions.*

---

a We express our opinions and beliefs about the future (often with words like *I think, I'm sure, maybe/perhaps/probably/definitely*).
b We make uncertain predictions or guess.
c We make predictions based on evidence in the present situation.

---

5 Find more examples of each form in the text.

b pollution

Future Health (3.23)

What will be the main threats to our health in the 21st century?

The climate is getting warmer and bugs love high temperatures so they are going to spread faster than ever. For example, tropical diseases, like malaria, may move into colder regions. Also, I'm certain that new diseases will appear, like Bird Flu (H5N1) and Swine Flu (H1N1). And there may be another global threat like AIDS soon.

But we have vaccines and drugs ...

The problem is that we have over-used antibiotics in the last fifty years. Many diseases, like tuberculosis, have become resistant to our drugs so it is going to be really difficult to treat infectious diseases. And vaccines may not work because bugs change quickly. Flu is a good example of that.

Does pollution create any health threats?

Oh, yes. Pollution causes allergies and serious problems like asthma. And I'm sure more allergies will develop because pollution won't disappear in the near future.

What problems does our lifestyle cause?

Well, I think the most serious threat is obesity. Twenty percent of British kids are obese and because of that, they are going to have all sorts of health problems, such as diabetes.

c obesity

Is there any good news?

Oh, yes. Today, we live thirty years longer than a hundred years ago and I'm sure modern medicine will help us live even longer.

d germs

56

Practice

↘ LANGUAGE CHOICE 36

6 Use the expressions in brackets to write predictions for these situations.

1 Mary has toothache.
(not come to the party tonight / may)

She may not come to the party tonight

2 Mark is very pale and has stomachache.
(be sick / going to)
3 Peter has got a cold.
(sure / be okay next week / will)
4 Carol has broken her leg.
(need an operation / may)
5 Alex reads a lot about medicine.
(be a doctor / going to)
6 Tess has got a bad cold.
(have to take antibiotics / will)

7 Choose the correct verb forms to complete the sentences.

1 Maybe scientists *will* /*may* find a cure for AIDS soon.
2 Who knows? In ten years, cancer *may/is going to* be easy to cure.
3 Stop eating! You *are going to/may* put on weight.
4 Infectious diseases *may not/won't* disappear. There's no chance of that.
5 You sit in front of the computer all day – you *are going to/may* have problems with your eyes.
6 I'm sure doctors *may/will* use antibiotics carefully in the future.

↘ LANGUAGE CHOICE 37

8 Look at the pictures (1–4). Make predictions for each situation using the correct forms of *will*, *may* and *be going to*.

Grammar Alive Predicting

9 **3.24** Listen to two dialogues. What are the people (1–3) doing? What predictions do these people make?

1 Amy   2 Luis   3 Sylvia

10 Work in pairs. Use the cues to describe the situation. Predict the future with *be going to*.

A: *There are dark clouds and strong wind.*
B: *It's going to rain.*

A starts	B answers
1 dark clouds, strong wind	1 rain
2 Mary / very pale, cold hands	2 faint
3 Mr Brown / old, pneumonia	3 go to hospital
4 car / going too fast	4 crash

B starts	A answers
5 Steve / stomachache, looks pale	5 be sick
6 Lisa / lying in the sun	6 get sunburnt
7 Chris / not do any exercise	7 put on weight
8 stars in the sky	8 weather be nice

11 **3.25** Listen to the dialogue. Complete the speakers' predictions with *will*, *won't* or *may* and the correct verbs below.

look for   ~~close~~   win   be   cancel (x2)

1 The authorities _may close_ the school because of the flu.
2 There _____ many students in class.
3 The teacher _____ the test today.
4 The school authorities _____ the football game on Saturday.
5 The school football team _____ the game on Saturday.
6 A person from Arsenal _____ young players on Saturday.

12 Make predictions about your life in five years' time. Use the cues or your own ideas and *will*, *won't* or *may*.

I won't be famous but I may have a career as a footballer.

study   have a job   be married
have a car   live on my own   travel a lot
work abroad   wear suits   have children
have my own flat   be famous

LESSON 21 SKILLS EMERGENCY

Warm Up

1 **Vocabulary** Work in pairs. Look at the network. Have you or has someone you know ever had an accident? Use the words to tell your partner.

Once, I had an accident in a football game. I broke my leg …

Accidents: break an arm/leg/finger, have a broken leg, be unconscious

Procedures: have an injection, an X-ray, an operation, stitches

Emergencies

Symptoms: have breathing problems, vomiting, diarrhoea, be bleeding, my arm/leg hurts

Medicine: take painkillers, pills, tablets

➤ LANGUAGE CHOICE 38: VOCABULARY PRACTICE

Listening

2 **3.26 3.27** Listen to an interview about emergency services in Britain. Choose the best answer to the questions.

1 What numbers do you need to ring for an emergency?
   a 999/112   b 999/121   c 999/212
2 How many students learn about first aid at school?
   a none   b a few   c a lot
3 How do people use the emergency services badly?
   a They don't phone.   b They phone too late.
   c They make silly calls.

3 **3.28 3.29** Listen again. Are the sentences true (T) or false (F)?

1 A man called an ambulance because he had a sore throat. *T*
2 A woman called the fire brigade because her child was in a tree.
3 A man called the police because he didn't want tomatoes on his pizza.
4 Silly emergency calls are not a problem for the emergency services.
5 Chest pains, bad bleeding and broken bones are real emergencies.
6 British people need to learn more about first aid.

4 **Your Culture** Ask and answer the questions in Exercise 2 about your country.

5 DVD 7 Look at the photos (a–c). Then watch a documentary without sound. Try to guess what happened in the emergency.

6 DVD 7 Watch, listen and check your guesses.

7 DVD 7 Watch the DVD again. Are the sentences true (T) or false (F)?

1 The purpose of the documentary is to train doctors. *F*
2 Danny's situation is so serious because his leg is broken in different places.
3 When he gets to the hospital, he has an X-ray.
4 The operation is difficult because they have to amputate his leg.
5 He gets over the operation quite quickly because he is young.
6 After six months, Danny can run and do sport.

8 Have you ever been to hospital? What was it like?

Watching and Speaking

9 3.30 DVD 8 Listen to or watch the dialogue at the doctor's. What are the woman's symptoms? Would you like to go to this doctor? Why/Why not?

10 3.31 DVD 8 Listen or watch the dialogue again. Complete the expressions in the Talk Builder. <u>Underline</u> expressions for giving advice.

> **Talk Builder** At the doctor's
>
> A: So, what's the ¹_____ ?
> B: I've got a stomachache and I ²_____ a bit sick.
> A: Where does it ³_____ ?
> B: Here.
> A: ⁴_____ vomiting?
> B: Yes, I've ⁵_____ sick twice.
> A: What ⁶_____ diarrhoea?
> B: Yes, that too.
> A: How ⁷_____ have you had these symptoms?
> B: ⁸_____ yesterday afternoon.
> A: I'm ⁹_____ you've got a stomach infection. You should ¹⁰_____ plenty of water. You shouldn't drink ¹¹_____ or fizzy drinks. Take these pills ¹²_____ times a day.
>
> → SKILLS BUILDER 47

11 3.32 Pronunciation Listen and repeat the expressions.

12 Imagine you are going to the doctor. Choose symptoms and write notes about them.

I feel … I've got … I've had it for …

13 Work in pairs. Take turns to be a doctor and a patient. Act out situations.

A: What's the problem?
B: I've got a pain in my arm and feel a bit …

14 What treatment did your partner recommend? Was he/she a good doctor? Tell the class.

Your Choice

Language Review Modules 6 and 7

1 Music/Health **Complete the descriptions with the correct words.**

I'm not really into music: I can't play ¹_____ guitar, I ²_____ stand rap and heavy metal, I hate listening ³_____ pop. But I'm crazy ⁴_____ jazz – I ⁵_____ love the sound of the saxophone.

When you ⁶_____ weak, your eyes ⁷_____ and you are ⁸_____ pain, you probably ⁹_____ flu. You don't need to go ¹⁰_____ hospital. Just stay in bed. If you ¹¹_____ a headache, ¹²_____ a painkiller. Rest a lot and don't ¹³_____ any exercise. **/13**

2 Verbs and adjectives/Multi-part verbs/Confusing words **Choose the correct words to complete the dialogues.**

A: Can we turn ¹⁴on/off the TV? I'd like to watch a programme about cooking.
B: Cooking? It doesn't sound very ¹⁵interesting/interestingly.
A: ¹⁶Actually/Now, I've started cooking for myself. I don't eat junk ¹⁷meals/food anymore and I feel really great.
B: Okay, let's stop talking and turn the volume ¹⁸up/down.

A: Your hair looks ¹⁹fantastic/fantastically and it feels ²⁰soft/softly.
B: I wash my hair in egg yolks and lemon juice. Shampoos ²¹damage/hurt your hair.
A: That's a ²²big/great idea. And quite cheap, too.
B: Come on, I was just joking. But try lemon juice and don't ²³use/wear hats all the time. **/10**

3 have to/not have to, can/can't **Complete the text with the correct modals.**

I am a medical student and I work very hard. I ²⁴_____ attend classes at the hospital every day and I ²⁵_____ miss more than a few days every term. I ²⁶_____ take some time off at the weekend because I ²⁷_____ go to university on Saturday and Sunday. But I ²⁸_____ study medical books all the time. In summer, I ²⁹_____ go away on holiday because I ³⁰_____ work in the hospital. **/7**

4 may, must, must not **Complete the hospital rules with the correct modal verbs.**

31 Patients _____ smoke. Smoking is not allowed in the hospital building.
32 Patients _____ follow doctors' orders.
33 Patients _____ buy papers and cosmetics in the hospital shop.
34 Visitors _____ wash their hands before entering the hospital.
35 Visitors _____ see patients between 3 p.m. and 8 p.m. The hospital is closed to visitors until 3 p.m. **/5**

5 Predictions **Choose the correct expressions to complete the sentences.**

36 He's got a stomachache but he won't/may perform in tonight's concert.
37 The clouds are dark – it it is going to/will rain.
38 He's got a cough – it's not serious but he will/may go to hospital.
39 She's pregnant – she may/is going to have a baby in June.
40 Our band is very good – I'm sure we will/may win the competition. **/5**

6 Agreeing/Disagreeing **Complete the dialogues.**

A: I love jazz. → (agree) **B:** Me ⁴¹_____ .
A: I'm really into Sugababes. → (disagree) **B:** I ⁴²_____ .
A: I don't really like hip hop. → (agree) **B:** Me ⁴³_____ .
A: I don't enjoy big concerts. → (disagree) **B:** I ⁴⁴_____ . **/4**

7 At the doctor's **Complete the dialogue with the correct words (one gap=one word).**

Doctor: So, what's the ⁴⁵_____ ?
Patient: Well, I ⁴⁶_____ tired all the time and I've got a stomachache.
Doctor: Where does it ⁴⁷_____ ?
Patient: Here.
Doctor: I'd like to ⁴⁸_____ your temperature.

★ ★ ★

Doctor: You've got flu. You ⁴⁹_____ stay in bed for two days. Take these pills three ⁵⁰_____ a day. **/6**

Self Assessment

3.33 **Listen and check your answers. Write down the scores. Use the table to find practice exercises.**

Exercise	If you need practice, go to
1	Language Choice 28 and 34
2	Language Choice 31, 32 and 35, p.55
3	Language Choice 29 and 30
4	Language Choice 33
5	Language Choice 36 and 37
6	SB p.52, ex. 5
7	SB p.59 ex.9

LEARNING LINKS: 1 Check Your Progress 7 → MyLab / Workbook page 63. Complete the **Module Diary**.
2 Sound Choice 4 → MyLab / Workbook page 64. Choose three pronunciation activities to do.

60

8 NATURE

Objectives: Listen, **read** and **talk about** nature; **write** a formal email; **make** suggestions and arrangements; **learn about** conditionals, time clauses and *all, most, many, some, no/none*.

TOPIC TALK

1 Look at the photos (a–c). What other endangered animals do you know about in the world and your country?

2 3.34 3.35 Listen to a radio interview. Complete the factfile.

🌍 THE PLANET
Nature in London

Green space/water (% of area): ¹ <u>66</u> %
Number of private gardens: ² _____ million
Number of bird species: ³ _____
Number of fish species: ⁴ _____
Days with dangerous air pollution: ⁵ _____

3 3.36 Pronunciation Listen and write down the numbers. Then listen again and repeat them.

4 3.37 3.38 Listen again to the interview. Complete the network.

Environment

In our area, there are lots of ¹ <u>green spaces</u> .
You can see interesting varieties of ² ____ .
My favourite animals are ³ ____ .
My least favourite animals are ⁴ ____ .
Our climate is ⁵*definitely*/*probably* changing.
The biggest environmental problems are ⁶ ____ and ⁷ ____ .

Places
gardens, green spaces, lakes, nature reserves, parks, rivers, woods

Wildlife
birds, mammals, reptiles, insects

Animals
alligators, bats, bears, bees, deer, foxes, hippos, jellyfish, monkeys, mosquitoes, rats, scorpions, sharks, spiders, snakes, toads, wolves, worms

Problems air/water pollution, climate change, habitat loss, noise, over-fishing, hunting, traffic

➤ LANGUAGE CHOICE 39: VOCABULARY PRACTICE

5 Your Culture Work in groups. Use the network to talk about *your* environment.

a black crested macaque

b Eurasian lynx

c great white shark

SPECIES AT WAR

TOAD INVASION

(3.39)

In 1935, Australian farmers brought cane toads from Hawaii to protect their sugar cane from beetles. Unfortunately, the toads did not eliminate the beetles and there are now more than 200 million cane toads in Australia. This has become one of Australia's worst environmental disasters.

The toads' skin is poisonous. 'Lizards, birds and snakes eat cane toads and then often die,' explains Dr Ben Phillips, of Sydney University. 'Some species may soon disappear, if we don't get rid of the toads.'

Recently, scientists have discovered a worm that attacks toads' lungs and kills them. They are planning to use the worm to fight the cane toad. But they are cautious: 'Before we use it, we will do more research.'

First, the scientists will need to answer some important questions. 'What will happen when we put this worm into the Australian environment?' asks team leader Professor Rick Shine. 'If the worm only kills the cane toads, it will be good news. But if it attacks other animals, it will destroy species we want to protect.'

At the same time, nature has found a solution. In the last 70 years, the heads of two species of snakes have become smaller. 'Snakes with small heads eat smaller toads and smaller toads are less poisonous. If natural selection works, in twenty years most snakes will have smaller heads. It's great that nature can solve its problems.' said Dr Phillips.

GREYBACK CANE BEETLE

c RED-BELLIED BLACK SNAKE

b CANE TOAD

Warm Up

1 Look at the photos (a–c). What do you think links these animals?

a People brought them to Australia.
b They are all dangerous to people.
c They eat each other.

2 Read the text and check your predictions from Exercise 1. Then answer the questions.

1 What problem do cane toads create in Australia?
2 What solution have people found to the problem and what solution has nature found?

3 Your Culture What do people do to save endangered animals in your country?

Future Conditional

4 Read the sentences (1–2) from the text and complete the rule.

1 Some species **may** soon **disappear, if** we **don't get** rid of the toads.
2 **If** it **attacks** other animals, it **will destroy** species we want to protect.

> **if** + _____ tense , **will/may** + infinitive
> (condition)   (consequence)

5 Find more sentences with the Future Conditional in the text. <u>Underline</u> the correct word in the rule below.

• We use the Future Conditional to talk about *possible/impossible* situations in the future.

Practice

6 Complete the conditional sentences with *will* and the correct forms of the verbs in brackets.

1 Cane toads _will eliminate_ (eliminate) a lot of species if their number _doesn't go_ (not go) down.
2 Great white sharks _____ (disappear) if over-fishing _____ (continue).
3 Sit still! The cat _____ (not come) to you if you _____ (not be) very quiet.
4 Animals in the Arctic _____ (be) in danger if the climate _____ (get) hotter.
5 You have to clean the aquarium. The fish _____ (get) ill if you _____ (not do) it regularly.

➡ LANGUAGE CHOICE 40

7 Use the cues to make sentences with the Future Conditional.

1 Australian animals – not adapt
➡ the cane toad – become the most common species in Australia

If Australian animals don't adapt, the cane toad will become the most common species in Australia.

2 we – use clean energy
➡ we – save the planet
3 the climate – hotter
➡ some birds – stop moving to colder regions in summer
4 farmers – use more chemicals
➡ many insects – die
5 people – not stop killing whales
➡ they – disappear

8 Look at the Sentence Builder with *before* and *when*. Do the verbs in **bold** talk about the present or the future?

> **Sentence Builder** Time clauses
>
> **Before** we **use** it, we will do more research.
> We will do more research **before** we **use** it.
> **When** we **find** a solution, we'll tell people.
> We will tell people **when** we **find** a solution.

9 Complete the sentences with *when* or *before* and the words in brackets.

1 Scientists won't use the worm _before they are certain that it is safe_. (they – certain that it is safe)
2 The zoo will buy an elephant ... . (they – have enough money)
3 Scientists will test the new drug on animals ... . (they – give it to people)
4 ... we will warn the neighbours. (we cut down the tree)
5 Ecologists will inform the media ... . (they – see any injured whales)

Grammar Alive Negotiating

10 **3.40** Listen to the conversation. What does Amy's mother want her to do? What will happen if she doesn't do it?

11 Work in pairs. Use the cues to make dialogues.

A: *Can you feed the dog?*
B: *I'll feed him when the game ends.*

A starts	**B** answers
1 feed the dog?	1 the game / end
2 repair my bike?	2 finish homework
3 iron this shirt?	3 find the iron
4 help me prepare for the test?	4 have some time
5 turn off the computer?	5 finish writing emails

B starts	**A** answers
6 tidy your room?	6 it / be really messy
7 clean the aquarium?	7 the fish complain
8 do homework?	8 everyone / go to sleep
9 do the washing up?	9 have nothing to do
10 lend me your mobile?	10 finish texting my friend

12 Work in pairs. Use the cues and take turns to make a chain of sentences with the Future Conditional.

A: *Will you help me with my maths homework?*
B: *I'll help you if you come to the cinema with me.*
A: *I'll come to the cinema with you if you lend me your new jacket.*

A: help me with maths ➡
B: go to the cinema with me ➡
A: you lend me your new jacket ➡
B: give back my CDs ➡
A: invite me to your birthday party ➡
B: bring something to eat ➡
A: help me prepare it ➡
B: buy the food ➡
A: come to the cinema with me ➡

No Comment

'The scientific name for an animal that doesn't either run from or fight its enemies is lunch.'

Michael Friedman, American philosopher

SKILLS
DEADLY ANIMALS

Warm Up

1 Which of the actions (1-6) do you think are the right things to do in the situation?

Reading

2 Read the article and check your guesses from Exercise 1.

3 Read the article again. Are the sentences true (T), false (F) or is no information given(?)?

1 Sharks sometimes attack people. *T*
2 Alligators are good runners.
3 Big cats sometimes get scared.
4 Female bears are very dangerous.
5 Bees are good swimmers.
6 Wild turkeys attack people.

A BEGINNER'S GUIDE TO

Dangerous Predators (4.1)

An Australian teacher, Jason Cull, was swimming in the sea last week when a great white shark bit his leg. 'I hit its eye,' said Cull, 'and then it let go.' However, most people don't know how to react to a hungry shark and you don't want to give a four-metre shark more reasons to dislike you. But what about other animals? What is the best thing to do if one attacks you?

When you meet an angry alligator, you should run away from it because alligators can't go very far on land. If it catches you, hit its eyes and nose. In 2006, Corey Workman of Florida did this and survived because he learnt the trick from Discovery Channel.

Never run away from a big cat like a puma. Stand there, look at it directly and try to look big. Open your coat or stand on a rock, show your teeth and make aggressive noises. Prepare to fight back with a stick or rocks. You must act like the more aggressive predator.

The general rule is: stay away from bears. They normally don't go near humans but if you come across a mother bear with cubs, she will probably attack you. Don't try to get away – bears can run fast and climb trees. Don't try to fight back. Some experts say you should 'play dead' but you have to be brave to do this!

4 Vocabulary **Look at the words in blue in the text. Match the verbs in bold in the Word Builder with the meanings (a-f).**

a don't go near   b escape   c go fast in the opposite direction
d move more slowly   e be aggressive, too   f meet by chance

> **Word Builder** Multi-part verbs (3)
> 1 You should **run away** (from it). *c*
> 2 Prepare to **fight back**.
> 3 **Stay away** from them.
> 4 If you **come across** a mother bear, …
> 5 Don't try to **get away**.
> 6 Try to **slow** them **down**.

→ LANGUAGE CHOICE 41: VOCABULARY PRACTICE

5 Work in pairs. Ask and answer questions about dangerous animals.

A: *What should you do when a shark attacks you?*
B: *You should fight back and hit its eye.*

You'll be pleased to hear that when killer bees attack you, you can run away. But don't hit them; it makes them angry. If you can't get indoors, run through bushes to slow them down. Don't jump into a river; the killer bees will just wait for you to surface.

Wild turkeys have recently caused problems in Boston in the USA. Groups of the 1.5 metre–tall turkeys run after joggers and schoolchildren. According to wildlife officials, you should fight back with an open umbrella. Don't be a victim. Be the dominant turkey!

Listening

6 **4.2** **4.3** Listen twice to a TV travel programme and complete the table.

TOP ten most dangerous animals

	Animal	Deaths
10	bears	
9		100
8		100+
7	hippos	
6		500+
5	alligators	
4		800+
3	scorpions	
2		50,000
1		

7 Vocabulary **4.4** **4.5** → SKILLS BUILDER 5 Listen again and use the strategies in the Skills Builder to guess the meanings of the words and expressions (1–8).

1 **creepy crawlies:** a deadly animals b poisonous animals c insects/spiders/snakes
2 **cute:** a friendly b pretty c lazy
3 **hind legs:** a large legs b front legs c back legs
4 **venom:** a bite b teeth c poison
5 **laid-back:** a dangerous b relaxed c beautiful
6 **bedding:** a under a bed b sheets and blankets c room to sleep in
7 **tiny:** a very big b very small c very dangerous
8 **long-sleeved:** a covering the head b covering arms c covering legs

8 Look at the Sentence Builder. What does *it* refer to in 1? Does *it* refer to anything in 2 and 3?

Sentence Builder *it*

1 At number seven is the hippo. **It** looks laid-back.
2 **It** is six o'clock and **it** is raining outside.
3 **It** is dangerous to go swimming.

→ LANGUAGE CHOICE 42

9 Use the cues to write sentences with *it*.

1 raining / very windy

It is raining and it is very windy.

2 dangerous / meet a mother bear
3 10 April 2012
4 difficult / learn a language
5 the elephant / dangerous / because / is / very big
6 dark / at five o'clock

10 Choose one of the options (a–c) below. Write notes about it.

a dangerous animals in your country / advice about them
b scary animals / why you are scared of them
c a nasty experience you have had with an animal / what happened

11 Work in groups. Tell your group your topic. Ask and answer questions.

A: *Why are centipedes dangerous?*
B: *Because they're poisonous. You should be careful when you have a picnic.*

Your Choice

No Comment

'Biologically speaking, if something bites you, it is probably female.'

Desmond Morris, British biologist

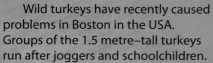

4.6

Bees are one of the most important species on our planet.

Of course, all species are important but none of them compares to bees. Who wants a world without honey, flowers and chocolate? Bees first appeared on Earth 150 million years ago and now there are 20,000 bee species around the world. They pollinate about 250,000 species of plants. Many of these plants, like apples and cotton, are very important to world agriculture. In addition, some important medicines come from plants.

But bees are not useful only for people. Many birds and small mammals eat plants that need bee pollination. If these animals die of hunger, their predators, the next animals in the food chain, will die, too.

Although there are other pollinating insects – like butterflies and wasps – none of these species is a true pollinating machine like bees.

Unfortunately, most bees are in danger at the moment. Modern farming has changed their habitat and many flowers have disappeared so bees do not have enough pollen to eat. Some bees are also killed by diseases.

Some people say that if bees disappear, then humans will only have four years to live. No bees means no pollination, no plants, no animals, no humans.

Warm Up

1 **Look at the photos. What do you know about bees?**

2 **Read the text. What have you learnt about bees? What other animals are useful to our planet? Why?**

all, most, many, some, no/none

3 **Read the sentences (1-5) from the text. Match them with the diagrams (a-e).**

1 *All* species are important. *d*
2 *Most* bees are in danger.
3 *Many* birds eat berries and seeds.
4 *Some* medicines come from plants.
5 *None of the* species is a true pollinating machine./*No* bees, *no* pollination, *no* plants, *no* animals, *no* man.

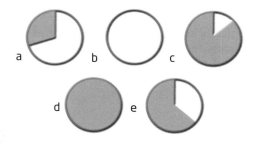

a   b   c

d   e

4 **Read the rules. Which of the nouns below do not go with *many*?**

- We use *all, most, some, no* and *none of the* with plural countable and uncountable nouns.
- We use *many* with plural nouns only.

animals   honey   bees   water   apples
chocolate   people   danger   insects

↘ LANGUAGE CHOICE 43 AND 44

5 **Look at the results of a class survey. Make sentences with *all, most, many, some,* or *none of the*.**

Some students are vegetarian.

10%	are vegetarian
85%	don't go to the zoo
100%	watch nature films on TV
15%	don't like playing with animals
0%	wear natural furs
60%	don't buy cosmetics tested on animals
70%	have a pet
0%	work for an animal charity

Writing Workshop 4

oxenboldnature@uk.co

Wild foods Collect, and cook plants and wild mushrooms, catch fish and animals.

Survival Make shelters and fires, collect water, cook wild food.

Wood crafts Cut down trees and make things from wood.

Wildlife watching Identify different species of plants, trees, animals and birds.

Three-day courses (May to September) for £300 (food included). Bring a tent.

1 Read the brochure about a nature school. What three questions would you ask to get more information about the courses?

2 Read the letter. Which of your questions from Exercise 1 does Bruce ask?

---

¹ Dear Sir/Madam,

² I am writing to ask for information about your wood-crafts course.

³ First, is it more difficult than the other courses? Do you need to have any previous experience? I am from London and do not know a lot about the countryside. Second, do I have to bring any equipment? Another question is about the groups. How many other students are there?

⁴ I have also got some practical questions. Does the price include all food? What kind of food is there? I am a vegetarian. The other thing is the journey from Exeter station to your centre. Is transport included in the price of the course?

⁵ I look forward to hearing from you.

Yours faithfully,

Bruce Newtown

---

3 → SKILLS BUILDER 17 **Find formal expressions in the text with these meanings (1–4).**

1 All the best. *Yours faithfully*
2 Write soon.
3 Hi there!
4 I want to know about the course.

4 Look at the Sentence Builder. Match the words in **bold** with the meanings (a–d).

a the second   b one more
c the rest of the   d different

> **Sentence Builder** *another/other*
>
> 1 **Another** question is about the groups.
> 2 **The other** thing is transport.
> 3 How many **other** students are there in them?
> 4 Is it more difficult than **the other** courses?
>
> → SKILLS BUILDER 31

5 Complete the sentences with *another, other* or *the other.*

1 Does your centre have any __other__ courses, for example about wild mushrooms?
2 Do I have to sleep in the tent or is there _____ place to stay?
3 You have two centres. What _____ courses do you have at _____ nature centre in Scotland?
4 Have you got _____ nature schools outside Britain?

6 Write a letter asking for information about one of the other courses at the nature school.

↘ SKILLS BUILDER 32

1 Read the brochure in Exercise 1 again. Write notes for the questions you want to ask.

2 Use your notes to write the letter. Follow the format of the letter in Exercise 2 and use the words in Exercise 4.

3 Check your letter for spelling, vocabulary and grammar.

7 Work in pairs. Give your letter to your partner. He/she asks you the questions in your letter.

A: *How many students are there in the classes?*

Speaking Workshop 4

1 ⬤ `4.7` `4.8` ➡ SKILLS BUILDER 6 **Listen to the dialogue. Use the strategies in the Skills Builder to identify the style (formal or informal). What is the relationship between the two people?**

2 `4.9` `4.10` **Listen again and answer the questions.**

1 Why don't they phone for help?
2 Where do they decide to build the shelter?
3 What wild food do they decide to look for?
4 How can they start a fire?
5 What do they decide to cook for dinner?
6 Why is Tim an expert on survival?

3 `4.11` Pronunciation **Listen to words from the dialogue. Mark the silent letters.**

answer   asthma   battery   comfortable
dangerous   different   environment   every
favourite   fire   interesting   poisonous   sure
tired   Wednesday

4 `4.12` **Listen and complete the suggestions (1-6) in the Talk Builder with the words below.**

can   about   should   Let's   Why

Talk Builder Suggestions and short questions

Suggestions	Short questions
1 **I think we should** phone someone.	a What?
2 **We** ____ carry on walking and stop later.	b How?
3 ____ make a shelter.	c Who?
4 **What** ____ over there?	d Where?
5 **We** ____ collect wild food, too.	e Why?
6 ____ **don't we** start a fire?	f When?

➡ SKILLS BUILDER 48

---

5 `4.13` **Match the suggestions (1-6) with the short questions (a-f). Then listen and check.**

6 **Work in pairs. Practise making suggestions and replying with questions**

A: *Let's do something this weekend.*
B: *What?*
A: *Why don't we go for a walk?*

1 do something this weekend (what?)
2 go for a walk (where?)
3 go tomorrow morning (what time?)
4 meet up somewhere (where?)
5 go for a coffee before the walk (why?)
6 meet some friends afterwards (who?)

7 **Arrange to do something with your partner this weekend.**

➡ SKILLS BUILDER 48

1 **Write notes with ideas about these things:**

• what to do
• where to go
• when/how to get there
• who to meet
• when to come back home.

2 **Practise saying suggestions to yourself.**

Let's go to the cinema this weekend.

3 **Work in pairs. Make, reject and accept suggestions.**

A: *What about going dancing?*
B: *Where? All the clubs are terrible. Let's watch a film.*
A: *What film? I think we should see that new James Bond.*
B: *Okay. Let's meet at …*

8 **What did you decide to do? Tell the class.**

LEARNING LINKS: **1** Read Herman Melville's story, *Moby Dick*, in **Culture Choice 4** on page 108. Then do a project about an animal from your country.
2 **Check Your Progress 8** → MyLab / Workbook page 71. Complete the **Module Diary**.
3 **Exam Choice 4** → MyLab / Workbook pages 72-74.

Objectives: **Listen**, **read** and **talk about** flying and transport; **ask for** information at airports; **learn more about** passives.

TOPIC TALK

1 Look at the photos (a-d). Which of the machines would you like to go in? Why?

2 4.14 4.15 Look at the network below. Listen to three people (a-c) and answer the questions.

1 How do they get to work or school?
2 How do they go on holiday?
3 Which of them hates flying on big planes?
4 Which of them is the least worried about the environment?

3 4.16 Pronunciation Listen and repeat the words and expressions. Notice the stress and the spellings.

➡ LANGUAGE CHOICE 45: VOCABULARY PRACTICE

4 Work in groups. Use the network to talk about *your* journeys.

b hot air balloon

a microlight

c superjumbo

d flying car

Journeys

I go to school *on foot*.
It takes me about *fifteen minutes*.
I'd like to go to school *by motorbike*.

We go on holiday by train.
I've never been on an aeroplane.

I love planes because they are *convenient*.

I hate buses because of the *queues*.

by bike, boat, bus, canoe, kayak, helicopter, train, car, moped, motorbike, plane/aeroplane, tram

on foot, horseback, rollerskates, the underground

cheap, convenient, quick, exciting

delays, crowds, expensive tickets, long journeys, queues, uncomfortable seats

69

SKILLS
PIONEERS

Warm Up

1 Look at the photos of the three women (a–c) in the website. Answer the questions.

1 Why do you think they were unusual?
2 What do you think happened to them?

Reading

2 Read the website. Check your answers to the questions in Exercise 1.

3 → SKILLS BUILDER 18 Use the strategies in the Skills Builder to match the sentences (a–f) with the gaps (1–5) in the text. There is one extra sentence.

a Since then she has become an American legend.
b Because of that, Bessie went to France and got her pilot's license there.
c Five years after that, in 1937, she tried to fly around the world but disappeared somewhere in the Pacific.
d She learnt to fly there and became an experienced pilot.
e After the war, she started flying and was the first woman to parachute from a plane.
f She didn't die but she was never the same.

4 Read about the three pilots again. Which of the women, Bessie Coleman (BC), Sophie Pearce (SP) and Amelia Earhart (AH), are the sentences about?

1 had a difficult childhood   *BC, AE*
2 took part in World War I
3 had problems learning to fly
4 made an important solo flight
5 became famous in her lifetime
6 survived a bad aeroplane accident

5 Vocabulary Look at the adjectives in the Word Builder. Find their opposites in blue in the text.

Word Builder Opposites

Adjective	Opposite	Adjective	Opposite
experienced	1 *inexperienced*	usual	6 _____
possible	2 _____	happy	7 _____
conventional	3 _____	accompanied	8 _____
reliable	4 _____	known	9 _____
lucky	5 _____		

→ LANGUAGE CHOICE 46: VOCABULARY PRACTICE

WOMEN IN HISTORY   4.1

HOME   ABOUT US   PILOTS   SITE MAP   CONTACT US

In the 1920s and 30s, there was an incredible generation of young women pilots. A group of adventurous and unconventional women were pioneers in the male world of flying. These brave women flew primitive, unreliable aeroplanes and a lot of them died young in accidents.

A

BESSIE COLEMAN (1892–1926)

5 Bessie was born into a very poor African American family. She wanted to take lessons at a flying school but it was impossible; none of them wanted her because of her colour. [1]_____ Back
10 home, Bessie did acrobatics at air shows to make money and planned to start a school for African American pilots. However, Bessie died before she could open it. In an unlucky accident, she fell hundreds of metres from her plane. Americans were horrified and thousands came to her funeral. [2]_____
15

LADY HEATH (SOPHIE PIERCE) (1897–1939)

B

Sophie was Irish but moved to England when she was a young girl. She was a motorbike messenger for the army there during World War 1
20 and in the 1920s became quite a successful athlete. [3]_____ In 1928, Sophie made the first ever solo flight from Britain to South Africa. For the trip, Sophie took some
25 unusual luggage with her: a gun, tennis rackets, evening dresses and a fur coat. Sophie became a celebrity but in 1929 she had a plane crash. [4]_____

6 Your Culture **Work in pairs. Ask and answer the questions.**

1 Which of the three women do you think was the most interesting?

2 Do you know any famous pilots from your country?

3 What other famous women from your country do you know about? What did they do?

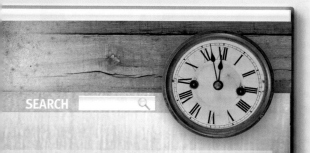

SEARCH

AMELIA EARHART (1897–1937)

Amelia Earhart was born in the USA in 1897 and had an unhappy
30 childhood. When she was twenty-three she went in an aeroplane for the first time and loved it. Immediately, she wanted to fly and in 1922 made her first
35 unaccompanied flight. Six years after that, Amelia became the first woman to fly across the Atlantic but she was quite inexperienced and did not pilot the plane alone. However, four years
40 later, she made another trip across the Atlantic, this time on her own and immediately became world-famous.
⁵ _____ The cause of Amelia's death is unknown but her plane probably ran
45 out of fuel and crashed into the sea.

C

Writing

7 → SKILLS BUILDER 33 **Read about reference words. What do the words (1–10) refer to in the website?**

1 *women aviators*

1 these brave women (line 3), 2 them (line 4), 3 it (line 7), 4 them (line 8), 5 her (line 9), 6 she (line 13), 7 it (line 13) 8 thousands (line 15), 9 there (line 19), 10 the trip (line 24), 11 that (line 36), 12 she (line 37),

8 **Read the information about the Wright Brothers. Replace the words in *italics* with the reference words below.**

that (x 2) they it there one their

1 *it*

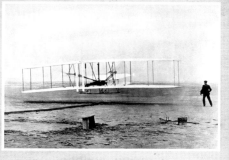

In 1878, Milton Wright gave his two sons, Wilbur and Orville, a toy helicopter. The boys loved playing with ¹ ***the helicopter*** and ² ***Wilbur and Orville*** soon began to make models. In 1892, the brothers started a bicycle workshop. ³ ***In their workshop***, they experimented with a model aeroplane. After ⁴ ***the experiment***, they tested real aeroplanes and built their first powered aeroplane, *Flyer I*. On 17 December 1903, Orville made the first powered flight of 36.5 metres in 12 seconds. After ⁵ ***the first flight***, they made a flight of 60 metres and a final ⁶ ***flight*** of 260 metres. In 1905, ⁷ ***Orville and Wilbur's*** third model, *Flyer III*, flew 39.4 kilometres.

9 **Work in pairs. Student A look at page 114 and Student B look at page 128. Choose four questions about the history of flight. Ask and answer your partner's questions.**

10 **How many questions did you get right? Tell the class.**

Your Choice

No Comment

'There are only two emotions in a plane: boredom and terror.'

Orson Welles, American film director

a **solar system**

planet

satellite

astronaut

spacecraft

b **spacewalk**

c **space junk**

science world

Space Junk (4.18)

In November 2008, a bag was lost in space by astronaut Heidemarie Stefanyshyn-Piper, during repairs outside the *International Space Station*. The incident was reported by the media all over the world.

In fact, this happens quite a lot. A glove was lost during the US astronauts' first spacewalk in 1965 and a camera disappeared in space during the *Gemini 10* mission in 1966. These objects in space are called space junk.

There is a lot of junk in our solar system. It is found on Venus and Mars and twenty tons of it have been left by Americans on the Moon since the first Moon landing! Since 1957, when the first satellite, *Sputnik*, was launched by the Soviet Union, more than 4000 satellites have been sent into orbit. So it isn't surprising that some rubbish has been left behind!

Space junk travels as fast as 36,000 kilometres per hour and is very dangerous for spacecraft and satellites. Space Shuttle windows are often damaged and have been replaced over eighty times so far!

A lot of work is needed to clean up the space junk. Who knows, 'space junk collector' may be an important job in the future!

Warm Up

1 Look at the photos (a-c) and answer the questions.

1. What do people use satellites for?
2. What planets in the solar system have people reached so far?
3. Why do astronauts go outside spacecraft?

2 Read the text. What is space junk? Is it dangerous?

3 Would you like to travel in space? Why/Why not?

The Passive

4 Look at the text again. Complete the sentences below with the correct form of the verb *be*. Name the tenses for a, b and c.

a _____ tense
*Many objects **were lost** during the spacewalk.*
*The incident _____ **reported** by the media.*

b _____ tense
*Space shuttle windows **are** often **damaged** by space junk.*
*A lot of work _____ **needed** to clean up the space junk.*

c _____ tense
*More than 4000 satellites **have been sent** into orbit.*
*Some rubbish _____ **left** behind!*

Practice

⇝ LANGUAGE CHOICE 47

5 Use the cues to write sentences in the Passive. Use the Present Simple, Past Simple or the Present Perfect.

1 The Hubble telescope / launched / in 1990

   The Hubble telescope was launched in 1990.

2 No life / discovered / on Mars / so far
3 The Moon landing in 1969 / watched / on TV all over the world
4 Different animals / regularly / sent / into space in spacecraft
5 No planet like Earth / found / so far
6 Different objects / often / lost / in space

6 Look at the Sentence Builder. What information do the phrases in **bold** give us?

> **Sentence Builder** *by* phrases
>
> 1 *Sputnik* was launched **by the Soviet Union.**
> 2 A lot of junk has been left **by Americans** on the Moon.

7 Complete the sentences (1–6) with the Passive forms of the verbs in brackets and add the correct phrases below.

by the USSR / by Leonardo da Vinci
by a piece of space junk / ~~by robots~~
by rings of rocks and ice / by American astronauts

1 The exploration of Mars _was carried out by robots_ . (carry out)
2 The first aeroplane _____ . (design)
3 An astronaut _____ (hit) during the spacewalk.
4 Saturn _____ . (surround)
5 Twenty tons of junk _____ (leave) on the Moon.
6 The first spaceship _____ . (launch)

⇝ LANGUAGE CHOICE 48

8 Complete the text with the verbs in the Passive. Use the Present Simple, Past Simple or the Present Perfect.

The Moon appeared over four billion years ago in a big collision. Its dry surface [1] _is covered_ (cover) by sand and rocks and [2]_____ (often hit) by meteoroids. During the day, it [3]_____ up (warm) to 117°C by the sun and at night the temperature falls to -169°C. In the 1950s and 1960's many spaceships [4]_____ (send) to the Moon. The first photographs of the far side of the Moon [5]_____ (take) in 1959. The first successful Moon landing [6]_____ (perform) in 1966 by the Soviet robot spaceship *Luna 2*. Since then, moon rocks [7]_____ (examine) by scientists from all over the world but no life [8]_____ (find).

Grammar Alive The news

9 4.19 Listen to the news item and answer the questions.

1 What did the astronauts lose during the last spacewalk?

   an expensive bag with tools

2 How many more spacewalks are they going to do on this mission?
3 What changes have been made on the *International Space Station*? Why?
4 Who/What can find the position of the bag?
5 What happens to objects in space when they enter the Earth's atmosphere?

10 Use the notes below to write a news item. Use correct tenses and the Passive where necessary.

The International Space Station *was hit by a piece of space junk last night.*

space station – hit by a piece of space junk – no astronaut hurt – some equipment damaged – only one signal received from the station since the accident – rescue mission sent from Earth

11 Imagine you are a journalist. Use the cues to make questions in the Passive about a space voyage.

1 How / food prepared?

   How is food prepared?

2 What / plates and spoons made of?
3 How / water obtained?
4 Where / oxygen stored?
5 How / illnesses treated?
6 Where / rubbish kept?
7 How / the space ship cleaned?

12 Work in pairs. Ask the questions from Exercise 11. Choose the correct answers (a–g).

A: *How is food prepared?*
B: *It is made on Earth.*

a It is thrown out into space.
b It is cleaned by robots.
c It is stored in tanks.
d They are made of plastic.
e It is made on Earth.
f The ship is equipped with medicines.
g A lot of it is recycled.

Warm Up

1 Vocabulary **Look at the airport plan. Answer the questions.**

1 Where do you have to go when you arrive at an airport to catch a flight?
2 What do you have to go through before you get to the departure lounge?
3 Where do you have to go first when you enter another country?

➙ LANGUAGE CHOICE 49 AND 50: VOCABULARY PRACTICE

Listening

2 4.20 4.21 **Listen to a documentary about Heathrow Airport in London. Are the sentences true (T) or false (F)?**

1 Heathrow has nearly seventy million passengers a year.
2 There are six passenger terminals.
3 A hundred and ninety airlines take off and land from Heathrow.
4 The airport is crowded because it is designed for fifty-five million passengers.
5 Airlines have short times to load and unload.
6 There are trains to London every five minutes.

DVD Choice

3 DVD 9 **Look at the photos (a–c) from a BBC documentary about Heathrow Airport in London. Guess which of the things below are mentioned. Then watch and check your guesses.**

a the number of passengers at Heathrow
b fines for airlines when flights leave late
c weight limits on baggage and cost of excess baggage
d animals in baggage

4 DVD 9 **Watch the documentary again and answer the questions.**

1 How many minutes late can a plane be without a fine?
   five minutes
2 What is the job of the duty officer of Qatar Airways?
3 What is the weight limit for hand baggage?
4 What do passengers usually do when they have excess baggage?
5 Does the flight finally leave on time? How do you think the duty officer feels?

5 **Have you ever had problems at an airport? What happened?**

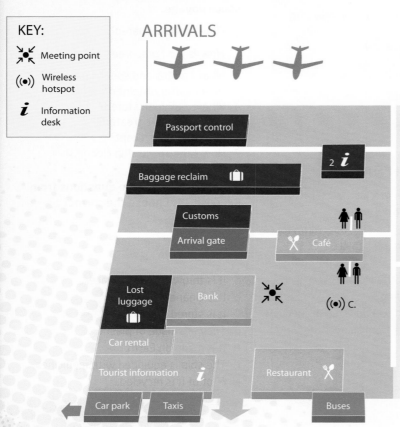

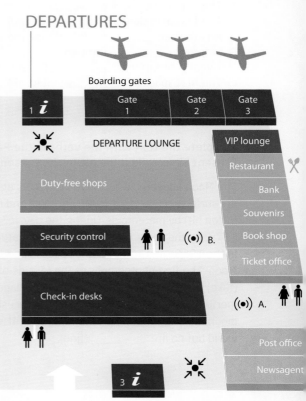

KEY:
⁕ Meeting point
((•)) Wireless hotspot
𝒊 Information desk

ARRIVALS

Passport control

Baggage reclaim 🧳

2 𝒊

Customs

Arrival gate

Café

Lost luggage 🧳

Bank

((•)) C.

Car rental

Tourist information 𝒊

Restaurant

Car park | Taxis | Buses

DEPARTURES

Boarding gates

1 𝒊

Gate 1 | Gate 2 | Gate 3

⁕ DEPARTURE LOUNGE

VIP lounge

Duty-free shops

Restaurant

Bank

Souvenirs

Security control ((•)) B.

Book shop

Ticket office

Check-in desks ((•)) A.

Post office

Newsagent

3 𝒊

8 `4.24` **Listen and match the questions and requests (1-7) with the replies (a-g) below.**

a Yes, of course. Here you are.
b Yes, I did.
c I'm sorry, I can't.
d Yes, certainly. Go through ... and turn right, go past the ... The ... is between the ... and the ... It's in front of the ...
e Just a moment.
f Aisle, please.
g Sure.

Talk Builder Airport situations

1 Good morning, sir. Could I have your passport and ticket, please?
2 Is that a window or aisle seat, Mr Macdonald?
3 Could you put your case here, please?
4 Could you help me with my case, please?
5 Could you pay the excess baggage at the ticket office?
6 Did you pack your case yourself, sir?
7 Could you tell me how to get to the nearest bank?

➔ SKILLS BUILDER 49

Watching and Speaking

6 `4.22` `DVD 10` **Listen to or watch the airport situation. Answer the questions.**

1 How many kilos over the limit is his suitcase?
   2 kilos
2 How much does he pay for excess baggage?
3 Where is the ticket office?
4 Where does he put the things from his suitcase?
5 Where and when does the flight start boarding?
6 What is the bank in front of?

7 `4.23` `DVD 10` ➔ SKILLS BUILDER 7 **Use the strategies in the Skills Builder to listen to or watch the dialogue again and find examples of formal style.**

9 `4.25` Pronunciation **Listen and repeat the polite requests and replies. Notice the intonation.**

10 `4.26` **Listen and choose the best reply to the phrases.**

1 a Give me a window seat. b Window, please.
   c I'd like a window.
2 a I can. b Not at all. c Sure.
3 a No, I didn't. b Of course I did. c Yes, I did.
4 a Here you are. b Here we are. c Here they are.
5 a Of course. b Not at all. c Right.

11 **Work in pairs. Look at the airport plan again. Ask for and give directions to these places from one of the information points:**

a café / a car park / a bookshop / tourist information / a bank / the arrival gate

12 **Work in pairs. Choose three of the situations (a-d) and act them out.**

a check in (no excess baggage)
b check in (passenger with excess baggage)
c an information desk (ask for buses)
d an information desk (ask for British Airways check in)

Your Choice

Language Review Modules 8 and 9

1 Environment/Journeys/Airports **Complete the texts with the correct words.**

In my city, there are a lot of green ¹_____ so we have some wild animals. But my favourite wild animals are polar ²_____ . Unfortunately, they are threatened by ³_____ change. I'm also interested in bees, the most useful ⁴_____ of insects in the world. I don't like ⁵_____ , like snakes and crocodiles.

Last summer I was coming home from Spain ⁶____ plane. All the planes were delayed because ⁷_____ a storm. It ⁸_____ us an hour to go through passport ⁹_____ . The departure ¹⁰_____ was so crowded that we had to stand. Then, we had to go to the plane ¹¹____ foot. The whole journey was a disaster. I was so happy when I finally saw my dad at the arrival ¹²_____ .

/12

2 Multi-part verbs/Opposites **Complete the gaps with the correct multi-part verbs or the opposites of the words in brackets.**

A: Is this new anti-insect spray ¹³_____ (unreliable)?
B: The best thing is always to stay ¹⁴_____ from insects. It is ¹⁵_____ (possible) to protect people against all of them. But this spray is quite ¹⁶_____ (usual) – it works on mosquitoes and flies.
A: And what about bees?
B: When you come ¹⁷_____ a bees' nest, don't touch it. If you are ¹⁸_____ (lucky) and get bitten, put some ice on the bite. There are some ¹⁹_____ (conventional) remedies, like raw onion, but their true effects are ²⁰_____ (known). */8*

3 Future Conditional and time clauses **Complete the sentences with the correct forms of the verbs in brackets.**

21 If I _____ (not get) the plane ticket, I _____ (go) by train.
22 He _____ (buy) some books in the airport shop before he_____ (get) on the plane.
23 If we _____ (not find) a cheap hotel, we _____ (stay) at the campsite.
24 I _____ (call) you when we _____ (land).
25 They _____ (inform) us if the departure time _____ (change). */5*

4 The Passive **Use the cues to write sentences with the Passive.**

26 A unique spider / discover / in Central America
27 I / bite / my neighbour's dog / last week
28 Coffee / produce / in South America and Africa
29 The theory of evolution / develop / Darwin
30 Snakes / threaten / cane toads / in Australia */5*

5 *all, most, many, some, no/none, another/other* **Choose the correct words to complete the text.**

I hate planes. I always choose ³¹*some/another* means of transport, if I can. Last summer, I was flying to New York. ³²*All/Most* passengers looked relaxed but the two people next to me were really nervous. One was an elderly woman and ³³*another/the other* was a young man. The woman chatted to ³⁴*none/most* people around her but the man ignored ³⁵*some/the other* passengers. He took ³⁶*other/some* medicine but ³⁷*most/none* of it helped him relax. When we landed, ³⁸*some/most* police cars drove up to the plane and the man was arrested. ³⁹*All/Many* the passengers had to wait until they took him away and ⁴⁰*none/most* of us were informed what was going on. */10*

6 Suggestions/Airport situations **Complete the dialogue with the correct words.**

Officer: Good morning. Could I ⁴¹_____ your passport, please?
John: Of course, here you are.
Officer: Window or ⁴²_____ seat?
John: Window, please.
Officer: I'm afraid your baggage is ⁴³_____ the limit, sir. You'll have to pay ⁴⁴_____ baggage.
Amy: John, why ⁴⁵_____ you take out some of the books?
John: Okay.
Officer: Here is your ⁴⁶_____ pass, ⁴⁷_____ . Have a good flight!
John: And where are the gates?
Officer: Go ⁴⁸_____ the pharmacy and you'll see the gates ⁴⁹_____ the restaurant and the newsagent's. I think you ⁵⁰_____ go there right now. It's quite late. */10*

Self Assessment

4.27 Listen and check your answers. Write down the scores. Use the table to find practice exercises.

Exercise	If you need practice, go to
1	Language Choice 39, 45, 49, 50
2	Language Choice 41, 46
3	Language Choice 40, SB lesson 22 ex 8
4	Language Choice 47, 48
5	Language Choice 43, 44

LEARNING LINKS: 1 Check Your Progress 9 → MyLab / Workbook page 81. Complete the **Module Diary**.
2 Sound Choice 5 → MyLab / Workbook page 82. Choose three pronunciation activities to do.

Objectives: Listen, read and **talk about** islands and holidays; **write** a postcard and **ask for** and **give** information; **learn more about** conditionals and articles.

TOPIC TALK

1 **Match the photos (a–c) with the places (1-3). Which of the places would you like to visit? Why?**

   1 The Pacific 2 The Adriatic 3 Scotland

2 4.28 4.29 **Listen to three people talking about holidays. Where do they usually go – Majorca, Elba or Ireland? Which of the islands in the photos are their dream destinations?**

3 4.30 4.31 **Listen again to the first person. Complete the information in the network.**

Holidays

I usually go on holiday ¹ *to the coast* . _____

I go ² _____ . _____

We stay ³ _____ . _____

I often ⁴ _____ . _____

My dream is to go to Mull because it's got ⁵ _____ . _____

> abroad, **to the** coast, country, mountains
> **with** my family, friends, the school

> **at** a campsite, **in** an apartment/hotel, **with** family

> **beautiful** beaches, coral reefs, forests, hot springs, lagoons, mountains, rivers, sea, streams
> **old** castles, churches, villages
> **a** cool, sunny, tropical **climate**

> **go** bird-watching, cycling, diving, hiking, kayaking, sailing, sightseeing, snorkelling, sunbathing, surfing, wind-surfing

4 4.32 Pronunciation **Listen and repeat the words and expressions from the network. Notice the ending (-ing) and the unstressed words.**

➤ LANGUAGE CHOICE 51: VOCABULARY PRACTICE

5 **Work in groups. Use the network to talk about *your* holidays and *your* dream destination.**

DESERT ISLAND

Warm Up

1 Look at the advertisement. Would you like to take part in this reality show? Why/Why not?

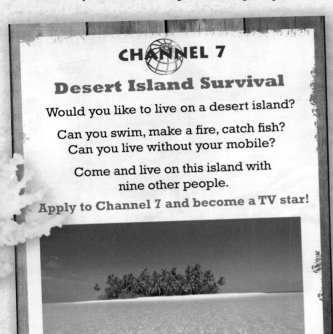

CHANNEL 7

Desert Island Survival

Would you like to live on a desert island?

Can you swim, make a fire, catch fish?
Can you live without your mobile?

Come and live on this island with
nine other people.

Apply to Channel 7 and become a TV star!

2 **4.33** Colin wants to take part in the reality show. Read and listen to the interview. Tick (✓) the things he can do on the application form.

APPLICATION FORM

Name: Colin Jones

Age: nineteen

Occupation: student

I can:

make a fire ☐

make a shelter ☐

catch fish ☐

cook ☐

collect fresh water ☐

INTERVIEW

Interviewer: Hi, Colin. So, you are nineteen, you're a student and you don't work.

Colin: That's right! If I had a job, I wouldn't have time to watch lots of reality shows.

I: Oh, I see. Okay. We'd like to ask you a few questions. In our programme, a group of young people spend three months on a desert island.

C: Sounds great!

I: Well ... You won't have MP3 players, mobiles, books or ... food! So, first question: How would you get fresh water?

C: Erm ... I suppose I'd find a stream.

I: Imagine there is no stream!

C: Oh, I don't know ... erm ... If there wasn't a stream, I would drink sea water.

I: Sea water ... hmm. And what about food?

C: If there were trees, I'd look for fruit. And if there was no forest, I could catch fish and cook it on the fire. My granddad taught me to catch fish.

I: How would you make the fire if you didn't have any matches?

C: No problem! I'd use dry wood. If I wasn't a boy scout I wouldn't know how to make a fire. I've been a scout since I was ten, you see.

I: Right. And do you know how to make a shelter?

C: No, not really. But I wouldn't need any shelter if I was on a tropical island! It's nice and warm there, isn't it?

I: Thank you, Colin. We'll get in touch with you.

3 Do you think Colin is a good candidate for the desert island reality show? Why/Why not?

Unreal Conditional

4 Read the sentence and answer the questions.

If I wasn't a boy scout, I wouldn't know how to make a fire.

1 Is Colin a boy scout?
2 Does Colin know how to make a fire?

5 Look at the pattern and find similar sentences in the text.

if + Past Simple tense, (condition)	*would/could* + infinitive (result)

6 Look at the conditions in sentences (1-2) and match them with the situations (a-b).

1 *If I wasn't a boy scout, I wouldn't know how to make a fire.*
2 *I would drink sea water if there wasn't a stream.*

a an imaginary situation about the **future**
b a **present** situation which is not true

Practice

↘ LANGUAGE CHOICE 52

7 **Look at the picture. Which sentences (1–4) could the boy say?**

1 If I didn't have these exams, I would go on holiday.
2 If I was a student, I would have to study a lot.
3 If I had a laptop, I could find information on the internet.
4 If I took my laptop to the island, I could study on the beach.

8 **Imagine you and your friends are going on the reality show. Match conditions (1–6) and results (a–f) to make sentences with the Unreal Conditional.**

If we didn't have fresh water, we would collect rain water.

1 not have fresh water — a catch fish
2 meet a dangerous animal — b eat only fruit
3 not have food — c collect rain water
4 not have matches — d send smoke signals
5 see a plane — e run away
6 not know about poisonous fish — f make a fire with my glasses

9 **Imagine these situations (1–5) on a desert island. What would you do? Make two sentences about each situation.**

1 There is a storm.

If there was a storm, I would hide under a tree.
If there was a storm, I would collect rain water.

2 You lose all your tools (knife, etc.).
3 Someone breaks their leg.
4 You have no clothes.
5 You find some treasure.

Grammar Alive Dreaming

10 **4.34** **Listen to the conversation between participants in a desert island reality show. Match the people (1–3) with the statements (a–c).**

1 Colin   a can cook
2 Julia   b tries to change someone's habits
3 Dave   c loves meat

11 **Work in pairs. Use the cues to make dialogues.**

A: *Would you like to go to a desert island?*
B: *Yes, if I went to a desert island, I'd get a nice sun tan.*

A starts | **B answers**
1 go to a desert island | 1 get a nice sun tan
2 do an island survival course | 2 learn how to make a shelter
3 learn to dive | 3 see a coral reef
4 have a yacht | 4 go on a sailing holiday

B starts | **A answers**
5 be a pirate | 5 be rich and free
6 sail around the world | 6 become famous
7 take part in a 'desert island' reality show | 7 learn some survival tricks
8 work on a ship | 8 travel all over the world

12 **What dreams do you have? Think about your life (school, home, family, town, etc.) and write conditional sentences explaining your dreams.**

I would like to live in Scotland. If I lived in Scotland, I could eat seafood all the time.

No Comment

'Man can live about forty days without food, about three days without water, about eight minutes without air but only one second without hope.'

Hal Lindsey, American writer

SKILLS
PARADISE?

Warm Up

1 Look at the online travel guide to the Maldives in the Indian Ocean. Guess the answers to the questions.

1 What do you think the climate is like?
2 Why is it probably a good place for a holiday?
3 What activities is it probably good for?

Reading

2 Read the travel guide and check your guesses from Exercise 1.

3 Read the travel information again. Match the headings (a-g) with the paragraphs (1-6). There is one extra heading.

a Things to do   5
b How to get there
c Islands in the Maldives
d A paradise destination
e The people
f Places to stay
g Geography

4 Vocabulary ➔ SKILLS BUILDER 19
Use the strategies in the Skills Builder to work out the meanings of the words in blue in the text.

5 Why do you think the people (1-4) would like to go to the Maldives?

1 James is a keen cook and is interested in nature.
   James would like the food and would enjoy …

2 Michelle and Gavin are a young couple. They want to chill out and have a good time.
3 Sue is going with some friends from her local sports club.
4 Charles and Maria are in their sixties with health problems especially in the winter.

THE MALDIVES
4.3

1 Imagine your paradise holiday location. Warm, sunny weather. Clear, blue sea. Tall palm trees. White, sandy beaches. Turquoise lagoons and colourful coral reefs. You can find all this and more in the Maldives.

2 There are over 1000 coral islands in the Maldives and ninety percent of the country's 90,000 square kilometres is covered by sea. The climate is warm and tropical all year round, with an average temperature of 29ºC.

3 The population of the Maldives is just over 300,000 and a third of the people live in the capital, Malé. The Maldives has been a Muslim country since 1153. Maldivians are open and friendly and English is spoken widely. The local food is absolutely delicious with Arab, Indian and Sri Lankan influences; fish curry is the national dish.

4 There are luxury resorts on uninhabited islands where you can stay in a deluxe bungalow built over a lagoon and they are building more every year. On other islands, you can chill out on the beach, relax with a massage at the health spa or enjoy dancing at the discotheque.

5 The Maldives is one of the best dive sites in the world. You can discover a beautiful underwater world of seventy different kinds of coral and 700 species of fish. Canoeing, wind-surfing and sailing are also available at most resorts and if you like surfing, there are good waves on some of the islands. You can go dolphin watching or stay in the resort and work out in the gym, join in a game of beach volleyball or play badminton or tennis.

6 There are direct flights to the capital, Malé, from many European countries and transfer from the airport to your resort is by seaplane or speedboat.

For more information: www.visitmaldives.com

6 Look at the Sentence Builder. Which of the words in **bold** is a verb and which are nouns?

> **Sentence Builder** *-ing* forms
> 1 **Canoeing, wind-surfing** and **sailing** are available.
> 2 You can enjoy **dancing** at the discotheque.
> 3 They are **building** more every year.

7 Work in pairs. Use the expressions to say sentences about activities from the brochure.

I love playing volleyball. Playing volleyball is good fun.

- I love/like/can't stand …
- … is good fun/relaxing/boring/exciting

➤ LANGUAGE CHOICE 53

Listening

8 **4.36** **4.37** Look at the photo. Listen to a news programme and choose the best headline (1-3) below.

1 New president looks for new country

2 **Rising sea level destroys coral reefs**

3 Maldives builds artificial island

9 **4.38** **4.39** ➔ SKILLS BUILDER 8 Listen to the programme again. Use the strategies in the Skills Builder to complete the notes below.

> Population of the Maldives: ¹ *370,000*
> Number of islands: ²_____
> Sea level rise: ³_____
> Highest point in the Maldives: ⁴_____
> Future rise in sea level: ⁵_____
> Year of the tsunami: ⁶_____
> The tsunami destroyed: ⁷_____
> Solutions: buy another ⁸_____
>   build ⁹_____

10 **Vocabulary** Look at the Word Builder. Match the verbs in **bold** with the meanings (a-f).

a happen b leave the house
c return d rise e fall f continue

> **Word Builder** Multi-part verbs (4)
> 1 People are not **going out** and are staying at home. *b*
> 2 What's **going on** in the Maldives?
> 3 In the last few years, the sea level has **gone up**.
> 4 It's not going to **go down** again.
> 5 People still have not **gone back** to their homes.
> 6 Sea levels will go up if climate change **goes on**.

➤ LANGUAGE CHOICE 54: VOCABULARY PRACTICE

11 Work in pairs. Choose one of the options (a-c) to talk about. Give reasons for your decisions.

a What activities would *you* do if you were in the Maldives on holiday? What month would you go there? Do you think you would like it? Why/Why not?
b What would *you* do if you were the president of the Maldives now? What solution would you choose?
c If *you* were the president of your country, what would you do to stop climate change?

A: *What would you do if you were in the Maldives on holiday?*
B: *I would go diving …*

Your Choice

Warm Up

1 Look at the map and the photos. Why is New Zealand an attractive tourist destination?

2 Read the text. What can you do in these places?

- Mt Cook
- the Waikato River
- Auckland

DISCOVER NEW ZEALAND

(4.40)

NEW ZEALAND, 2000 KILOMETRES SOUTHEAST OF AUSTRALIA, WITH ITS SOUTH AND NORTH ISLANDS, OFFERS LOTS OF ACTIVITY HOLIDAYS.

100miles

Aukland
Waikato River
Lake Taupo
Huka Falls
Mt Ruapehu
Rangitikei River
Southern Alps
TASMAN SEA
Wellington
Okarito Lagoon
PACIFIC OCEAN
Aoraki (Mt Cook)
Mt Aspiring National Park
Queenstown

- Kayak in the **Okarito Lagoon** and enjoy some rare bird-watching and beautiful views of **the Southern Alps**.

- Cycle across **the South Island**: from **the Tasman Sea** to **the Pacific Ocean**.

- Hike in **Mt Aspiring National Park** and climb up snow-capped **Aoraki** (Mt Cook) 3754 m, the highest mountain in New Zealand.

- Explore **the North Island** with its active volcanoes, hot springs and waterfalls.

- Walk up New Zealand's longest river – **the Waikato** – to the impressive **Huka Falls** and see **Lake Taupo** in Rotorua, the biggest volcanic crater in the world.

- Travel with Aragorn and Frodo: raft down **the Rangitikei River** and see the sites where *The Lord of the Rings* was filmed, hike around **Mt Ruapehu**, where Mordor was set – a real treat for all *LOTR* fans.

- Visit **Auckland**, **Wellington** and **Queenstown**, New Zealand's main towns and enjoy the local culture.

- Our website (www.explorenz.com) provides information about flights from **the United States** and **Europe**.

the in geographical names

3 Complete the table with geographical names from the text and your own ideas. Which names take *the* and which do not?

	examples
continent	
country	*Australia*
the + country	*the United States*
city	
river	
lake	
sea/ocean	
mountain	
mountain range	
island	*New Zealand*

4 Complete the sentences with *the* or (–).

1 _–_ London is the capital of _the_ United Kingdom.
2 ___ Danube flows through some capital cities in ___ Europe, including ___ Budapest and ___ Belgrade.
3 Eight of the highest mountains in ___ Himalayas, including ___ Mount Everest, are in ____ Nepal.
4 ___ Cuba is the largest island in ___ Caribbean Sea.
5 ___ Poland, ___ Latvia, ___ Lithuania and ___ Estonia have important towns on ___ Baltic Sea.
6 To get from ___ Switzerland to ___ Italy you have to cross ___ Alps.
7 You can cross ___ United States going down ___ Mississipi, from ___ Lake Itasca to ___ New Orleans.
8 ___ Lake Victoria is the largest lake in ___ Africa and Kilimanjaro is the highest mountain.

LANGUAGE CHOICE 55

5 Write about five places to visit in your country.

You can visit Dubrovnik, a beautiful old town in the south of Croatia and swim in the Adriatic Sea.

SKILLS
Writing Workshop 5

1 **Read the postcard. Use your general knowledge and Lesson 30 to correct the four <u>underlined</u> mistakes with the words (1–4).**

1 Mt Ruapehu 2 Huka Falls
3 January 4 North Island

Rotorua, NZ, 2 July

Hi Katy,

Having a great time. It's quite hot here because it's the middle of summer. Now in Auckland in the <u>South Island</u> for two days – the nightlife's great! Yesterday, we were in Rotorua. Saw the hot springs and geysers and went to the <u>Okarito Lagoon</u> – AMAZING!!! Last week, stayed on my aunt's farm near Wellington. Saw lots of places from The Lord of the Rings – <u>Mt Aoraki</u> very scary – like Mordor in the film! Going sailing tomorrow. Back on Thursday. See you next weekend.
Take care, Sally xxxxxx

Ms K. Simons,

23 Castle Road,

Orleton, SY1 1GH

GREAT BRITAIN

Text Builder

2 **→ SKILLS BUILDER 20** **Find informal expressions in blue in the postcard with these meanings (1–4).**

1 With best wishes, 2 We are enjoying New Zealand.
3 Dear …, 4 Look forward to seeing you on …

3 **Answer the questions (1–5) about punctuation.**

1 Why does Sally use CAPITAL LETTERS for words?
   a for names b to emphasise something
2 What examples of contractions does Sally use?
3 Why does Sally use dashes? (–)
   a to comment on something mentioned
   b to start a new sentence
4 When does Sally use exclamation marks? (!!!!!)
   a to emphasise something b for questions
5 What does 'xxxxxxx' mean?
   a good luck b kisses

4 **What words does Sally leave out? Complete the sentences.**

1 _I_ _am_ having a great time.
2 ___ ___ now in Auckland.
3 ___ saw the hot springs and geysers.
4 ___ stayed on my aunt's farm.
5 Mt Aoraki ___ very scary.
6 ___ ___ ___ back on Thursday.

5 **→ SKILLS BUILDER 34** **Use the model to write a postcard to a friend at home.**

1 **Imagine you are on holiday somewhere exotic. Write notes about the things below:**

- where you are
- the weather
- why it's great/terrible
- what you did yesterday
- what you did last week
- what you are going to do tomorrow
- when you are coming back

2 **Use your notes to write your postcard.**

3 **Check your postcard for style and punctuation.**

6 **Work in pairs. Read each other's postcard. Would you like to visit his/her place? Why/Why not? Tell the class three things.**

Monika's postcard is from Iceland. She went horse-riding yesterday. Last week she saw some amazing waterfalls. Tomorrow, she is going to go whale-watching.

Speaking Workshop 5

1 Look at the photo of Manhattan Island.

1 What do you know about it?
2 Would you like to go there?

2 5.1 5.2 Listen to a dialogue in a travel agent's and complete the notes.

Weather in September: ¹ _hot_
Student discounts: flights/hotels/² _____ /theatres
Needed to enter the USA: a ³ _____
Places to visit: the Empire State Building/the Statue of Liberty/ ⁴ _____
Price of a hostel: ⁵$_____ a night
Total price for a week: ⁶$____

3 5.3 5.4 Listen again. Complete the questions (1–10) with the words below.

do you   anything   aren't there   right
please (x 2)   yeah   isn't it   don't you

Talk Builder Asking for information

Requests

1 **Could you** give me some information about New York, _please_ ?
2 **Could you** tell me about places to visit there, ____ ?
3 **Do you** know ____ about the nightlife?
4 Which of these hostels **do you** recommend?

Question tags

5 That's a good time of year, _____ ?
6 You give discounts for students, _____ ?
7 You don't need a visa for the States, _____ ?
8 There are lots of things to see, _____ ?
9 Breakfast is included in the price, _____ ?
10 So this is the total price for a week, _____ ?

➔ SKILLS BUILDER 50

4 5.5 **Pronunciation** Look at the words in bold in the Talk Builder. Listen to two versions of them: a very slow and unnatural b normal speech. What differences can you hear?

5 5.6 Listen again. Repeat the requests.

6 Choose the correct alternatives (a or b) to complete the questions.

1 Could you tell me about flights to Istanbul, a right? (b) please?
2 It's not very cold there in May, a right? b isn't it?
3 You don't need a visa for Turkey, a do you? b don't you?
4 It's got great food, a has it? b hasn't it?
5 There are some great places to see in Istanbul, a are there? b aren't there?
6 Breakfast is included, a yeah? b doesn't it?

7 Work in pairs. Use the cues to ask and answer questions about New York. Use question tags.

A: *You don't need a visa for the States, do you?*
B: *No. Not if you're British.*

- hot in early September
- cheap flights for students
- Statue of Liberty - cool
- lots of places to visit
- Central Park - great
- student discounts
- need a visa
- great art galleries
- hotels - expensive
- good nightlife

8 Give tourist information about your city.

➔ SKILLS BUILDER 50

1 Write notes about the things below:

- visa
- where to stay
- places to eat out
- transport in the city
- what the weather is like
- when to visit
- what to see
- places for nightlife
- transport to the city

2 Work in pairs. Take turns to be a travel agent and a customer. Ask for and give information about your city. Use requests and question tags.

9 Tell the class when to visit, what to see, where to go out, etc. Agree and disagree.

A: *We think the best place for nightlife is …*
B: *We don't agree. We think the best place is …*

LEARNING LINKS: 1 Read an extract from *Robinson Crusoe* by Daniel Defoe in **Culture Choice 5** on page 110. Then do a project about things you would miss from your country.
2 Check Your Progress 10 ➔ MyLab / Workbook page 89. Complete the **Module Diary**.
3 Exam Choice 5 ➔ MyLab / Workbook pages 90–92.

MODULE 11 FRIENDS

Objectives: Listen, read and talk about friends and friendship; make telephone calls; write descriptions of people; learn more about future tenses.

Curtis · Simon · Fatima · Kirsty · Silvia

TOPIC TALK

1 Work in pairs. Use the network to describe the looks of the people in the photo.

Curtis is short but quite well-built. He's got short, dark hair and he's about nineteen. He looks very easy-going.

2 5.7 5.8 Listen to the descriptions of three people (1–3) and find them in the photos above.

3 5.9 5.10 Listen again to the first person. Complete the information in the network.

4 5.11 **Pronunciation** Listen to words from the network. <u>Underline</u> the stress.

hard-<u>working</u>

➜ LANGUAGE CHOICE 56: VOCABULARY PRACTICE

5 Work in groups. Use the network to talk about *your* friends.

People

(She) is a very good friend of mine. We've known each other for
¹ *four/ fourteen* years.
She's very ² _____ .
She's got ³ _____ .
She's usually ⁴ _____ .
Sometimes she's a bit ⁵ _____ .

Looks

attractive, good-looking, handsome ♂, pretty ♀, ugly
- -
overweight, short, slim, skinny, tall, well-built,
- -
dark-, fair-, pale- **skinned**

short/long, curly/straight/wavy, blond/dark/fair/red/dyed **hair**

Personality

confident, easy-going, enthusiastic, friendly, funny, hard-working, helpful, honest, impatient, kind, lazy, moody, outgoing, quiet, romantic, sensitive, sensible, shy, sociable, talkative, tidy, untidy, unhappy

85

Warm Up

1 Match the descriptions (1–4) with the people (a–d) below.

1 not very confident and unhappy *c Tim*
2 a good teacher with a strong personality
3 handsome, sporty and outgoing
4 pretty, intelligent and hard-working

My Movie blog 5.12

The Wave
(Die Welle) (2008)

Rate this film

Director: Dennis Gansel

Summary:
It's project week at a German high school and Rainer Wenger (Jürgen Vogel) is teaching a class about autocracy. Everyone in the class gets bored quickly. Not this stuff again! We could never have a dictator in Germany now, could we?

The class is a typical group of high school kids. Marco (Max Riemelt) is handsome and sporty, one of the best players in the school water polo team. He's popular and outgoing but has problems at home. Marco's going out with Karo (Jennifer Ulrich). She's sensible, intelligent and hard-working and always gets good marks. Karo's best friend, Lisa (Cristina do Rego), is pretty but not as confident as Karo. Another student, Sinan (Elyas M'Barek), is Turkish-German. He's as good-looking and sociable as Marco and a good water polo player too, but they both fight all the time. Tim (Frederick Lau) is an unhappy loner with no friends. He's brilliant with computers but doesn't get on with his family.

The enthusiastic and hard-working Mr Wenger starts an experiment. First, he moves around the desks and the students. Everybody has to stand up when they speak and sit down again immediately. They do relaxation exercises together. They march in time next to their desks to annoy the class downstairs. They choose a name,

The Wave, for their group. Everybody has to get a uniform (white shirt and jeans) to get rid of differences between them. They think of a symbol and a salute for the group.

Most of the students enjoy the class. They're not as divided as before. It doesn't matter if they're rich or poor, good or bad students. They're all part of the group now. Even Marco and Sinan start getting on better in the water polo team. Tim is the keenest – he loves the discipline. Only Karo and a friend refuse to wear the uniform; they don't like what is going on in the class. Karo argues with Marco and Lisa about it. They don't understand her negative attitude.

Then, The Wave spreads outside the school. They paint their symbol all over the town and have parties only for group members. Fights start between Wave members and other local groups. At the end of project week, Mr Wenger's little experiment ends up in a real tragedy.

5 Comments

a Karo

b Marco

c Tim   **d Mr Wenger**

Reading

2 Read the film blog. Check your guesses from Exercise 1.

3 ➡ SKILLS BUILDER 21 Use the strategies in the Skills Builder to answer the questions (1–3).

1 Where would you find the film summary?
   a in a newspaper
   b in a film magazine
   c in a film blog
2 What style (formal/informal) does the writer use? Give examples.
3 What is the purpose of the summary?
   a to tell people what the film's about
   b to express opinions about the film
   c to tell the people about the ending of the film

4 Read the blog again. Answer the questions.

1 Do the students like the group experiment in the beginning? Why/Why not?
2 What does Mr Wenger make the group do?
3 Why do most of the students like it?
4 Why do you think Tim is so keen on the group?
5 Why do Marco and Lisa get angry with Karo?
6 What does the film show about groups of people?

5 Vocabulary Look at the Word Builder. Match the uses of *get* (1–6) with meanings (a–f).

a have a bad relationship with
b have a good relationship   c eliminate
d buy/find   e become   f achieve

Word Builder *get*

1 Everyone in the class **gets** bored. *e*
2 She always **gets** good marks.
3 Everybody has to **get** a uniform.
4 He **doesn't get on with** his family.
5 They do it to **get rid of** differences between them.
6 Marco and Sinan start **getting on** better.

➥ LANGUAGE CHOICE 57: VOCABULARY PRACTICE

6 Work in pairs. Ask and answer the questions.

1 When do you get bored?
2 Why do you get angry?
3 What marks do you get at school?
4 Where do you get your clothes?
5 Who do you get on with/not get on with?
6 What things in your school timetable would you like to get rid of?

Writing

7 Match the sentences (1–2) in the Sentence Builder with the correct definition (a or b). How do you say the sentences in your language?

1 a Sinan is more sociable than Marco.
   b Sinan and Marco are both sociable.
2 a Lisa is more confident than Karo.
   b Lisa is less confident than Karo.

Sentence Builder *as* for comparisons

1 Sinan is **as** sociable **as** Marco.
2 Lisa is **not as** confident **as** Karo.

➡ SKILLS BUILDER 35

---

8 Use the cues to write sentences about the characters in *The Wave*. Then write two more sentences about the characters with *as/not as*.

1 Tim / sporty / Marco

   Tim is not as sporty as Marco.

2 Sinan / good at water polo / Marco
3 Marco / outgoing / Sinan
4 Marco / interested in The Wave / Lisa
5 Lisa's personality / strong / Karo's personality
6 Sinan / unhappy / Tim

9 Work in pairs. Choose one of the options (a–b) and write a list of people.

a five boys or five girls you both know (but not from this class)
b five male or five female celebrities you know about

10 Write sentences about a person on your list. Use adjectives from the Topic Talk.

He is not as tall as Tom but he is slimmer.
His hair is not as long as Paul's and it is darker.
He isn't as tidy as Ricky but he is more outgoing.
He is more hard-working than Tim but he isn't as confident.

11 Work in pairs. Read out your sentences. Guess your partner's person.

No Comment

'Democracy is the worst form of government except all the others that have been tried.'

Winston Churchill, former British Prime Minister

Your Choice

32

GOODBYE

| Home | Links | Revision | Forum | Car |

LizA  **Party Time!** As you know, Maria is leaving us next week. The surprise goodbye party is on Friday. Who can help with the food? I'm making spaghetti bolognese.

A-Man Who is bringing Maria to the party? I could do that ☺☺☺☺☺

LizA I know you'd love to do it, A-Man but it's already been arranged.

Mickey I'm going to make a potato salad. What time are we meeting on Saturday?

LizA Thanks Mickey, we can have your salad as a starter. Is anybody doing a dessert? Anna is bringing Maria at 7.30 (her concert finishes at 6.30). So we all have to be there around 7 p.m.

Brad99 Who else is coming? And what are we going to do? Hope it will be fun.

Mickey ☺ Well, Brad99, Chelsea play Arsenal on Saturday night so we can all have fun in front of the telly! Isn't that a perfect idea for a farewell party?

A-Man Hope you are joking! Maria won't like that! She hates football.
Is anyone going to see her off at the airport? Her plane takes off at 10.45 on Sunday. I'm going to be there. With flowers …

LizA I can't be at the airport, I'm looking after my mood younger brother all weekend. ☹

Brad99 A-Man, she's going away on Sunday. Forget about her! Be sensible.

A-Man I am, Brad99! Why don't you log off? ☹

Good Luck back home in Prague – Kevin

Sorry you're leaving

Hope you like the goodbye gift
(once you find time to listen to it) - Lisa

Good luck with your musical career, master violinist – Sandy

It's been a great six months, studying, playing and having fun together - Keith

We'll miss you here. London is going to be sad without you – Andy and Mike

Warm Up

1 Read the goodbye card for Maria, an exchange student. Answer the questions.

1 Where is Maria from?
2 What does she do?
3 What did she do in London?
4 What present did she get?

2 Read the messages on a students' forum about a goodbye party for Maria. Who is:

1 the main organiser of the party?
2 in love with Maria?
3 not very pleasant?

3 Where would you like to do an exchange? Why?

Intentions and arrangements

4 Read the sentences (1-3) from the text. Match them with the meanings (a-c).

1 Chelsea **play** Arsenal on Saturday night.
2 Anna **is bringing** Maria at 7.30.
3 I'm **going to make** a potato salad.

a It's been arranged with family/friends.
b It's a fixed event. I can't change the date or time.
c I have an intention to do that.

5 Find more examples of a-c in the text.

Practice

6 Use the text, the cues and *(not) be going to* to say what Maria's friends are planning to do on Friday night.

LizA is going to cook something.

- LizA: cook something, look after her younger brother on Sunday
- Mickey: prepare some food, watch the match on Saturday
- A-Man: go to the airport on Sunday, kiss Maria goodbye

7 Look at Maria's diary for this week. Use the Present Continuous to make sentences about her arrangements.

She is seeing the exchange supervisor at 4 p.m. on Monday.

Monday	4 p.m.	see the exchange supervisor
Tuesday	7 p.m.	go to the cinema with Andrew
Wednesday	7 p.m.	have dinner with other exchange students
Thursday	8 p.m.	go to film club meeting
Friday	3 p.m.	meet Anna for a goodbye chat
Saturday	5 p.m.	play a concert in the school club
Sunday	8 a.m.	leave for airport

➥ LANGUAGE CHOICE 58

8 Use the Present Simple and the verbs below to write sentences about fixed events from Maria's future.

take off   land   come back   ~~finish~~
have got   begin   start

1 The summer term _finishes_ on Friday.
2 My plane on Saturday _____ at 10.45 and _____ in Prague at 14.00.
3 My family _____ from their holidays on 20 August.
4 The autumn term _____ on 1 September.
5 I _____ my first violin class on 2 September.
6 Orchestra rehersals _____ on 30 September.

➥ LANGUAGE CHOICE 59

Grammar Alive Arrangements

9 **5.13** Listen to the conversation and answer the questions.

1 Why is Jamie calling Jo?
2 What reasons does Jo give for not meeting Jamie? Tick (✓) the ones you hear.
  ☐ meeting someone
  ☐ going to the cinema/theatre/concert
  ☐ seeing a doctor/dentist
  ☐ going away
  ☐ helping someone
3 Do you think Jo wants to meet Jamie?

10 Work in pairs. Use the cues and the Present Continuous to make dialogues.

A: *Are you doing anything next Saturday? We could go to the cinema.*
B: *I'm afraid I can't. I'm going away for the weekend.*

A	**starts**	**B**	**answers**
1	next Saturday; go to the cinema	1	go away for the weekend
2	tomorrow night; go swimming	2	watch my favourite TV series
3	tonight; go to a club	3	go to a concert
4	on Friday night; go to the theatre	4	help my dad to repair my bike

B	**starts**	**A**	**answers**
5	at the weekend; go camping	5	paint my room
6	on Saturday; go to a concert	6	go out with some friends
7	in the afternoon; go for a walk	7	meet my friends to work on a history project
8	on Sunday morning; go cycling	8	have a tennis lesson

11 Write down your arrangements for this afternoon and this evening.

I'm having a Spanish lesson at 4 p.m.

12 Work in pairs. Arrange to do something together today. Use your notes from Exercise 11 and agree on the best time.

A: *Are you doing anything after school?*
B: *I'm having a Spanish lesson at 4 p.m. But we could meet at 6 p.m. and go to the cinema.*
A: *I can't, I'm meeting my mum to buy a present for my dad. Let's meet at 8 p.m. and go swimming.*

Warm Up

1 Vocabulary **Look at the network about social networks. Can you add any more advantages or disadvantages?**

Advantages
keep in touch with friends and make new ones
post comments on your friends' homepages
post photos/videos/music on your homepage

Social networks

Disadvantages
suffer from cyber-bullying
(e.g. nasty/aggressive messages)
give away personal information
Strangers **view** your information or try to meet you.

➤ LANGUAGE CHOICE 60: VOCABULARY PRACTICE

Listening

2 **Look at the internet safety tips. What advice do you think is true (T) or false (F)?**

1 Don't be nasty and aggressive online. *T*
2 Think before you post personal photos online.
3 Don't worry. You can always delete things online.
4 You should reply to messages from cyber-bullies.
5 You shouldn't get friendly with strangers.
6 It's okay if everybody can view your personal information.
7 Use a sentence to remember your password.
8 Give your password to your best friend.

3 5.14 5.15 **Listen to the interview. Check your guesses from Exercise 2.**

4 Your Culture **Work in pairs. Ask and answer the questions.**

1 How popular is social networking in your country?
What websites are the most popular?
What problems are there?
2 How else do young people keep in touch (e.g. text messages, instant messaging, phone)?

myngo

All · photos · blog · frie

Polly Crabtree Photos

Latest Me, my

Top lists

5 DVD 11 **Watch the BBC News report. Put the people in the order they start talking.**

a the creator of the website
b the girls
c journalist

6 DVD 11 **Watch again. Match the people (a–c) in Exercise 5 with the things they say.**

1 Teenage socialising has changed because of social networks.
2 Bebo is great because you can personalise it.
3 You can see your friends' and their friends' homepages.
4 It's not very nice when strangers ask you for your email.
5 The school stopped students using Bebo on their network.
6 There is lots of safety advice on the website.
7 Schools are worried about students' safety online.

7 **What problems have you had on social networking sites?**

quiz

Search....

d friends

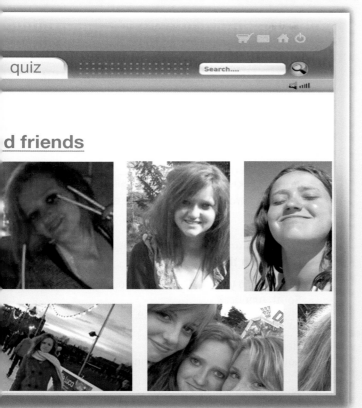

Watching and Speaking

8 [5.16] [DVD 12] → SKILLS BUILDER 9 **Listen to or watch two phone conversations. Match the people with their intentions (1-5).**

Judy / Adam / Mrs Williams / the receptionist

1 would like the caller to be quick *Mrs Williams*
2 wants to help the boy
3 needs help from his mum
4 wants to leave a message (x 2)
5 would like to arrange a meeting

9 [5.17] [DVD 12] **Listen to or watch the dialogues again. Write down the messages.**

10 **Look at the Talk Builder. Match the formal and informal expressions.**

> **Talk Builder** Telephoning
>
> | Formal | Informal |
> |---|---|
> | 1 Good morning. | a Can I speak to ... ? |
> | 2 Could I speak to ... ? | b Sorry, he's out. |
> | 3 Hold on a moment. | c Hi/hello. |
> | 4 I'll put you through. | d Thanks a lot. |
> | 5 I'm afraid she's not available at the moment. | e Hang on a sec. |
> | 6 Thank you very much. | f I'll get him for you. |
>
> → SKILLS BUILDER 51

11 [5.18] **Pronunciation Listen and repeat the expressions. Notice the words that come together.**

12 **Choose the best reply to the requests.**

1 Can I help you?
   a Of course you can. b Yes, please. c No, please.

2 Could I speak to Mr Smith, please?
   a Okay, I'll tell him. b Sorry, he's out with his dad.
   c Of course. Hold on, please.

3 Could I leave him a message, please?
   a Yes, of course. b Yes, no problem, love.
   c Sorry, you can't.

4 Thank you very much.
   a Of course. b Not at all. c Bye.

5 Do you want to leave him a message?
   a Yes, I want to. b Yes, I'd like. c Yes, please.

13 **Write two messages to leave (one formal/ one informal). Choose one of the ideas (a-d) for each message.**

To: Alice
Meet me outside the cinema at eight o'clock.
Bring your new boyfriend.

1 *Informal (for friend):*
   a arrange to go out somewhere
   b ask for something
   c invite someone to your house
   d arrange a party

2 *Formal (for a teacher):*
   a you've lost something/missed a bus/train
   b there's been an accident
   c you're ill
   d ask for help/money

14 **Work in pairs. Act out phone calls. Take turns to leave and take messages. Write down your partner's message.**

Your Choice

Language Review Modules 10 and 11

1 Holidays/People **Complete the texts with the correct words.**

I like going ¹_____ the coast in summer. I can ² _____ snorkelling and ³wind-_____ there. I like staying ⁴_____ a campsite ⁵_____ my family. I'm lazy – I don't like ⁶sight_____ and my favourite activity is ⁷sun_____ .

Claire is a ⁸*handsome/pretty* young woman with dark ⁹*curly/slim* hair. She is quite ¹⁰easy-_____ and has a lot of friends. She keeps in ¹¹_____ with them by email. She met her boyfriend when he ¹²_____ a comment on her homepage. Claire is a ¹³hard-_____ person – she works in a gallery part time.   **/13**

2 Phrases with *go* and *get* **Replace the words in *italics* with an expression with *go* or *get*.**

14 What is *happening* at the beach?
15 The people *returned* home after the storm.
16 The number of non-smokers is *increasing*.
17 If you *continue* criticising people, you'll lose all your friends.
18 My phone book was old so I *threw it away*.
19 I tried to watch the film but I *became* bored.
20 Mary and I always *have a good time together*.   **/7**

3 Unreal Conditional **Complete the sentences with the correct forms of the verbs in brackets.**

21 If we _____ (be) rich, we _____ (go) on a round-the-world trip.
22 I _____ (watch) this game if I _____ (have) more time.
23 If students _____ (study) harder, they _____ (get) better marks.
24 I _____ (buy) new clothes if I _____ (have) some money.
25 If our team _____ (play) better, we _____ (win) the World Cup.   **/5**

4 Arrangements and intentions **Complete the sentences with the correct future forms of the verbs in brackets.**

26 Hurry up! The lesson _____ (start) in two minutes.
27 I can't go out. Maria _____ (come) to see me.
28 I love languages so I _____ (study) French.
29 I _____ (fly) to Paris at the weekend. I bought the ticket this morning.
30 The train _____ (leave) at 2.35.   **/7**

5 *the* in geographical names **Complete the text with articles where necessary.**

³¹____ Africa is the world's second largest continent. It is surrounded by ³²____ Atlantic to the west and ³³____ Indian Ocean to the east. It includes some island countries, like ³⁴____ Madagascar. Its highest mountain is ³⁵____ Kilimanjaro, its longest river is ³⁶____ Nile and its largest lake is ³⁷____ Lake Victoria. The largest country is ³⁸____ Sudan, with its capital ³⁹____ Khartoum, and the smallest is ⁴⁰____ Seychelles, a group of islands off the east coast.   **/10**

6 Asking for information/Telephoning **Complete the dialogue with the correct words.**

A: Hello. Could you ⁴¹_____ me about trips to South America?
B: ⁴²_____ on a moment, please. I'll put you ⁴³_____ to a colleague.
C: Hello. Can I ⁴⁴_____ you?
A: Could you give me some information about Peru, ⁴⁵_____ ?
C: When would you like to go?
A: Spring is probably the best time to go, ⁴⁶_____ it?
C: Right.
A: Could you ⁴⁷_____ any good hotels in Lima?
C: I can send you our catalogue. You use email, ⁴⁸_____ you?
A: Sure. And do you know ⁴⁹_____ about trips to Machu Picchu?
C: Yes, of course. You are interested in visiting Cusco as well, ⁵⁰_____ you?   **/10**

Self Assessment

5.19 **Listen and check your answers. Write down the scores. Use the table to find practice exercises.**

Exercise	If you need practice, go to
1	Language Choice 51, 56
2	Language Choice 54, 57
3	Language Choice 52
4	Language Choice 58, 59
5	Language Choice 55
6	SB p.84, ex. 3, 6; SB p. 9 ex.11

LEARNING LINKS: 1 Check Your Progress 11 → MyLab / Workbook page 99. Complete the **Module Diary**.
2 Sound Choice 6 → MyLab / Workbook page 100. Choose three pronunciation activities to do.

Objectives: **Listen**, **read** and **talk about** emotions; **write** short notes and **talk about** happy experiences; **learn about** relative clauses and reported requests and orders.

a Slumdog Millionaire

TOPIC TALK

1 Look at the photos (a–d). Guess how the people are feeling. Use the network below.

2 5.20 5.21 Listen and check your answers from Exercise 1. Match the descriptions (1–4) with the films (a–d).

3 5.22 5.23 Listen to someone talking about their feelings. Complete the information in the network.

Feelings

I'm usually in a ¹ *bad/* *good* mood.
When I see a new film, I often feel (a bit) ² ___ .
When I'm with my friends, I feel ³ ___ .
When I'm on my own, I sometimes get (a bit) ⁴ ___ .
I find arguments with people ⁵ ___ .
Doing tests and exams is ⁶ ___ .
Doing my favourite hobby is ⁷ ___ .

angry, annoyed, bored, calm, confused, down, enthusiastic, excited, happy, interested, irritated, lonely, nervous, relaxed, sad, scared, shocked, stressed out, surprised, terrified, upset, worried

amusing, annoying, boring, confusing, depressing, exciting, interesting, relaxing, scary, shocking, stressful, surprising, terrifying, upsetting, worrying

b Babel

4 5.24 Pronunciation Listen and repeat the words. Notice the different endings.

LANGUAGE CHOICE 61: VOCABULARY PRACTICE

5 Work in groups. Use the network to talk about *your* feelings.

c The Messengers

d (500) Days of Summer

GRAMMAR
34 CRYING

Warm Up

1 Look at the photos in the article (a–c). Why are the people crying? Why do you cry?

2 Read the text. How has people's attitude to crying changed over the years?

3 Your Culture What is your opinion about crying in public? Are there different rules for men and women in your country?

Defining relative clauses

4 Read the examples (1–6) from the text and complete the rules about relative clauses with *who, which, that, whose* or *when*.

1 men **who** cry
2 a study **which** examined people's attitudes to crying
3 people **that** only knew her from TV
4 the music **that** came after it
5 a decade **when** many male pop stars cried
6 the house **where** she had lived

- We use _____ or _____ when we talk about people.
- We use _____ or _____ when we talk about things.
- We use _____ when we talk about places.
- We use _____ when we talk about time.

Boys Don't Cry? (5.25)

To older generations of British people, expressing emotions was a sign of weakness. Men in particular had to control their feelings.

The changes started in the 1950s. With rock 'n' roll and the music that came after it men could express the emotions they previously hid. The 1960s was a decade when many male pop stars cried during their performances.

When Diana, Princess of Wales, died in a car crash in 1997, the whole nation burst into tears. For weeks, people that only knew her from TV brought flowers and lit candles in front of the house where she had lived.

Nowadays, we cry all the time. Footballers cry on TV after a game they have lost or a penalty they have missed and surprisingly, they become more popular for doing it. The people we watch on TV reality programmes all cry, no matter if they win or lose.

A recent study which examined people's attitudes to crying shows that men's tears are becoming more acceptable; we believe that men who cry are expressing honest emotions. And crying, as all babies know very well, is actually a powerful weapon. Surely, you'd forgive a big man with tears running down his cheeks? ☹

Nowadays, we cry all the time.

94

5 Read the sentences (1–4) and the <u>underlined</u> words. Then complete the rules with the correct options (a or b).

1 *Men who/that <u>cry</u> express their emotions.*
2 *There is a study which/that <u>examined</u> people's attitudes to crying.*
3 *Footballers often cry after a game (that/which) <u>they</u> have lost.*
4 *People (who/that) <u>we</u> watch on TV reality programmes all cry.*

- We can leave out the relative pronoun *who, which* or *that* when it comes before
  a a noun or a pronoun   **b** a verb.
- We cannot leave out the relative pronoun *who, which* or *that* when it comes before
  a a noun or a pronoun   **b** a verb.

Practice

6 <u>Underline</u> relative clauses and ⟨circle⟩ relative pronouns. ~~Cross out~~ pronouns where possible.

1 The book ⟨which⟩ <u>I'm reading at the moment</u> is really funny.
2 I don't like people who cry in public.
3 According to a study that has been done of British teenagers, girls cry more than boys.
4 I don't understand strong emotions that people have about football.
5 Boys that I know never cry.
6 Things which people say during an argument are often really upsetting.

➜ LANGUAGE CHOICE 62

7 Complete the text with pronouns. Put brackets around relative pronouns which are not necessary.

The life of a person ¹ *who* can't help crying is not easy. I cry when people tell me about problems ² _____ they have or when I see a boy ³ _____ is in tears because he can't get the toy car ⁴ _____ he wants. I cry during the news, when they show people ⁵ _____ have lost their homes or poor children ⁶ _____ beg in the streets of big cities. There are so many things ⁷ _____ make me cry! I'm waiting for a time ⁸ _____ life is boring and unemotional!

Grammar Alive Descriptions

8 **5.26** Listen to the conversation and answer the questions.

1 What is James doing during this conversation?
2 What do the girls remember about Martha?
3 What do the girls think about Martha and James?

9 Work in pairs. Student A think of a person from your class and describe him/her. Use the cues, your own ideas and relative clauses. Student B guess who the person is.

A: *It's the girl who is never late for school.*
B: *Is it Carla?*
A: *Yes, it is.*

- he/she plays the guitar
- he/she smiles all the time
- he/she gets the best grades
- he/she didn't come to school today
- he/she always wears black
- all teachers like him/her

10 Use the cues and relative clauses to prepare a survey about crying. Add your own questions.

Do you cry when you read books that have unhappy endings?

Do you cry when you …

- read books – have unhappy endings
- see a cat/dog – is homeless
- watch programmes – show people in love
- remember a time – you were very unhappy
- go back to a place – you were very happy

11 Work in pairs. Ask each other the questions. How sentimental is your partner?

She cries when she watches programmes where people talk about their hard lives.

12 Quiz Work in pairs. Student A look at page 114 and Student B look at page 128. Prepare the quiz questions. Then ask and answer the questions.

year – Princess Diana died then (1997)

What was the year when Princess Diana died?

HAPPINESS

Warm Up

1 **Which of the ideas (1-9) are illustrated in the pictures (a-d)?**

1 being with friends 2 doing physical exercise
3 making lots of money 4 being in a steady relationship
5 doing things for other people 6 having a nice car
7 belonging to a group 8 being successful

2 **Which two things in the list in Exercise 1 do *not* make people happy? Check your answers on page 114. Discuss the results with the class.**

Reading

3 **Read the article. Would you like to have 'well-being' classes? Why/Why not?**

4 **Read the article again. In which paragraphs (1-3) can you find the things (a-e)?**

a useful things learnt in the happiness classes *3*
b student behaviour in the classes
c opinions about happiness
d opinions about education
e activities in happiness lessons

5.27 *Can you actually teach happiness? At Wellington College, a secondary school in England, they think you can actually make people happy. For the last two years, 'well-being' classes have been taught to fifteen and sixteen-year-old students.*

1 The Headmaster

Anthony Seldon, head teacher at Wellington, does not really like schools nowadays. 'They should be places of happiness. At the moment, they are too much about tests and exams. We should help students discover who they are, what they love in life and what they really want to be in life.' Dr Seldon thinks that we should make an effort to teach teenagers more about their minds and bodies. 'Teach people about these things when they are young and they will have them for life,' he says.

2 The Teacher

In the classes, Ian Morris teaches students meditation to help with stress and techniques for dealing with anger. Another classroom activity is 'count your blessings': pupils make lists of things which they are grateful for. 'Most of our pupils like the lessons,' says Ian. 'But once I sent one boy out of class for playing around. He complained, "I was sent out of happiness class for laughing," which I thought was funny.'

3 The Students

To start with, the students at Wellington were not very sure about their 'happiness' classes. 'But our happiness classes are actually well-being classes,' says Felix Cook. 'The school wants to prepare us so that when we are sad we can deal with it constructively rather than use drugs and alcohol. We learn that some things are not so important. For example, if you don't do well in a subject at school, it's not the end of the world. You can be less stressed out and do better in a subject because of it.' Another student, Charlie Maugham thinks the classes have made a big difference to his everyday life. 'The meditation techniques help me control my nerves before an important game or exam.' Charlie also thinks that the lessons have helped him make decisions and changed his opinions about life. 'Our culture is dominated by adverts about money and cars. People think that to be happy you have to be rich. I think we have lost contact with true happiness.'

5 Read the article again. Match the people with the statements below.

AS (Anthony Seldon)   CM (Charlie Maugham)
IM (Ian Morris)   FC (Felix Cook)

1 'I'm more relaxed when I do sport now.' *CM*
2 'Since I started the classes I'm not so worried about schoolwork.'
3 'Students enjoy my classes but sometimes they don't take them seriously.'
4 'Being rich does not bring happiness.'
5 'We need to teach students to be happy.'
6 'We learn what to do when we feel unhappy.'

6 Vocabulary **Look at Exercise 1 and the words in blue in the text. Complete the Word Builder with the words below.**

~~money~~ well a difference exercise better an effort decisions a list things (for other people) people happy

> **Word Builder** *make* and *do*
>
> **make** *money, ...*_____
>
> **do** _____

LANGUAGE CHOICE 63: VOCABULARY PRACTICE

7 Work in pairs. Ask and answer the questions.

1 What things make you happy?
2 What makes you sad or angry?
3 How many hours of exercise do you do a week?
4 What have you done for somebody else recently?
5 In what school subjects do you do well and which should you do better at?

Listening

8 5.28 5.29 SKILLS BUILDER 10 **Listen to three situations. Use the strategies in the Skills Builder to match the information (a-c) with the situations.**

1 Where is the dialogue taking place?
   a bus stop ☐ b doctor's surgery ☐1
   c school cafeteria ☐
2 Who is speaking in each of the three dialogues?
   a schoolmates ☐ b doctor/patient ☐1
   c two neighbours ☐
3 What time of day is it?
   a about 10 a.m. ☐ b lunch time ☐
   c in the evening ☐1
4 In which dialogue does somebody:
   a ask for advice ☐1
   b make a request for something? ☐
   c complain about something? ☐

9 Look at the Sentence Builder. How do you say the sentences in your language?

> **Sentence Builder** *not enough/too*
>
> I'm **not** relaxed **enough to** do maths.
> I'm **too** busy **to** do a lot of exercise.

10 Work in pairs. Use the cues to make sentences with *too* and *not enough*.

1 tired / do homework today

   We're too tired to do homework today.

2 old / get a job
3 nervous / do well in exams
4 shy / meet people at parties
5 tall / be a good basketball player
6 young / vote in elections
7 impatient / play chess
8 rich / buy a car

 LANGUAGE CHOICE 64

11 Choose two of the options (a-f). Write notes about your problems.

personality: too impatient/don't like people who are late

a personality
b school (e.g. exams/homework)
c money
d social life and friends
e health/exercise/food
f sport/hobbies

12 Work in pairs. Share your problems and give each other advice.

A: *I'm too impatient. I get angry when people are late.*
B: *You should do meditation exercises.*

No Comment

'What's the use of happiness? It can't buy you money.'

Henny Youngman, American comedian

Your Choice

EXAM STRESS

① Read the exam tips. Which of these things do you do?

Exam Tips

Revision:

Prepare a revision timetable – don't leave revision to the last minute.
Don't study all the time, take breaks.
Don't drink too much coffee, tea and fizzy drinks – they'll make you too excited.
Take regular exercise – it will give you energy and reduce stress.
Don't revise the night before an exam.

On the exam day:

Eat breakfast before the exam.
Go to the toilet before the exam starts!
Don't panic! Take deep breaths to deal with stress.

② Read the email. What does Peter think of the exam tips? How well do you think he will do in the exam?

Hi John,

The exam is in two days and I'm really nervous. Our teacher gave us some exam tips. She told us to prepare a revision timetable – a bit late for that, isn't it? She also advised us not to drink coffee or coke! How can you do that if you have to study all night? She told us not to panic – easier said than done – and to breathe deeply. I breathe all the time and it doesn't help me much! And she advised us to go to the toilet before the exam starts – that's a good one!
I'm just hoping for some luck.

Take care,

Peter

Reporting advice, orders and requests

③ Complete the table with Peter's report of the exam tips. Then complete the rule.

Advice	Peter's report
1 *Prepare a revision timetable.* 2 *Don't drink coffee or coke!* 3 *Don't panic.*	*She told us …*

- When we report people's advice, order or requests we use this pattern: *ask/tell/want/advise* someone + (not) + _____ + infinitive.

④ Read the reported sentences (1–4). Write the original advice, orders or requests in two different ways.

1 My brother asked me to repair his bike.

   Can you repair my bike? / Please, repair my bike.

2 My mum wanted me to go to bed earlier.
3 A friend advised me not to study so much.
4 The teacher told us not to fall asleep in her lessons.

➤ LANGUAGE CHOICE 65

⑤ Report the tips from Exercise 1 which are not reported in Peter's email.

   The teacher advised us to take regular exercise.

⑥ Read the tips a friend has given you about what to do when your boyfriend/girlfriend breaks up with you. Report them and comment on their usefulness.

1 Don't think about the past.

   She told me not to think about the past. I think this is good advice.

2 Go out and meet some friends.
3 Don't phone or write to your girlfriend/boyfriend.
4 Watch a comedy.
5 Don't tell anyone about how you feel.
6 Throw away all photos, letters, etc. that remind you of your girlfriend/boyfriend.

Writing Workshop 6

1 Read the notes. Match the requests (1-2) with the replies (a-b).

1
Hi C,
A quick note to ask you something – I've just been on the phone with Sam and he is going away all summer. Maybe he wants to finish our relationship!!!!!!! I'm feeling really DOWN and just don't know what to do. Can we meet to have a chat about it tomorrow after school? I'd really like to hear what you think. I'll be out tonight. Please, leave a message on my mobile.
Thanks a lot. D.

2
Hi there,
You know we've got that French oral exam next week? Well, I'm really nervous about it. I'm completely STRESSED OUT!!!!!! Can you do me a favour? You're much better at French than me. Can you meet up with me tomorrow evening so that you can help me practise the interview? We can meet up at that café near your school. Give me a ring (I'm at home) or send me a message. I'll be here with my French textbook!
All the best, F

a Sorry, I can't tomorrow – I've got a judo match. What about the weekend? I can come round to your place to work on it there.

b No problem. That's terrible. Poor you! Let's meet up at that café near your school so that we can have a good chat.

Text Builder

2 Read the notes (1-2) again. In what order do the writers do these things?

a say how to contact them ☐
b explain the situation ☐1☐
c request help ☐
d arrange to meet up ☐
e describe feelings ☐

3 Find examples of informal writing in the two notes.

4 Look at the Sentence Builder. How do you say the words in **bold** in your language? Find two examples of the structures in the replies (a-b) in Exercise 1.

> **Sentence Builder** Purpose linkers
>
> Can we meet **to have a chat** about it tomorrow after school?
> Can you meet up with me tomorrow after school **so that we can have a chat** about it?
>
> ➡ SKILLS BUILDER 36

5 Use the cues to write requests with *to* and *so that*.

1 borrow your guitar / practice for the school concert
Can I borrow your guitar so that I can play in the school concert? Can I borrow your guitar to practice for the school concert?

2 meet up tomorrow / study for the history exam
3 ring me / talk about a problem I've got
4 come shopping with me / help me choose a new jacket for the party
5 send me the photos / put them on my home page

6 Write a note to a friend asking for something.

➡ SKILLS BUILDER 37

1 Look at Exercise 2. Write short notes with ideas about the things below:
   • the situation
   • your feelings
   • the request
   • where to meet
   • how to contact you.

2 Use your notes to write the message to your friend.

3 Check your notes for spelling mistakes.

7 Work in pairs. Give your note to your partner. Your partner writes a short reply to it.

8 What did you ask for? Did your partner agree? Tell the class.

Sandra asked me to meet up to talk about something. We agreed to meet up at the weekend.

Abba forever!

1 Look at the poster of the ABBA tribute band. Answer the questions.

1 Are there any tribute bands (groups that play a famous groups' music) in your country? What groups do they imitate?
2 Would you go to a concert of an ABBA tribute band? Why/Why not?
3 What tribute band would you like to watch?

2 5.30 5.31 Listen to a dialogue and answer the questions.

1 What kind of event was it? *an ABBA concert*
2 When was it?
3 Who was there?
4 What was the best moment?
5 What happened?
6 Was it good fun? Why?

3 5.32 5.33 Listen to the dialogue again. Which of the questions (1–8) in the Talk Builder:

a show interest/surprise? b ask for clarification?

Talk Builder Active listening

1 An ABBA concert? *b*   5 *Mamma Mia?*
2 With your grandma?   6 Did she?
3 Was it?   7 Really?
4 Were they?   8 Have you?

➔ SKILLS BUILDER 52

---

4 5.34 Pronunciation Listen to the questions again and repeat them. Notice the intonation.

5 Complete the dialogues below with *are, were, do, did* or *has*.

1 A: I was at a concert on Saturday.
   B: _Were_ you? Lucky you!
2 A: We won the game at the weekend!
   B: _____ you? That's great!
3 A: Sue's won that music prize.
   B: _____ she? Brilliant!
4 A: I'm going to be in the football team on Saturday.
   B: _____ you? Congratulations.
5 A: I take part in chess competitions.
   B: _____ you? That sounds really interesting.

6 ➔ SKILLS BUILDER 53 Work in pairs. Take turns to say things using the cues below. Use the strategies in the Skills Builder to react to your partner.

A: *On Saturday, I took part in a debate.*
B: *Really? Did you?*
A: *Yeah, it was about climate change.*
B: *Climate change?*

go to an event (a concert/a football game/a celebration/a film/a play/an exhibition)

take part in something (a competition/a debate/ a game/a concert/a play)

7 Tell your partner about a happy experience at an event.

➔ SKILLS BUILDER 43

1 Look at the questions in Exercise 2. Write notes to answer them.

2 Use your notes to rehearse your story of the event.

3 Work in pairs. Take turns to tell your partner about the event. Listen actively!

8 Tell the class about your partner's event.

Javier went to a football match with his dad on Sunday. It was between Atlético and Real Madrid. Atlético won 4–3 in the last moment. Javier had a great time because he's an Atlético supporter!

Language Review Module 12

1 Emotions **Complete the text with the correct words.**

Most people hate Mondays. They often ¹____ angry and ² *depressing/depressed*. I think Mondays are ³ *excited/exciting*. After a long, ⁴ *boring/bored* weekend, you can do new ⁵ *interesting/interested* things. So I am usually in a good ⁶ _____ on Monday morning. Actually, I find Sundays a ⁷____ stressful and ⁸ *upset/upsetting*. Spending all day with my family is sometimes ⁹ *irritating/irritated*. I often get quite ¹⁰ *annoying/annoyed* on Sundays. **/10**

2 *make* and *do* **Complete the sentences with *make* or *do*.**

The students are ¹¹_____ much better now – having well-being classes ¹²_____ a big difference. Some people ¹³_____ a lot of money but it doesn't ¹⁴_____ them happy. ¹⁵_____ an effort and ¹⁶_____ more exercise. **/6**

3 *not enough/too, to/so that* **Use the words in brackets to rewrite the sentences.**

17 I'm not very strong. I can't lift this box.
I am not _____ . (*enough*)
18 He is very tired. He can't do his homework now.
He is _____ . (*too*)
19 We are saving money. We want to buy a computer.
We are _____ . (*to*)
20 I'll phone you to discuss the project.
I'll phone you _____ . (*so that*)
21 We are too poor to buy a yacht.
We aren't _____ . (*enough*)
22 It's very dark. We can't read the map.
It's _____ . (*too*)
23 I am studying. I want to improve my marks.
I am _____ . (*to*) **/7**

4 Reporting advice, orders and requests **Use the verbs in brackets to rewrite the sentences.**

24 'Don't go there!'
The teacher _____ . (*ordered*)
25 'Can you help me with this bag?'
The woman _____ . (*asked*)
26 'I'd like you to wash up.'
My mother_____ . (*wanted*)
27 'Call me tomorrow, please!'
The doctor _____ . (*told*)
28 'Don't eat so much chocolate!'
My mum _____ . (*told*)
29 'Can you open the door, please?'
The man _____ . (*asked*) **/6**

5 Defining relative clauses **Rewrite the sentences. Change the sentence in brackets into a relative clause.**

30 The boy is in hospital. (He had an accident.)
31 The day was beautiful. (We arrived in Venice on that day.)
32 Most people don't smoke. (I work with these people.)
33 The book is a bestseller. (It talks about dinosaurs.)
34 I don't know the club. (Our band is playing there.)
35 The restaurant is really fantastic.
(It won the 'Best Dessert' competition.) **/6**

6 Active listening **Complete the dialogues with *were, do, did, have* or *has*.**

36 **A:** I went to Peru last summer.
B: _____ you? Lucky you!
37 **A:** We were at home last night!
B: _____ you? No one answered the phone.
38 **A:** I've found the money.
B: _____ you? Where was it?
39 **A:** I love football.
B: _____ you? I prefer basketball.
40 **A:** My dad has won some money in the lottery!
B: _____ he? How much? **/5**

Self Assessment

5.35 **Listen and check your answers. Write down the scores. Use the table to find practice exercises.**

Exercise	If you need practice, go to
1	Language Choice 61
2	Language Choice 63
3	Language Choice 64; SB p.99 ex. 4, 5
4	Language Choice 65
5	Language Choice 62
6	SB p.100, ex. 3, 5

LEARNING LINKS: **1** **Check Your Progress 12** → MyLab / Workbook page 107. Complete the **Module Diary**.
2 **Exam Choice 6** → MyLab / Workbook pages 108-110.
3 Find out about cultural differences and listen to a song in **Culture Choice 6** on page 112. Then do a project with advice for people coming to your country.

Culture Choice 1

1 Which of the world's major festivals (1–4) can you see in the photos (a–b) on page 103? Do you celebrate any of them?

1 Diwali (Hindu) 2 Chinese New Year
3 Eid al-Fitr (Muslim) 4 Christmas

2 Vocabulary Look at the words below. Which of these things can you see in the photos?

Decorations
lights, candles, plants
(Christmas tree/mistletoe)

Activities
dance, have parades/parties,
give presents,
pull crackers, send cards,
watch fireworks

Festivals

Food
desserts (cake, pudding,
mince pies), roast meat (turkey/
lamb), sweets

3 Work in pairs. Try to answer the quiz.

1 **Which two festivals are related to Christmas?**
a Halloween (Celtic) b Yule (Scandinavian) c Saturnalia (Roman)

2 **When did people begin to celebrate Christmas on 25 December?**
a 1st century AD (Palestine)
b 2nd century AD (Greece)
c 4th century AD (Rome)

3 **Where does the name 'Santa Claus' come from?**
a Father Christmas (England)
b Saint Nicholas (The Netherlands)
c Odin (Scandinavia)

4 **Where did people first have Christmas trees?**
a Scotland/Ireland b the USA/Canada
c Germany/Scandinavia

5 **What special food do the British eat at Christmas?**
a fish soup, turkey, Christmas pudding
b mince pies, turkey, Christmas pudding
c mince pies, turkey, apple pie

4 6.1 6.2 Listen to the radio programme. Check your answers to the quiz in Exercise 3.

5 6.3 6.4 Listen again and answer the questions.

1 Why did people celebrate mid-winter festivals?
2 When did the Dutch go to America?
3 What do people eat at Christmas in the USA?

6 Read the information about Adrian Henri. Then read through the first two verses of the poem and find words related to Christmas.

stocking …

7 6.5 Use the glossary to read the whole poem. What is it about?

a how he enjoyed Christmas and New Year
b his love for a woman he misses
c his plans for this year

8 Answer these questions. Find sentences and expressions to explain your answers.

1 How does he feel?
2 Who does he miss?
3 What do you think has happened?
4 What celebrations does he enjoy?
5 Why is he sad about the future?

9 Read the poem again. Which of these things do you think are *not* true?

1 British people get presents on Christmas morning.
2 People sing songs at Christmas lunch.
3 People eat and drink a lot at Christmas.
4 People give presents at New Year.
5 People sing a song at New Year.

My Culture Project

10 Choose an important festival in your country. Make notes to answer the questions. Use vocabulary from Exercises 2 and other words. It is sometimes impossible to use an English word! e.g. *panettone (Italian Christmas cake)*

1 When do you celebrate and who with?
2 What decorations are there?
3 What special meals do you have?
4 Do you give/receive presents? Who to/from?
5 What other things do you do (e.g. dance/sing)?

11 Work in pairs. Imagine you are telling a visitor to your country about the festival. Take turns to ask and answer the questions.

A: *What is your celebration? When do you celebrate?*
B: *We celebrate Eid al-Fitr. The date changes every year. We celebrate the end of Ramadan. That's a time when you don't eat or drink during the day …*

Talking After Christmas Blues

Adrian Henri (1932-2000) was a talented painter, poet and musician. Adrian became famous in the 1960s and was one of the 'Liverpool poets'. He knew the Beatles, John Lennon and Paul McCartney, and had his own band 'The Liverpool Scene'. He wrote popular poems about everyday life.

Well l woke up this mornin' it was Christmas Day
And the birds were singing the night away
I saw my stocking lying on the chair
Looked right to the bottom but you weren't there
there was*
   apples
     oranges
       chocolates
         ... aftershave
but no you.

So I went downstairs and the dinner was fine
There was pudding and turkey and lots of wine
And I pulled those crackers with a laughing face
Till I saw there was no one in your place
there was
   mince pies
     brandy
       nuts and raisins
         ... mashed potato
— but no you.

Now it's New Year and it's Auld Lang Syne
And it's twelve o'clock and I'm feeling fine
Should Auld Acquaintance be Forgot**?
I don't know girl, but it hurts a lot
there was
   whisky
     vodka
       dry Martini (stirred
        but not shaken)
... and twelve New Year resolutions
- all of them about you.

So it's all the best for the year ahead
As I stagger upstairs and into bed
Then looked at the pillow by my side
... I tell you baby I almost cried
there'll be
   Autumn
     Summer
       Spring
         ... and Winter
- all of them without you.

Glossary

aftershave: (n) perfume for men
ahead: (adv) in front of you
Auld Lang Syne: a traditional Scottish song, sung at New Year
crackers: (n) decorated paper tubes containing a small gift and a joke that make a noise when you pull them - traditional at British Christmas dinner
downstairs: (adv) to the lower floor of a house
pillow: (n) a soft object - you put your head here in bed
resolution: (n) a promise about the future
stagger: (v) walk with difficulty
(Christmas) stocking: (n) a big sock with presents in it

*   informal (correct = there were)
** first line of the song = is it a good idea to forget old friends?

Culture Choice 2

1 **Vocabulary Complete the sentences (1-5) with the words below.**
- to be **in debt** (to someone)
- to **owe** money to someone
- to **borrow** money from someone/to **lend** money to someone
- to **make** money
- to **make a fortune** (a lot of money)
- to **win**
- to **lose** money (e.g. by gambling)
- to **inherit** money from your family
- to **invest** money in something (e.g. buy shares)

1 Tim _inherited_ some money from his grandma when she died last year. He ____ it in shares and ____ a fortune.
2 Sally ____ £1 million on the lottery but she ____ it all at the casino.
3 Sam bought a fantastic car but now he's in ____ to the bank.
4 My friend ____ £10 from me last week and she still ____ me £6.
5 I ____ a lot of money from a holiday job and I ____ some of it to my brother.

2 **6.6** **6.7** **Listen to a lesson about the writer Charles Dickens' early life. Complete the text.**

On his [1]-_twelfth_ birthday, Charles Dickens went to work in a factory. Soon afterwards, his family went to a prison for people in debt because his father owed [2] £____ . Charles lived in a different part of [3] ____ and only saw his family on [4] ____ . After [5] ____ months, everything changed and Charles went back to [6] ____ . When he was [7] ____ , Charles got a job in an office and later became a journalist. Charles wrote [8] ____ novels and made a lot of money but he never forgot his early experiences.

3 **Look at the drawings (a-d) from the story, _Little Dorrit_. Try to guess the order. Then read the story quickly and check your guesses.**

4 **6.8** **Read and listen to the story. Answer the questions.**

1 Why were the Dorrits in prison?
   William Dorrit owed money to different people.
2 Why did Amy need to look after her father?
3 Why did people call her 'Little Dorrit'?
4 How did the Dorrits suddenly become rich?
5 How did Amy's family change with the money?
6 How did the Dorrits and Arthur lose their money?
7 Why did Arthur realise that Amy loved him?
8 How did Arthur get out of Marshalsea?

5 **Work in pairs. Discuss the questions. Then tell the class your answers.**

1 Did you like the story? Why/Why not?
2 Would you like to watch the film of the story?
3 Why do you think Dickens wrote _Little Dorrit_?
4 How did Dickens' early experiences help him write the book?

6 **Your Culture** **Work in pairs. Read the proverbs (1-4). Which of them do you agree with? Tell the class your answers.**

1 'The best things in life are free.' (English)
2 'Money goes where money is.' (Spanish)
3 'With money you can buy a house but not a home.' (Chinese)
4 'The best way to stay poor is to be an honest man.' (French)

7 **What proverbs about money are there in your language? Try to translate them into English.**

My Culture Project

8 **Work in pairs. Find out about the life of a famous writer from your country. Write notes to answer the questions.**

1 Where was he/she from? What kind of family did he/she come from?
2 What early experiences did he/she have?
3 What job did he/she do?
4 What things did he/she write?
5 How did his/her early life influence his/her writing?
6 How successful was he/she?

9 **Tell the class about your writer.**

Miguel de Cervantes was born in Alcalá de Henares but his family moved to different cities. His father was a doctor but he had money problems and was sometimes in prison because he was in debt.

LITTLE DORRIT

It was a hot summer's day in Marshalsea Prison in London. The prison was noisy and smelly and a lot of the prisoners and their families were hungry. One young family, the
5   Dorrits, were new to the prison. The father, William Dorrit, was not a criminal but he owed money to different people. William was not worried: 'I'll soon pay the debt and we'll be out of here,' he said.

10 That afternoon, Mrs Dorrit had a little baby girl, Amy, in the prison. A few weeks later, Mrs Dorrit died and left her husband with three young children. Time passed and, when they were older, the Dorrit children went out of the
15 prison every day to work. Unfortunately, Amy's brother was lazy and her pretty older sister wanted to be a dancer, so Amy needed to work hard to get money for her family and to look after her father too.

20 When Amy was twenty-two, she was small and thin; a lot of people thought she was still young and called her 'Little Dorrit'. She still looked after her father in the prison and went out to work in an old lady's house. One day, Amy met
25 the old lady's son, Arthur. He was twenty years older than Amy but he felt sorry for her and wanted to help her family. Amy started to fall in love with this quiet, sensitive man.

A few months later, the Dorrits inherited a lot
30 of money and suddenly became rich. The family immediately left Marshalsea Prison and moved into a big house. Amy's father, brother and sister loved their new life with rich food, fine clothes and lots of parties but they were frightened that
35 people would discover their past at Marshalsea. Only Amy did not change because of the money; she still looked after her father and she still loved Arthur.

Amy's sister married a rich but stupid young
40 man and her brother lost money by gambling. Then things got worse. Amy's father died and there was a terrible financial scandal in London. The Dorrits had money in a bank but its owner was a criminal and they lost a lot of it.
45 Because of the scandal, Arthur's business owed money to different people and they put him in Marshalsea Prison.

Arthur became very ill but Amy went to the prison every day to look after him. Arthur
50 started to realise that Amy loved him and that he loved her, too. Luckily, Arthur's business partner then returned to London after making a fortune and their business immediately recovered. Arthur left Marshalsea and soon got
55 better. A few months later, on a beautiful sunny morning Arthur and Amy got married.

Culture Choice 3

1 **6.9 Quiz** Listen to five extracts of traditional music (1–5) and match them with the photos (a–e). Which music do you like best?

2 **6.10 6.11** Listen to an interview about Irish music. Complete the notes.

ORIGINS:
- music - from ¹*hundreds* of years ago
- words of songs - from the ²_____ century.

INSTRUMENTS:
- traditional - ³_____ , harp and violin
- modern - guitar and ⁴_____ .

IRISH MUSIC NOW:
- traditional - The Chieftains
- ⁵_____ - The Corrs
- new age - Enya
- rock - Van Morrison/U2/ The Cranberries
- ⁶_____ - The Pogues

3 Read about the famous Irish song *The Fields of Athenry*. Match the words in blue in the text with the meanings (1–6).

1 to fight authority *rebel*
2 when people do not have enough food
3 a royal government (with a king or queen)
4 an area of land
5 independent from control by another country
6 to leave your country

The Fields of Athenry

In the 1840s, there was a terrible famine in Ireland because a disease killed most of the potatoes. A million people died and a million emigrated because of the famine. Some of them had to go on British prison ships to the colony of Botany Bay in Australia.

At the time, Ireland was part of the United Kingdom but the government did not do very much to help and in 1848 some young Irish people rebelled against the British crown. Ireland finally became free from the UK in 1922.

In 1979, an Irish singer and song-writer, Pete St John, wrote *The Fields of Athenry* about the famine. The song was a hit in the 1980s and many different Irish and American groups have recorded it, including the punk-rock group, Dropkick Murphys. Fans at Irish rugby and football games often sing the song.

b

a

4 Read the song lyrics and use the glossary to help you. Then order the pictures (a–c).

The Fields of Athenry [1]

By a lonely prison wall,
I heard a young girl calling:
'Michael, they are taking you away,
For you stole Trevelyn's [2] corn,
So the young might see the morn.
Now a prison ship lies waiting in the bay.'

Low lie the fields of Athenry
Where once we watched the small free birds fly
Our love was on the wing
We had dreams and songs to sing
It's so lonely round the fields of Athenry.

By a lonely prison wall,
I heard a young man calling
'Nothing matters, Mary, when you're free.
Against the famine and the crown,
I rebelled, they cut me down.
Now you must raise our child with dignity.'

By a lonely harbour wall,
She watched the last star falling
As the prison ship sailed out against the sky
Sure she'll wait and hope and pray
For her love in Botany Bay
It's so lonely round the fields of Athenry.

Glossary
by: (prep) next to
corn: (n) cereal to make bread
dignity: (n) calm, serious behaviour
field: (n) area of land
for: (conj) because
harbour: (n) where ships can stay
low lie: (v) to be a flat area
morn: (n) morning
on the wing: (adj) flying
pray: (v) ask God for help
raise a child: (v) look after/educate
rebel: (v) to fight authority
the young: (n) their children
the crown: (n) the UK government

1 a town in western Ireland
2 an English lord living in Ireland

5 **6.12** Listen to two versions of the song (traditional and punk-rock). Which one do you prefer?

6 Read the lyrics again and choose the best answer to the questions.

1 Who is the girl in the story?
  a Michael's sister (b) Michael's wife
  c Michael's daughter
2 Why did Michael steal the food?
  a His children were hungry.
  b He hated Lord Trevelyn.
  c He wanted a free Ireland.
3 What memories does the girl have of Athenry Fields?
  a of being lonely b of the small birds
  c of happy times with Michael
4 What does Michael tell the girl?
  a 'The soldiers cut my leg.'
  b 'I want to be free.'
  c 'Look after our child.'
5 What did the girl feel?
  a She wanted to go to Botany Bay.
  b She prayed for Michael's return.
  c She felt okay without her husband.

7 Your Culture Work in pairs. Discuss the questions. Then tell the class your answers.

1 What traditional songs from your country do you like? How many can you sing?
2 When do people usually sing traditional songs? (e.g. family celebrations)
3 Is folk music popular with young people in your country?

My Culture Project

8 Work in groups. Prepare a short presentation for the rest of the class.

1 Choose a song (traditional or modern) from your country and find a recording of it.
2 Make notes about these things:
  • what kind of song it is: folk song/ pop song/love song
  • what the song is about: who is singing/what happens in the song
3 Translate the chorus or a couple of lines.
4 Think about why you like it/why it is important to you.

9 Give your presentation to the class and play the song. Which is your favourite song? Have a class vote.

Culture Choice 4

Moby Dick

a red fox
b wild boar
c red squirrel
d grey wolf
e otter
f butterfly

1 Look at the photos (a–f). Are there any of these animals in your country?

2 6.13 6.14 Listen to a radio programme. Match the animals in the photos (a–f) with the descriptions (1–6).

1 going down in numbers *f*
2 extinct
3 endangered
4 going up in numbers
5 became extinct but now re-introduced
6 common

3 6.15 6.16 Listen again. Answer the questions.

1 Why is British wildlife endangered? What four reasons does the report mention?
2 What animal have people traditionally hunted in the UK?
3 What kind of hunting is now illegal in the UK?

4 Your Culture Work in pairs. Think of six species of animals in your country. Describe them as in Exercise 2.

5 Read the information about the American writer Herman Melville. Then read the story quickly and answer the questions.

1 What is it about?
2 How do you think Melville's personal experiences helped him to write the story?

Call me Ishmael. I'm a sailor from Manhattan and I'm going to tell you a strange story. You may believe it or you may not but every word of it is true. One dark stormy night, I arrived in the town of New Bedford. I was tired and hungry and went to a small hotel. Unfortunately, I had to share a room with another sailor. I went to sleep. I woke up when a strange dark man, covered in tattoos, came into the room. He was frightening at first but soon I became friends with Queequeg, a Polynesian whaler, and the next day we went together to Nantucket to look for work on a whaling ship.

We got work on a ship called *The Pequod* and sailed out on Christmas Day. The crew was friendly but there was no sign of the captain. Then, after several days, Captain Ahab appeared. He was the strangest man I've ever seen; he had an enormous scar on his face and one leg made of whale bone. Captain Ahab called the crew together and talked to us. A few years before, a white whale called Moby Dick destroyed Ahab's ship and bit off his leg. Now our captain wanted to find the whale and kill him.

One day, Queequeg became very ill. He thought he was going to die so he made his own coffin. Luckily, my friend got better after some days but after that he always slept in his coffin. We spent several months hunting whales and the crew wanted to return home but Ahab was obsessed with his enemy, the white whale. One night, Ahab somehow smelt Moby Dick and the chase began.

Glossary
coffin: (n) long box for a dead person
crew: (n) people working on a ship
float: (v) to stay on the surface of liquid
harpoon: (n) a weapon like a spear
overturn: (v) turn something over
scar: (n) permanent mark from a cut
whaler: (n) ship to hunt for whales

Herman Melville (1819–1891) was born in New York City and went to sea when he was seventeen. In 1841, he joined a whaler and travelled around the world. He left his ship in Polynesia and stayed there for several months. Eventually, he got back to Boston and started to write novels.

On the first day, the enormous whale came to the surface and looked at us calmly. We lowered our boats from the ship but Moby Dick disappeared underwater. Then, suddenly, the whale came up fast and bit Ahab's boat in half. We rescued Ahab and the other men but the whale escaped. On the second day, we saw Moby Dick again and this time the whale overturned another boat and escaped again.

On the last day, we saw the whale again and chased it. Ahab threw a harpoon into Moby Dick's side but the whale became angry and attacked our ship with his enormous head. Ahab threw a harpoon at the whale but the animal pulled him into the sea. The ship started to sink and I was the only person to survive. Somehow, I swam away from the ship and, when I saw Queequeg's coffin floating near me, I got on to it. I floated for a day and a night and eventually a ship picked me up. Because of that, I am here to tell you this story.'

6 **6.17 Read and listen to the story. Order Ishmael's experiences (1–7).**

1 Another ship rescues him.
2 He meets Queequeg and they become friends. *1*
3 He sees Moby Dick attack them.
4 He sees Moby Dick for the first time.
5 He meets Captain Ahab and hears about Moby Dick.
6 He gets a job on *The Pequod*.
7 He escapes from *The Pequod* on Queequeg's coffin.

7 **Read the story again and answer the questions.**

1 Why was Ishmael frightened at the hotel?

because a strange man covered in tattoos came into his room

2 Why was Captain Ahab strange?
3 Why was Captain Ahab obsessed with Moby Dick?
4 How did Queequeg act strangely?
5 What was Moby Dick`s first reaction to the sailors?
6 What did Captain Ahab try to do?
7 Why did *The Pequod* sink?
8 How did Ishmael escape?

8 **Work in pairs. Discuss the questions. Then tell the class your answers.**

1 Melville's story is about (rare) attacks by whales on whale ships. Why do you think they attack ships?
2 Some countries still hunt and eat whales for food. Do you think it is right or wrong?
3 Should people hunt animals for fur (e.g. seals) or for pleasure (e.g. wild boar)?

My Culture Project

9 **Choose an interesting animal. Find out these things about it:**

- status (endangered/common, etc.)
- can people hunt it?
- its size/appearance
- its habitat/food/habits
- why you like it

10 **Work in groups. Tell your group about the animal you have chosen.**

The blue whale is an incredible animal. It's the biggest animal on Earth. Now it's endangered and there only a few thousand blue whales.

Culture Choice 5

1 Work in pairs. Ask and answer the questions.

1 Have you read any books or seen any films about desert island survival? Did you like them? Why/Why not?
2 Would you like to spend time alone on a desert island? Why/Why not?

2 (6.18) (6.19) Listen to the interview about Daniel Defoe and *Robinson Crusoe*. Order the events (a-g).

a Defoe probably spoke to Selkirk and other castaways on desert islands.
b He wrote the book *Robinson Crusoe*.
c He became a journalist and a writer.
d He went to prison again because of one of his articles.
e After that, he wrote other famous novels like *Moll Flanders* and *Roxana*.
f Daniel Defoe was born in London. *1*
g He went to debtors' prison because he owed a lot of money.

3 (6.20) (6.21) Listen again and answer the questions.

1 Why was *Robinson Crusoe* an important book?
2 How much money did Defoe owe?
3 What did he do after he left prison?
4 Why did an article put him in prison again?
5 How were Robinson Crusoe and the real sailor, Alexander Selkirk, different?
6 Why were Defoe's novels, *Moll Flanders* and *Roxana*, unusual for the time?

4 (6.22) Read and listen to the extract from *Robinson Crusoe*. Choose the best title for it. Use the glossary to help you.

a My happy island life
b Alone on the island
c Not alone on the island

Glossary

bone: (n) one of the hard parts of the body
cave: (n) a hole in the ground
footprint: (n) a mark made by a foot or shoe
gun: (n) a weapon which fires bullets
native: (n) people living in a place when foreigners arrived
servant: (n) a person who lives in your house and cleans, cooks and does other jobs
tame: (adj) not afraid of people (for an animal)
wall: (n) a structure to divide one area from another
wreck: (n) a badly damaged car, plane or ship

Robinson Crusoe

Robinson Crusoe was shipwrecked on a small island near the coast of Venezuela. Robinson was the only survivor but he collected useful things from the ship before it sank: tools, seeds and guns. He made his home in a cave, planted corn and had tame goats for milk and meat. He was happy on his island until one day he saw something ...

'This afternoon, I was walking along the beach when I saw the footprint of a man in the sand! I listened and I looked round me but I couldn't hear or see anything. I was frightened and ran home to my cave on the other side of the island. That night, it was impossible to sleep; I was thinking all the time, "Who was this person? What was he doing on my island?"

The next day, I decided that the footprint was probably that of a native from the mainland. What would happen if these natives found my boat or my fields? I was so afraid that I stayed in my cave for three days and three nights. Then, I started to go out to collect food and to milk my goats but started building a wall around my cave for protection.

A few months later, I was exploring the other side of the island when I saw some bones on the beach. There were human heads, hands and feet! The natives were cannibals and they came to my island to eat their prisoners. I became more careful than before and always carried my gun and three pistols. I made plans to kill them and to rescue their prisoners but what could one man do against thirty or forty natives? I decided to live quietly and not to visit the other side of the island.

A few months later, there was a storm and I heard the noise of a ship's gun. Immediately,

I ran to the top of the hill and made a fire to attract the ship's attention. However, the next day I saw the wreck of the ship near some big rocks. I went out to the ship in my small boat but there were no survivors. I found some boxes and took them back to my cave. When I opened them, I found clothes and food and also lots of gold and silver. I was now rich, but all this gold and silver was worth nothing to me, alone on my island.

One day, I saw some canoes on my side of the island. Through my telescope, I watched the cannibals with two prisoners. Suddenly, one of them escaped and ran along the beach very fast and came towards my cave. Two of the cannibals ran after him, but I decided to try to save the poor man's life. I went out with my guns and killed the two cannibals.

The man was frightened, but finally he came to me. I took him to my cave and gave him food and water. Soon, he fell asleep and when he woke up I began to talk to him and teach him to speak to me. I called him Friday, because it was the day I saved his life. Finally, I was not alone on the island and now I had a servant, too.'

⑤ **Read the extract again. Are the sentences true (T) or false (F)?**

1 Robinson Crusoe was a good survivor. T
2 He was happy when he saw the footprint.
3 The natives came to the island to find food.
4 A ship was wrecked on the island with no survivors.
5 Robinson found useful things like gold on the ship.
6 The cannibals were going to kill and eat their prisoners.
7 Robinson saved Friday's life and took him home.
8 Robinson decided to learn Friday's language.

⑥ **Answer the questions about the extract.**

1 What things helped Robinson survive on the island?
2 How did the footprint on the beach change his life?
3 Why was the gold and silver no use to him?
4 Why did he decide to save Friday's life?
5 What was Robinson's attitude towards Friday?

⑦ **Work in pairs. Discuss the questions.**

1 If you had to live on a desert island like Robinson Crusoe what five useful objects would you take? Give your reasons.
2 If you could take five books or records, what would you choose?
3 If you could choose five people to go with you, who would you choose?
4 What would you do to survive? How good would you be at survival?
5 Would you try to escape? How would you do it?

⑧ **Tell the class your answers.**

First, we would take a good, big knife. Then we would take …

My Culture Project

⑨ **Imagine you had to live on a desert island. What things would you miss from your country? Make a list of five things (not people). For example:**

- the radio and TV in my country
- my home town (the buildings/the shops)
- some food (e.g. special cheese)
- my house/bedroom
- the green countryside

⑩ **Work in groups. Tell your partners about the things that you would miss.**

111

a   b   c   d   e   f

1 Look at the drawings (a–f). Match them with the emotions (1–6).

1 scared *a*   2 sad   3 angry   4 happy
5 disgusted   6 surprised

2 Try to match the cultures (1–4) with the 'typical' behaviours (a–d).

1 Japanese   a show a lot of emotion.
2 Northern Europeans   b show quite a lot of emotion.
3 North Americans   c don't show a lot of emotion.
4 Mediterraneans and   d show very little emotion.
  Latin Americans

3 **6.23** **6.24** Listen to a talk about cultural differences. Check your guesses from Exercise 2.

4 **6.25** **6.26** Listen again. Are the sentences true (T) or false (F)?

1 People have different feelings in
  different cultures. *F*
2 Japanese people show emotion in their faces.
3 Japanese emoticons (happy ^.^ or sad ;_;) show
  the eyes but Western ones (happy : -) or sad : - ( )
  show the eyes, nose and mouth.
4 In Northern Europe, laughing is okay in
  most situations.
5 American babies show less emotion than
  Asian babies.
6 In the USA, you should always smile at strangers.
7 Mediterranean people use more gestures than
  those from Northern Europe.
8 North Americans stand closer together than South
  Americans.

5 Your Culture Work in pairs. Answer the questions.

1 Have you met people from other cultures? Did
  they appear 'cold' or 'excitable' to you? Why?
2 What differences in showing emotion and
  communication are there between your culture
  and those below?
  • the Japanese • the Italians
  • the British   • people from the USA

6 Read about Joan Armatrading and the lyrics of *Show Some Emotion*. What kind of culture do you think she comes from in terms of showing emotion?

7 **6.27** Listen to the song and read the lyrics. What ways of showing emotion does the singer mention?

8 Read the lyrics again. What does the singer advise you to do if you feel happy or sad?

My Culture Project

9 Work in pairs. Imagine a brother and sister are coming to live in your country from the USA or Britain. Write notes to answer the questions below.

1 What should I do when I meet someone new?
  (shake hands/kiss)
2 Should I smile and say hello to strangers?
3 Should I cry or show I'm angry in public?
4 In what situations is it okay to laugh out loud
  and make jokes?
5 When I'm talking to someone, how much
  should I look at them?
6 Is it okay to use gestures to show
  my feelings?
7 How close to other people should I sit
  or stand?
8 What should I do if I want to go out
  with someone?

10 Tell the class your advice. Do you all agree?

Show Some Emotion

Joan Armatrading was born on the Caribbean island of St Kitts and moved to Britain when she was young. She started writing songs, singing and playing the guitar in the 1970s. She has had hit songs and albums in the UK and the USA like *Show Some Emotion* and *Drop the Pilot*.

Show some emotion,
Put expression in your eyes,
Light up, if you're feeling happy,
But if it's bad then let those tears roll down.
Some people hurting,
Someone choking up inside,
Some poor souls dying,
Too proud to say they got no place to lie.
And there's people if they hear a joke,
Can't keep the laugh out of their eye.
I said, show some emotion,
Put expression in your eyes,
Light up, if you're feeling happy,
But if it's bad, then let those tears roll down.
Some people in love,
But all they got is a photograph.
How can they get it?
Too scared to open their mouth, to ask.
I said, show some emotion,
Put expression in your eyes,
Light up, if you're feeling happy,
But if it's bad, then let those tears roll down,
Come on try,
Learn to bleed when you get a bad fall,
Light up, light up, light up, if it's nice,
But if it's bad, then let those tears roll down.

Glossary
bleed: (v) to lose blood
choke up: (v) feel very upset
light up: (v) show happiness in your eyes
no place to lie: (n phr) nowhere to stay/ nobody to be with
poor soul: (n) unlucky person
roll down: (v) fall

113

STUDENT A

M3, Lesson 8, Exercise 13

1 Yes = not extravagant - 0 points, No = 1 point
2 Yes = not extravagant - 0 points, No = 1 point
3 Yes = extravagant - 1 point, No = 0 points
4 Yes = not extravagant - 0 points, No = 1 point
5 Yes = extravagant - 1 point, No = 0 points
6 Yes = extravagant - 1 point, No = 0 points
7 Yes = extravagant - 1 point, No = 0 points
8 Yes = extravagant - 1 point, No = 0 points

0-2 points - not extravagant at all
3-5 points - not very extravagant
6-8 points - quite extravagant
9-10 points - very extravagant

M5, Lesson 14, Exercise 12

Ask about these facts:

How long / the United States / be an independent country?
How long / internet/ be around?
How long / European countries / use the euro?
How long / Mona Lisa / be a symbol of beauty?
How long / California / belong to the USA?

Give information about these facts:

Albert Einstein / be dead / 1955
The Beatles / be popular / 1960s
Doctors / know penicillin / 1930s
The world / know Harry Potter / 1997
People / admire the Egyptian pyramids / 25 BC

M7, Lesson 19, Exercise 9

Read the remedy then answer your partner's questions.

First, take some yoghurt and mix it with three tablespoons of coffee.
Second, put the mixture in the fridge for four hours.
Third, put the mixture on your head with a brush.
Finally, cover your hair with a plastic bag. Now, you are ready to go out!

M9, Lesson 25, Exercise 9

Flight quiz

1 Who designed the first drawings of a flying machine and a parachute?
   a Michelangelo ⓑ Leonardo da Vinci c Newton
2 Who made the first powered flight in 1903?
   a Wilbur Wright b Katharine Wright ⓒ Orville Wright
3 When did Louis Blériot fly across the English Channel?
   a 1903 b 1905 ⓒ 1909
4 When did Charles Lindbergh make the first non-stop solo flight across the Atlantic?
   a 1917 ⓑ 1927 c 1937
5 Which country launched the first spaceship in 1957?
   a the USA b China ⓒ the USSR
6 Valentina Tereshkova was the first woman to go into space. When did she go?
   a 1953 ⓑ 1963 c 1983

M12, Lesson 34, Exercise 12

1 year - Armstrong first walked on the moon then (1969)
2 medicine - you take it to kill bacteria (antibiotics)
3 game - it was the most successful PC game ever (*The Sims*)
4 town - running of the bulls is organised there every year (Pamplona)
5 actor - he wore clothes that were too big (Chaplin)
6 animal - it produces honey (bee)
7 town - Camden market is there (London)
8 decade - mobile phones appeared then (1980s)

M12, Lesson 35, Exercise 2

Things that make people happier:

- Being in a steady relationship or being married - single people are less happy.
- Being religious - people who believe in God are happier than those who do not.
- Belonging to a club - people with more social contact are usually happier.
- Doing physical exercise - afterwards you feel better and more relaxed.
- Doing something nice for someone else makes you feel better and happier.
- Spending time with family and friends - people are usually happier when with other people than when they are alone.

Things that don't make people happier:

- Being successful - successful people are not actually any happier.
- Having a nice car/a big house/expensive clothes - richer people are not actually happier.

IRREGULAR VERBS

Infinitive	2nd form (Past Simple)	3rd Form (Past Participle)
be	was/were	been
become	became	become
begin	began	begun
break	broke	broken
bring	brought	brought
build	built	built
burn	burned/burnt	burned/burnt
buy	bought	bought
catch	caught	caught
choose	chose	chosen
come	came	come
cost	cost	cost
cut	cut	cut
dig	dug	dug
do	did	done
draw	drew	drawn
dream	dreamed/dreamt	dreamed/dreamt
drink	drank	drunk
drive	drove	driven
eat	ate	eaten
fall	fell	fallen
feed	fed	fed
feel	felt	felt
fight	fought	fought
find	found	found
fly	flew	flown
forget	forgot	forgotten
forgive	forgave	forgiven
get	got	got
give	gave	given
go	went	gone
grow	grew	grown
have	had	had
hear	heard	heard
hide	hid	hidden
hit	hit	hit
hold	held	held
hurt	hurt	hurt
keep	kept	kept
know	knew	known
lead	led	led
learn	learned/learnt	learned/learnt
leave	left	left

Infinitive	2nd form (Past Simple)	3rd Form (Past Participle)
lend	lent	lent
let	let	let
lie	lay	lain
light	lit	lit
lose	lost	lost
make	made	made
mean	meant	meant
meet	met	met
pay	paid	paid
put	put	put
read	read	read
ride	rode	ridden
ring	rang	rung
run	ran	run
say	said	said
see	saw	seen
sell	sold	sold
send	sent	sent
set	set	set
shine	shone	shone
show	showed	shown
shut	shut	shut
sing	sang	sung
sit	sat	sat
sleep	slept	slept
smell	smelled/smelt	smelled/smelt
speak	spoke	spoken
spend	spent	spent
spill	spilled/spilt	spilled/spilt
stand	stood	stood
steal	stole	stolen
swim	swam	swum
take	took	taken
teach	taught	taught
tear	tore	torn
tell	told	told
think	thought	thought
throw	threw	thrown
understand	understood	understood
wake	woke	woken
wear	wore	worn
win	won	won
write	wrote	written

🎧 Listening

1 Matching with pictures (the main idea)
Page 5, Exercise 2

- Before you listen, look at the drawings or pictures. Try to answer these questions: What is in the picture? Where is it? Who is in it? What is happening?
- Make a list of possible words and expressions (e.g. *wake up/alarm clock/feel tired*).
- When you listen to something, listen out for these words to help you identify the main idea. Then match the people with the pictures.

2 Multiple choice (specific information)
Page 17, Exercise 8

- Before you listen, read the questions carefully.
- Try to guess answers to the questions when possible. Use your knowledge of the world or any pictures there are.
- The first time you listen, listen out for the information. Sometimes it is in a different form (e.g. ¼ and not *25 percent*).
- When you listen again, try to get the rest of the information.
- When you don't know an answer, make a guess.

3 True/False (specific information)
Page 33, Exercise 7

- Read the statements. Identify important words or expressions (e.g. *treasure/rescue*).
- Read them again. Guess if the statements are true or false. Use any pictures there are to help you or use your general knowledge (e.g. about science fiction films).
- Listen the first time. Get the general idea and identify the important words or expressions or words with similar meaning.
- Listen again. Decide if the statements are true or false. Guess answers you don't know.

4 Matching (questions/parts of a text)
Page 49, Exercise 7

- Look at any pictures or photos related to the listening to help you get an idea.
- Read the questions and make guesses to answer them (e.g. *Where do you get music? – downloading/ buying CDs/from friends*).
- Think of words related to the topics in the questions (e.g. *getting music – downloading/ CDs/sharing*).
- When you listen, do not try to understand every word. Listen out for words from the questions or similar words (e.g. *get music/buy music*).
- Remember that texts will have some words related to different topics or questions to distract you.
- If you are not sure about the answers, make a guess.

5 Multiple choice (words/meanings)
Page 65, Exercise 7

- Look at the words and try to guess the meanings before you listen. Answer these questions:
  - Are there any words in your language that look similar?
  - Do you think the meaning is similar?
- When you listen, try to choose the answers. Use these things to help you:
  - the context (e.g. *long-sleeved shirt* (different kinds of shirts: summer/winter, etc.);
  - your general knowledge (e.g. *What do bears do when they are angry? They stand on their back legs*).
- Look at the three options (a-c) and choose the best one.

6 Identifying informal style

Page 68, Exercise 1

- Listen out for names:
  - *Mr Smith/Ms Jones* (formal)
  - *Mark/Sandra* (informal)
  - *Katy/Tim* (abbreviations = very informal)
  - *Darling/Sweetie* (expressions of affection = very, very informal)
- Notice colloquial words and expressions:
  - *Cool. Hey!/Oh stop it!/No problems./Oh no!/ Wow!*
- Pay attention to short forms:
  - *Who? (should we phone?)*
  - *(Are) You sure about this?*

7 Identifying formal style

Page 75, Exercise 7

- When you listen to dialogues you can tell formal style from this language (informal examples in brackets):

  Titles/names:

  Sir/Madam - only used by a shop assistant / waiter/airline employee, etc. *Mr Macdonald (Mike)/Ms Macdonald (Sue)*

  Expressions:

  Good morning. (Hi./Hello.)

  Excuse me? (Hey!)

  Not at all. (That's okay.)

  Requests:

  Could I have your bag, please? (Can I ... ?/ Give me your ...)

  Could you help me, please? (Can you ... ?/ Help me, please.)

8 Completing notes (specific information)

Page 81, Exercise 9

- Read the task first. Guess what kind of information you are listening for (e.g. a number, a measurement, a date, a place, an activity, an action).
- Make guesses about the information (e.g. *population of the Maldives = 1 million*). Use your general knowledge to help you.
- When you are listening, listen out for key words in the notes (e.g. *population*). Also listen out for words with the same meaning (e.g. *the number of people*).
- Use abbreviations to write down the information on a piece of paper (e.g. *1.5 m (metres)*).
- After listening, write out your answers. Make a guess when you are not sure.

9 Matching (speakers/intentions)

Page 91, Exercise 8

- Listen the first time to get the general idea of the situation. Who is speaking? Where are they?
- Listen again. Listen to the speakers' tone of voice. Are they friendly, relaxed or angry?
- Decide which of these things they want to do:
  - give information/tell somebody something
  - make a suggestion/give advice/give an opinion
  - ask for something (information/permission/ make a request)
  - react positively or negatively to requests/ suggestions
- Remember, that in English, people are not always very direct. They often say things indirectly, e.g. *It's cold. = Can you close the window?*

10 Multiple choice (focus on context)

Page 97, Exercise 8

- First, identify the basic situation (where it is and what is happening). Listen out for any sound effects (e.g. cars/telephones). Also listen out for important words related to different situations (e.g. *meeting/boss* = office).
- Think about the people. Who are they? What is the relationship between them? What do they call each other? What do they know about each other? What kind of language do they use (formal/informal)?
- Listen out for more information to find out the time and the intention of the speakers (e.g. words like *breakfast/lunch, morning/ evening* or expressions like *should/have to*).

 # Reading

11 Multiple choice (general idea)
Page 6, Exercise 2

- First, look at the text and any photos or drawings with it.
- Read the question and look at the options. Guess which one it is.
- Look through the text very quickly to check your guess.
- Do not read everything or try to understand all of the words.

12 Matching (general idea of parts of a text)
Page 6, Exercise 3

- Read all of the text first to get the general idea.
- Read each paragraph carefully, especially the first sentence. It usually introduces the topic of the paragraph.
- Underline important words in the paragraph. Then choose the heading from the list or think of a title for the paragraph.

13 Matching (words/meaning)
Page 16, Exercise 4

- Ask these questions to work out the meaning of the words:
  - What is the word: a verb, adjective, noun or adverb? (e.g. *simulation* = noun)
  - Are there any words that look similar to words in your language? Do you think the meaning is similar?
- Use the context to guess the meaning (e.g. *reviews of computer games*) and your general knowledge to help you (e.g. your knowledge of computer games).
- Match the words and the meanings. If you are not sure, make a guess.

14 True/False (specific information)
Page 22, Exercise 4

- Read the text to get the general idea.
- Read the statements. Guess if the statements are true or false. Use any pictures with the text to help you.
- Identify important words or expressions (e.g. *frugal/spend lots of money*).
- Find the place (or places) in the text with information about the questions. Read them closely and check your true/false guesses.
- If you are not sure, make a guess.

15 Matching (writer/intentions)
Page 38, Exercise 3

- Read the texts quickly to get the general idea. Identify the topics of each text (e.g. fashion/music/technology).
- Examples of language in the text depend on the author's intention:
  - to remember (talk about the past)
  - to give advice (imperatives e.g. *be careful/talk to her*)
  - to ask for help (questions e.g. *What is the best place to visit?*)
  - to describe/explain (give information to someone)
- Look for examples of this kind of language in the texts.
- Match the intentions with the authors. Make sure that the extra intention does not match with any of the options.

16 Multiple choice (specific information)
Page 55, Exercise 3

- First, read the text quickly to get the general idea.
- Read the questions and the options (a-d). Use your general knowledge to guess answers to them.
- Read the text again. Identify sentences with information for each question (e.g. 1 = a).
- Read that part carefully and choose an answer.
- Make sure the other alternatives are not possible answers.

17 Identifying formal style
Page 67, Exercise 3

- In formal, written English we do not use these features of informal writing:
  - contractions (e.g. *I'm okay now.*)
  - colloquial words and expressions (e.g. *It's so cool!*)
  - direct requests (*I want some information.* = *I would like some information.*)
- When you read letters, look for the following formal features:
  - *Dear Sir/Madam, Dear Mr/Ms Smith, Dear Editor*
  - *Yours faithfully/Yours sincerely/With best wishes*
  - *I am writing (to you) about .../I look forward to hearing from you.*

18 Sentence gaps (connections/ linking)
Page 70, Exercise 3

- Read the text to get the general idea. Identify the topic of the paragraphs.
- Read the example sentences and identify the topics.
- Carefully read the sentences before and after a gap. Look for clues about the missing sentences. Look at linkers (e.g. *however/later/ finally*) and reference words (e.g. *another/they/ then*) that refer back or forward to another word. See linkers in the writing Skills Builders and reference words in Skills Builder 33.
- Choose sentences for a gap. Check that it fits the sentences before or after it.
- Check that the extra sentence does not fit in one of the gaps.

19 Identifying difficult words
Page 80, Exercise 4

- Read the text quickly to get the general idea. Don't worry about words you don't understand.
- Read again and underline difficult words that are important to understand the text. Do not underline every new word for you.
- Read the part of the text with an underlined word again carefully. Use the strategies in Skills Builder 13 to help you work out their meaning.
- If you can't guess the meaning, use a dictionary to help you (e.g. *Longman Wordwise Dictionary*).

20 Identifying informal style
Page 83, Exercise 2

- Notes, emails, letters or postcards to friends or family have an informal style. Blogs and chats on the internet are also usually informal.
- Some features of informal style:
  - starting letters, etc.: *Hi/Hi there/Hello/How are things?/How are you?*
  - finishing: *Write soon/See you/Take care/All the best/Love*
  - colloquial words: *cool/mate/okay/anyway*
  - short forms: *(I'm) Having a great time./(I'll be) Back on Tuesday.*
  - punctuation: contractions (e.g. *can't*)/ AMAZING (capital letters)/ !!!!!!! (exclamation marks)/- (dashes)/ xxxxx (kisses at the end of a letter)

21 Focusing on context
Page 87, Exercise 3

- Before you read, look at the format and design of the text. What kind of text does it look like? (e.g. newspaper/magazine article, brochure, letter, website, blog).
- Read the text quickly to check your guess about the type of text.
- Think about what kind of reader the text is written for (age: child/young person/adult; occupation: job/studies; interests/hobbies).
- Look at the style. Is it formal (e.g. a newspaper article/formal letter) or informal (blog/ postcard/informal letter)?
- Read the text closely to find out what the writer is trying to do: give information/ give news/express opinions/tell a story/sell something/ask for something/complain about something.

 Writing

22 Linkers: *and/but/or/and then*
Page 7, Exercise 7

and
- makes lists
  *I like computer games, football **and** tennis.*
- joins two ideas
  I live in Spain. I come from Córdoba.
  *I live in Spain **and** (I) come from Córdoba.*
- describes actions
  *I get up **and** (I) have a shower (I get up and then have a shower).*
  *I have breakfast **and** (I) watch TV (at the same time).*

or describes alternatives
*On Sunday, I play football **or** (I play) tennis.*
*In the evening, I watch TV **or** (I) play computer games.*
but contrasts two ideas
*I like the cinema **but** (I) don't go very often.*
*I'm not very good at tennis **but** (I) like playing it.*
and then describes actions
*I get home **and then** do my homework.*

23 Purpose linkers
Page 19, Exercise 5

to + verb
*I'm having a party **to** celebrate my birthday.*
*We're organising a party **to** celebrate the end of term.*
for + noun
*We're raising money **for** charity.*
*We're having a party **for** our teacher.*

24 An invitation
Page 19, Exercise 7

25 Adjective order
Page 23, Exercise 8

We use adjectives in this order before a noun:

1 Opinion
nice/nasty/cool/expensive/cheap/interesting/boring difficult/easy

2 Size/Age
big/small/large/medium/extra-large old/new old/young

3 Colour
red/blue/green/yellow/orange/black/brown/grey/ purple/silver

4 Material
cotton/silver/metal/leather/wool

5 Make/Type
Calvin Klein jeans/French Connection top, men's/ women's/miniskirt/role-playing (game)

26 Story linkers
Page 35, Exercise 4

Describing *when* something happens
yesterday/last week/at three o'clock/on Friday evening/last year/during the lesson
Describing *the order* things happen
before *(lunch/the lesson)/**after that/at first/then/ later/in the end***
Describing *how* things happen
suddenly *(not expected)/**immediately*** *(with no delay)/**quickly/slowly***
Giving opinions
sadly/luckily/unluckily/amazingly

KEY
Purpose linkers

title

COME TO OUR SUMMER PARTY!

Tickets are ONLY £8!

price

what

We're having a party **to** celebrate the end of the year! We're also raising money **for** our camping trip in North Wales.

reasons

venue/time

The party is at the **School Gymnasium** at **9 p.m. on 23 July**.

Don't miss our fantastic resident DJ, Chaz, with some really cool dance music (house/electro/techno). And you can take part in our air guitar competition. Great prizes for the winners!

Snacks, soft drinks and party hats provided.

things included

Interested? Contact Amy Simons (09876538) or Katy Harris (01873045).

contact

KEY
informal style (e.g. personal feelings/
contractions)
story linkers
background (Past Continuous)

27 An email story
Page 35, Exercise 5

email information

Subject: car accident
To: *Anna* annabriercliffe@cmg.com
From: *Cathy* cpzjh@talknet.com

Hi Anna

informal beginning

introduction

How are things? Everything's okay here but something happened last week.

On Friday evening, I was coming back from the cinema with a mate. It was snowing and it was very
cold. Suddenly, we heard a loud noise and saw a car in a shop window. At first, I thought it was a robbery
but the man in the car was not moving. Immediately, I rang the emergency services. After that, I talked
to the man. He couldn't move and had a bad cut so I put a clean handkerchief on it. I didn't have time
to get scared. Luckily, the emergency people arrived quickly. They immediately opened the car and
took the man to hospital. In the end, the man was okay. Anyway, later the police asked us questions and
thanked us. I felt really proud.

story

Write soon. Love, Cath

informal ending

28 Contrast linkers
Page 39, Exercise 7

but links two parts of a
sentence
*He uses his computer every day
but he doesn't use the Net.
That dress is nice **but** (**it is**)
expensive.*
although links two parts of a
sentence
***Although** he uses his computer
every day, he doesn't use the Net.
He doesn't use the Net, **although**
he uses his computer every day.*
however links two sentences
*He uses his computer every day.
However, he doesn't use the Net.*

29 A letter to a magazine
Page 51, Exercise 5

KEY
formal style

Linkers:
1 = contrasting ideas
2 = reporting someone's opinions
3 = giving examples
4 = making conclusions

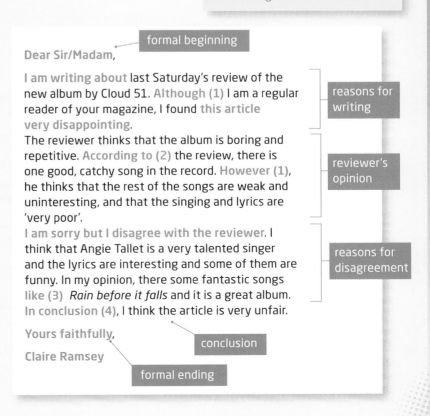

formal beginning

Dear Sir/Madam,

I am writing about last Saturday's review of the
new album by Cloud 51. Although (1) I am a regular
reader of your magazine, I found this article
very disappointing.

reasons for
writing

The reviewer thinks that the album is boring and
repetitive. According to (2) the review, there is
one good, catchy song in the record. However (1),
he thinks that the rest of the songs are weak and
uninteresting, and that the singing and lyrics are
'very poor'.

reviewer's
opinion

I am sorry but I disagree with the reviewer. I
think that Angie Tallet is a very talented singer
and the lyrics are interesting and some of them are
funny. In my opinion, there some fantastic songs
like (3) *Rain before it falls* and it is a great album.
In conclusion (4), I think the article is very unfair.

reasons for
disagreement

Yours faithfully,

Claire Ramsey

conclusion

formal ending

Writing

30 Listing/Ordering linkers

Page 55, Exercise 7

Listing information

There are some things you can do to avoid spots.
First, have a healthy diet and don't eat junk food.
Second, don't touch your face and wash your hands.
Third, wash your face with warm water twice a day.
Finally, use special creams on the spots.

Ordering instructions

First, pick four leaves from an aloe plant.
Second, squeeze the leaves into a cup.
Third, put the cup in the fridge.
Then, take out the cup after two hours.
Next, put the liquid on the sunburn for two hours.
Finally, wash off the liquid.

31 Reference: *another/ other*

Page 67, Exercise 4

another

I have **a question** about the food. When are meal times? I have **another question** about the classes. What experience have the teachers got?

Singular

What is the accommodation like? Do I have to bring a sleeping bag? **The other question** I have is about food. Do you offer vegetarian meals?

Plural

Where exactly is your nature centre? How can you get there by train? **The other questions** I have are about the classes. How many are there in the groups? How long are the classes?
You mention **courses** in the summer. What **other courses** are there in the winter?

32 A formal letter

Page 67, Exercise 6

formal beginning	Dear Sir/Madam,
reason for writing	I am writing to ask for information about your summer English courses in Norwich.
questions about courses	First (1), what kind of courses are there for teenagers? Are there any intensive courses or courses with sports? Second (1), do you organise any excursions or trips to places like (2) London or Cambridge? Another question is about the classes. How many students are there in the groups?
more questions	I have some other practical questions. Does the price include food and accommodation? What kind of accommodation is there at the school? What other kind of accommodation is there? Finally (1), are textbooks and materials included in the price of the course?
formal ending	I look forward to hearing from you. Yours faithfully, Soledad García

KEY
formal language
reference
linkers:
1 = listing
2 = example

33 Reference words

Page 71, Exercise 7

People

Amelia Earhart flew across the Atlantic but **she** did not pilot the plane on her own.
The cause of **Amelia's** death is unknown but **her** plane probably ran out of fuel.

Things

Her plane ran out of fuel and **it** crashed into the sea.
She made **the first transatlantic flight** on her own and **the trip** was difficult.
She made **a flight** in 1928, **another** (flight) four years later and a final **one** in 1937.

Situations

She **went in an aeroplane** and loved **it**. (it = going in an aeroplane)
She had **problems with fuel** and because of **that** crashed into the sea.
Amelia **became famous** and after **that** she tried to fly around the world. (that = becoming famous)

Time

She died in **1937** and since **then** has been a legend. (then = that time)

Place

After the war, she moved to **California** and learnt to fly **there**. (there = in that place)

Quantities

Americans were horrified and **millions** came to her funeral.
These **female pilots** were very brave and **many** died young.

34 A postcard
Page 83, Exercise 5

places

dates

Reykjavik, 11/06

informal beginning

Hi Katy,

~~I am~~ Having a great time in Iceland. ~~It is~~ Not hot here but it's only rained a bit. ~~I~~ Am now in the capital – the nightlife's cool and it NEVER gets dark! Last week, ~~I~~ went to the South – ~~There are~~ Some great waterfalls and geysers. ~~I~~ Went rafting but ~~I~~ didn't fall in luckily – the water's freezing. Yesterday, ~~I~~ went whale watching. ~~I~~ Saw a blue whale –AMAZING!!! Tomorrow, I'm going sea kayaking. ~~I'll be~~ Back on Thursday. See you next weekend.

Take care, Sally xxxxxx

informal ending

address

Ms K. Simons,
123 Castle Road,
Orleton, SY1 IGH
GREAT BRITAIN

35 *as* for comparison
Page 87, Exercise 7

Comparing two things/people
*She is **as** outgoing **as** her sister.* (They are both outgoing.)
*She is **not as** sporty **as** her sister.* (She is less sporty than her sister.)
Comparing two actions/activities
*She can run **as** fast **as** her sister.* (They both run at the same speed.)
*She doesn't play tennis **as** well **as** her sister.* (She plays worse than her sister.)

36 Purpose linkers
Page 99, Exercise 4

to + infinitive
*Can we meet **to** talk about the project?*
*We met **to** talk about the project.*
so that + *can*
*Can we meet **so that** we can talk about the project?*
*I would like to meet **so that** we can talk about the project.*

37 Short notes for requests
Page 99, Exercise 6

making a request

Hi Sam,
A quick note to ask you something. I'm going camping this weekend. I haven't got a cooker – you know, one of those gas things. Can you lend me yours for the weekend? I'll buy the gas and give it you back on Monday. Can I come round to your house to pick it up on Friday? Is four o'clock okay? Give me a ring on my mobile or send me a message. All the best, Cam

saying no

a Sorry, I can't. You see I gave it to my brother to use when he goes camping. You can ring him up to ask him, if you like.

agreeing

b No problem. But I won't be at home on Friday. Why don't we meet up in town so that I can give it to you.

💬 Speaking

38 Describing photos

Page 11, Exercise 9

Page 20, Exercise 8

Questions to ask about photos

What's this photo about?
Where is it from?
Why do you think that?
What's happening?
Who can you see in the photo?
What's he/she saying?
What's he/she feeling?
What time of year is it?
What else is happening?
What else can you see?

Describing position

*There are two people **in the middle of** the picture.*
*They are in **the foreground** and **behind them** you can see …*
*Then, **in the background**, there are …*
***On the left of the photo**, there is …*
***On the right of the photo**, you can see ….*

Making guesses

*Well, it's **probably** in the evening.*
*It's **definitely** in the summer **because** it's hot.*
*They are **definitely not** very happy.*
***Maybe** they're in France.*
***Perhaps** they're in the USA.*

39 Vague language

Page 20, Exercise 4

Similar to something

*It's **like** a big party. (a parade)*
*It´s **like** a big car. (a lorry)*

Part of a category

*There's **a sort of** walk. (parade)*
*He's **a sort of** artist. (painter)*
*It's **a kind of** skirt. (kilt)*
*She´s **a kind of** music organiser at a party. (DJ)*

40 Keep talking (strategies)

Page 20, Exercise 7

- When you don't know a word in English, never stop speaking! Use strategies to continue talking.
- Don't say a word in your language but you can make some words 'sound English'.
  I've got a camera video. (video camera)
- Use gestures and sounds to describe the word:

'guitar'

- Use vague language to describe the word.
  It's a musical instrument – a sort of a guitar.

41 Shopping

Page 27, Exercises 9 and 11

Shopkeeper: Hello. **Can I help you**?
Customer: Yes, **can I have a look at** those T-shirts, **please**?
Shopkeeper: **What size**?
Customer: Small. (*Small/Medium/Large/Extra large*)
Shopkeeper: **Here you are**.
Customer: Okay. **Can I try it on, please**?
Shopkeeper: **Of course**, the changing room is over there.
Shopkeeper: Do you like it?
Customer: Well, **it's a bit too** big. **How much is** this silk scarf?
Shopkeeper: Seven pounds fifty.
Customer: **Can I have this one, please**?
Shopkeeper: Thanks. **That's** two pounds fifty **change**.
Customer: **Could you wrap it up, please**? It's for a present.
Shopkeeper: **I'm sorry**. I haven't got any paper. **Here you are**.
Customer: **Okay, thanks**.
Shopkeeper: **Thank you. Bye**.

42 Telling stories

Page 36, Exercises 4 and 6

Hesitating
Umm ... You know, I didn't think it was serious.
Err ... Well, I was at my mate Sam's farm.
Linking events
But then it started to go red and swollen.
And then he couldn't breathe properly.
Going back to the story
Anyway, we stopped in a field.

43 Preparation strategies

Page 36, Exercise 6, Stage 2
Page 100, Exercise 7

- First, think of ideas about what to say. Use the Skills Builders to help you.
- Write short notes about what you want to say. (For this task, use your notes from the Writing Workshop).
- Don't try to translate directly from your own language. If you don't know the vocabulary or the grammar, do not try to say it or say it in a simpler way.
- Use your notes to practise. For example, use them to talk to yourself or aloud at home. It can be useful to record yourself and listen to yourself. Get a friend or member of your family to listen to you, too!

44 Opinions

Page 43, Exercise 10

A: **In my opinion**, eleven o'clock is a good time to come home. **What do you think**?
B: **Well**, **I'm sorry**, **I don't agree with you** – twelve o'clock is better!
A: **I disagree with that**. It's very late!

A: I've got a computer in my room. **I think** they're very useful for homework.
B: Yes, **I agree with you** about that. I **really think** computers in teenagers' bedrooms are okay.

A: **Personally**, **I think** three hours of TV a day is enough.
B: **You're right**. Too much TV's not very good for you.

A: **Do you think** five euros pocket money a week is okay?
B: Well, **I don't think** that's very good. **In my opinion**, ten is okay because everything is very expensive.

45 Agreeing and disagreeing

Page 52, Exercise 4

Agreeing with someone
A: *I like jazz.*
B: *Me too.* (*I like jazz, too.*)

A: *I don't like jazz.*
B: *Me neither.* (*I don't like jazz either.*)

Disagreeing with someone
A: *I like rock.*
B: *I don't.* (*I don't like rock.*)

A: *I don't like rock.*
B: *I do.* (*I do like rock.*)

46 Class discussions

Page 52, Exercise 7, Stage 2

- Choose a secretary to make notes of the group's decisions.
- Always try to speak in English.
- Don't interrupt other people. Wait till they finish speaking.
- Respect other people's ideas and ask them what they think.

47 At the doctor's

Page 59, Exercise 10

Doctor: Come in and sit down.
Patient: Thanks.
Doctor: So, **what's the problem**?
Patient: Well, **I've got a** stomachache and **I feel** a bit sick.
Doctor: **Where does it hurt**?
Patient: Here.
Doctor: **Any** vomiting?
Patient: Yes, I've been sick three times.
Doctor: **What about** diarrhoea?
Patient: Yes, I've had that, too.
Doctor: **How long have you had these symptoms**?
Patient: Since yesterday morning.
Doctor: **You've got** a high temperature. **I'm afraid you've got** a stomach infection.
Patient: Oh, no!
Doctor: **You should** drink plenty of water. **You shouldn't** drink coffee or cola. **Take these tablets** twice a day.
Patient: **Right**, thanks a lot, doctor.
Doctor: Not at all.

 Speaking

48 Suggestions and replies
Page 68, Exercise 4

should
I think we should phone someone.
I don't think we should wait.
We should carry on walking and stop later.
We shouldn't stop now.

let's
Let's make a shelter.
Let's not stop now.

what about
What about lunch?
What about having lunch?

can
We can have lunch now.
You can come at 6.00.

why don't
Why don't we start a fire?
Why don't you help?

Short questions
Who? (should we phone?)
Why? (should we wait?)
When? (should we stop?)
Where? (should we stop?)

Accept suggestions
Okay.
Right.
That's a good idea.
I agree.

Reject suggestions
Why? It's ... (early/late etc.)
I don't think that's a good idea.

49 Airport situations/Polite requests and replies
Page 75, Exercise 8

Employee: Good morning, *sir/madam*. **Could I have your passport and ticket, please**?
Passenger: **Yes, of course.** Here you are.
Employee: **Window or aisle seat**?
Passenger: Aisle, please.
Employee: **Could you put your case here, please**?
Passenger: **I'm sorry**, I can't. It's rather heavy. **Could you help me** with the bag, **please**?
Employee: Sure. I'm afraid it's over the limit. **Could you pay the excess baggage at the ticket office, please**?
Passenger: **Just a moment**. I'll take some things out.
Employee: **Did you pack your case yourself**, *sir/madam*?
Passenger: Yes, I did.
Employee: Okay. So, **that's gate** 25 at 11.20.
Passenger: One more thing. **Could you tell me how to get to** the nearest bank, please?
Employee: Certainly, *sir/madam*. **Go through** security control **and turn right**. **Go past** the toilets and a bookshop. The bank is **on your right**, **between** the souvenir shop and the restaurant. **It's in front of** the duty-free shops.
Passenger: Thanks a lot.
Employee: Not at all.

50 Asking for/Checking information
Page 84, Exercises 3 and 8

Requests
Could you give me some information about New York, please?
Could you tell me about places to visit there, please?
Do you know anything about the nightlife?
Which of these hostels *do you recommend*?

Question tags: Fixed tags
These are more informal and used by young people.
*That's a good time of year, **right**?*
*So this is the total price for a week, **yeah**?*

Question tags with auxiliaries
When the main part of the sentence is affirmative, the tag is negative.
*There are discounts for students, **aren't there**?* (to be)
*You need a visa for the States, **don't you**?* (Present Simple)
When the main part of the sentence is negative, the tag is affirmative.
*There aren't discounts for students, **are there**?*
*You don't need a visa for the States, **do you**?*

51 Telephoning

Page 91, Exercise 10

Formal

A: Good morning. **Can I help you?**
B: **Yes, please. Could I speak to** Mrs Wilson?
A: **Of course. Hold on a moment. I'll put you through.**
B: Thanks.

★ ★ ★

A: **I'm afraid she's** not available at the moment.
B: **Could I leave a message, please?**
A: **Yes, of course.**
B: **This is** Paul. I've missed the bus. Can she collect me?
A: **Okay, I'll repeat the message.** You've missed the bus and can she collect you?
B: **Yes, that's right. Thanks very much.**
A: Not at all.

Informal

A: **Hello**, 8735122.
B: **Hi**, Mrs Jones. **This is** Anne.
A: Oh, **hello**, Anne.
B: **Can I speak to** Tom, **please?**
A: **Of course. Hang on a sec. I'll get** him/her **for you.**
B: Thanks.

★ ★ ★

A: **Sorry**, he/she's out. **Do you want to leave a message?**
B: Yes, please. **Can you tell** him/her **this?** I've got the information for the homework. We're meeting tomorrow after school in the computer room. Can he come, too?
A: Right. Can Tom meet you in the computer room after school tomorrow?
B: Right.
A: Okay, **I'll tell** him/her. Bye.
B: Thanks a lot. Bye.

52 Listening actively

Page 100, Exercise 3

Asking for clarification

A: I went to an ABBA concert.
B: **ABBA?**
A: Yes, that old Swedish group. My gran loves them.
A: They played *Mamma Mia*.
B: *Mamma Mia?*
A: Yes, it's one of their best songs.

Showing surprise or interest

A: I went with my grandma.
B: **Your grandma?**

Echo questions

We use these to show attention, interest or surprise:

A: I'm English.
B: **Are you?** (affirmative)
A: I'm not very good at football.
B: **Aren't you?** (negative)
A: I play tennis at the weekend.
B: **Do you?**
A: I don't like that player.
B: **Don't you?**

A: I had a great time.
B: **Did you?**
A: I didn't see it.
B: **Didn't you?**
A: I've finished it.
B: **Have you?**
A: I haven't done it.
B: **Haven't you?**

53 Listening actively (strategies)

Page 100, Exercise 6

- When you are listening to someone, use gestures and facial expressions to show you are following.
- Also use expressions to show you are listening: *right/yeah/I see/okay*.
- Use expressions to show surprise (e.g. *Wow!/Oh no!*), interest (e.g. *Really?*) and sympathy (e.g. *Really?*).
- Repeat words and expressions to show interest or surprise (e.g. *With your grandma?*).
- When you are not clear about something, you can also repeat words (e.g. *ABBA?*).
- Use questions to show interest or surprise (e.g. *Were you? Did you? Have you?*).

STUDENT B

M1, Lesson 3, Exercise 12

M5, Lesson 14, Exercise 12

Ask about these facts:

How long / Albert Einstein / be dead?
How long / The Beatles / be popular?
How long / doctors / know penicillin?
How long / the world / know Harry Potter?
How long / people / admire the Egyptian pyramids?

Give information about these facts:

The United States / be an independent country / 1776
The internet / be around / 1969
European countries / use the euro / 2002
Mona Lisa / be a symbol of beauty / 1500
California / belong to the USA / 1850

M7, Lesson 19, Exercise 9

Read the remedy and answer your partner's questions.

First, mix two tablespoons of vinegar with six tablespoons of hot water.
Second, before you go to bed put the mixture on your hair with a brush.
Third, cover your hair with a scarf.
Finally, in the morning have a shower and wash your hair.

M9, Lesson 25, Exercise 9

Flight quiz

1 When did the Montgolfier brothers invent the first hot-air balloon?
   a 1583   b 1683   c 1782
2 When did Otto Lilienthal fly the first effective glider (aeroplane with no engine)?
   a 1785   b 1845   c 1891
3 Thérèse Peltier from France was the first woman to fly a plane solo. When did she do it?
   a 1908   b 1918   c 1928
4 When did Igor Sikorsky make the first successful helicopter flight?
   a 1909   b 1939   c 1959
5 Who was the first person to go into space in 1961?
   a Yuri Gagarin   b Alan Shepard   c Neil Armstrong
6 Who was the first person walk on the Moon in 1969?
   a Neil Armstrong   b Buzz Aldrin   c Michael Collins

M12, Lesson 34, Exercise 12

1 man – he designed the first aeroplane (da Vinci)
2 disease – people get it from birds (Bird Flu – H5N1)
3 actress – she wore a $26 dress at a film premiere (Angelina Jolie)
4 continent – there is a problem with toads there (Australia)
5 animal – you should never run away from it (puma/big cat)
6 woman – she crossed the Atlantic alone in a plane in 1932 (Amelia Earhart)
7 country – The Lord of the Rings was filmed there (New Zealand)
8 islands – they can be flooded by the sea soon (the Maldives)

WORD LIST

Module 1: Time
Page 5
Adjectives describing a person

organised	Jack is very organised about doing his homework.
relaxed	I felt more relaxed after the exam.
stressed	Don't get stressed about exams – try to relax.
tired	I feel so tired that I have to lie down.

Times

at night	Mum often feels tired at night.
at the weekend	At the weekend, I go to the park.
in the morning	I feel tired in the morning.
on Thursday	On Thursday, I go to the cinema.

Meals

breakfast	I usually have breakfast when I get up.
dinner	They have dinner at 8 p.m. every evening.
lunch	I always have lunch with my friend.

Daily routine

do homework	I don't like doing homework.
do jobs in the house	I do lots of jobs in the house.
get up	The children get up at 7 a.m. to go to school.
go to bed	My brother never goes to bed before midnight.
shower	I have a shower every morning.
sleep	I sleep eight hours a night.

Free time activities

basketball	Jan and Stefan play basketball.
cinema	I love going to the cinema.
computer game	He's into playing computer games.
cycling	We planned to go cycling at the weekend.
extra class	After school, I go to extra classes.
football	My brother plays football.
jogging	I agreed to go jogging with Zac on Sunday morning.
party	My children go to a lot of birthday parties.
sport	I love sport, especially football and tennis.
swimming	Do you want to go swimming on Thursday night?
family	I eat lunch with my family.
friend	I watch TV with my friend.
home	I spend the weekends at home.
Messenger	Lucy goes on Messenger every night.
park	We can walk in the park.
spend	She often spends time with her best friend.

Pages 6–7
Adjectives

adventurous	Your holiday was very adventurous.
aristocratic	Are your family aristocratic?
beautiful	The garden is beautiful in spring.
famous	Everybody knows him because he's very famous.
friendly	The students are very nice and friendly.
funny	The joke was very funny.
historic	We saw some historic buildings.
national	That is the national costume of Slovakia.
ordinary	Not much happened – it was a very ordinary day.
personal	My personal life is private.
professional	Daniel is a professional artist.
successful	My dad is a rich and successful businessman.
unusual	Martinez is an unusual name for an Englishman.
windy	It was cold and windy on Sunday.
wonderful	It was wonderful to see him again.
eccentric	My uncle is a real eccentric.
obligation	Doing my homework is one of my obligations.
plan	We planned a trip around Europe by train.

Pages 8–9

fast food	Don't eat too much fast food.
lifestyle	Young people have very busy lifestyles.
ready-made	Fay bought a ready-made meal at the supermarket.
sleepy	I felt sleepy today because I got up at 5 a.m.
stressed out	I think he's a bit stressed out about the exams.
tai chi	Tai chi helps me to relax.
unhealthy	Fast food is often unhealthy.
vegetarian	I don't eat meat – I'm vegetarian.
yoga	She practises yoga to help her to relax.

Pages 10–11
Races

athletics	I'm good at athletics, especially the 100m sprint.
cycling	Cycling is my favourite sport.
marathon	Roy's going to run the New York marathon.
road race	How far is the road race?
running	I go running to keep fit.
sprint	I prefer sprint races to marathons.

swimming	They went swimming this morning.
triathlon	Josh took part in the triathlon in Hawaii.

Equipment

ball	You play tennis with a small, yellow ball.
bike	He fell off his bike and hurt his arm.
boot	These football boots are very comfortable.
cap	Linda forgot her swimming cap.
goggles	Wear goggles to protect your eyes in the pool.
helmet	You have to wear a helmet to protect your head.
mountain bike	My dad gave me a mountain bike!
running shoe	I lost one of my running shoes in the mud!
shorts	It's too cold to wear shorts in the winter.
ski	I fell down the mountain and lost one of my skis.
sunglasses	It's sunny today so I'm wearing sunglasses.
swimsuit	Greta always wears a one-piece swimsuit.
water bottle	The cyclist took a drink from his water bottle.
wetsuit	Sarah put on her wetsuit and dived into the sea.

General sport

athlete	Professional athletes can earn a lot of money.
breaststroke	I prefer to swim breaststroke.
cyclist	This part of the road is for cyclists only.
exercise	It's good exercise so you will get fit.
finish	He was tired when he reached the finish.
freestyle	My son won the 100m freestyle.
mile	We ran 6 miles this morning.
muscle	Your muscles will feel tired afterwards.
Olympic	Triathlon is an Olympic sport.
PE	I have a PE lesson at 2 p.m.
Tour de France	The Tour de France is a cycling race.
track	The 800m race is twice round the track.
training	I do rugby training three times a week.
transition stage	I lost time in the transition stage of the triathlon.

Describing photos

behind	There is a car behind the cyclist.
in the background	In the background of the photo there is a forest.
in the foreground	I really like that tree in the foreground of the photo.
in the middle of	You can see a tree in the middle of the photo.
on the left	Wayne's dad is on the left of the photograph.
on the right	My house is on the right of the photo.
definitely	It's definitely in Italy.
maybe	Maybe the man is a scientist.
perhaps	Perhaps they are Spanish.
probably	He is probably talking to his wife.

Module 2: Fun
Page 13
Hobbies

acting	I love acting and I want to be in a film.
air guitar	Playing air guitar is great fun.
board game	Their parents don't enjoy playing board games.
chess	David really enjoys playing chess.
collecting coins	I enjoy collecting coins and I have a rare £5 coin.
collecting stamps	I like collecting stamps – I have 200.
computer game	Will likes playing computer games with the kids.
cycling	I like cycling in the countryside on my mountain bike.
dancing	We'd like to try dancing as a way of losing weight.
free running	I'm really into free running, but I try to be careful!
gymnastics	I don't enjoy doing gymnastics.
making jewellery	Sue wants to try making jewellery.
making model aeroplanes	Keith likes making model aeroplanes.
music DVDs	I'm into collecting music DVDs.
photography	Aidan is really into doing photography.
piano	I can't play the piano.
saxophone	Ola plays the saxophone.
singing	Are you good at singing?
sport	I love all sport, especially basketball.
stamp	I enjoy collecting stamps from letters from abroad.
yoga	I do yoga every morning – it's very relaxing.

Pages 14–15

comedian	He was one of the funniest comedians I've ever seen.
silent-film	Silent-films don't have any sound.
tramp	The tramp lives in the street and is very poor.
turkey	Would you prefer turkey or chicken for dinner?

Pages 16–17
Computer games

expansion pack	He bought an expansion pack for the game.
game-play	The game-play is really exciting.
gamer	My brother is a really serious gamer.

graphics	The latest computer games have brilliant graphics.
location	Let's try a new location for level 2.
role-playing	The role-playing games are great fun.
simulation game	He loved playing the simulation game.

Adjectives

amazing	Wow! The music in this game is amazing.
challenging	Level 1 was easy but level 2 is more challenging.
creative	Do you think it's creative?
fantastic	Your mum's food was fantastic.
perfect	It was a perfect evening – everything was great.
silly	It was silly to start playing the game at 10 p.m.
terrible	I don't like the food in that terrible restaurant.
wonderful	I was so happy because I had a wonderful holiday.

Modifiers

a bit	The geography lesson was a bit boring.
absolutely	I think the film's absolutely great.
quite	The book is not very long but it is quite good.
really	I don't think it's really interesting.
very	It's good but it's very sad.

Page 18

bull	There was a big, black bull in the field.
injure	Eight people were injured in the crash.
protest	There was a protest about the new law.

Page 19

Party

celebrate	We will celebrate Anya's birthday.
fancy-dress	I wore an alien costume to the fancy-dress party.
invitation	We got an invitation to their New Year's party.
raise	The school raised money for the storm victims.

Page 20

celebration	There was a big celebration on 1 May.
kilt	The Scottish man wore a kilt and big boots.
parade	We went into town to watch the parade.
St Patrick's Day	St Patrick's Day is an important day in Ireland.

Module 3: Money

Page 21

Money

bank account	I put the money into my bank account.
earn money	How much money do you earn a week?
get money	I get £25 pocket money a month.
good with money	I'm good with money.
job	Ben earns a little money from his part-time job.
pocket money	I get £10 pocket money every week.
save money	Cathy is saving money for a new coat.
spend money	I spend money as soon as I get it.

Places to shop

bookshop	I got that crime story at a bookshop.
charity shop	I enjoy looking for bargains at charity shops.
clothes shop	I bought a new dress in my favourite clothes shop.
computer shop	The computer shop sells batteries.
discount shop	Sally likes spending money in discount shops.
online	Look for a good price online.
shopping centre	Tom enjoys buying clothes at shopping centres.
street market	She enjoys shopping at street markets.
supermarket	I usually buy fruit at the supermarket.

book	Look at my new book.
CD	I'm looking for the latest CD.
cinema	The cinema closes at 8 p.m.
clothes	She has very nice clothes.
computer game	I don't like computer games.
cosmetics	She loves cosmetics, especially lipstick.
crisps	We don't spend much money on crisps or drinks.
drink	I bought a drink at the cinema.
DVD	I've got that film on DVD.
food	Food can be very expensive.
make-up	Janet often spends money on make-up.
mobile phone call	I spend money on mobile phone calls.
music download	I spend some of my money on music downloads.
part-time	Dick has a part-time job.
present	I spent too much money on Christmas presents.
second-hand	I found this second-hand shirt in a charity shop.
shampoo	I washed my hair with a new shampoo.
soft drink	Ray spent some money on soft drinks for the kids.
sweet	Eating sweets is bad for your teeth.

Pages 22-23

Quantities

a bit of	Can I have a bit of paper to write on?
a bottle of	The present was a bottle of perfume.

a bouquet of	The bride carried a bouquet of roses.
a box of	I bought mum a box of chocolates for her birthday.
a can of	He opened a can of cola very carefully.
a packet of	She gave her son a packet of crisps.
a pair of	Dad needs a new pair of trousers.

Adjectives describing products

comfortable	These jeans are very comfortable.
cotton	Kathleen wore a white, cotton dress.
good condition	The car is old, but it's still in good condition.
leather	Dad wears a leather jacket on his motorbike.
metal	These earrings are plastic, not metal.
silver	Those silver earrings were just what I wanted!

bargain	I got a bargain - a T-shirt for 5 euros.
check out	I checked out the price in three different shops.
crowd	It's stressful to shop when there are crowds.
film premiere	The stars will go to the film premiere.
fork out	I don't like to fork out money for presents.
frugal	He always looks for bargains. He is very frugal.
generous	It was very generous of Jack to buy us lunch.
half-price	All the shoes were half-price or less.
mean	He's very mean with money and never buys presents.
sales	She bought a new coat in the January sales.
top	I bought a new top to wear with my skirt.
valuable	The painting is valuable, it cost over 2000 euros.
vintage	Magda wore a vintage jacket from the 1960s.

Pages 24–25

costume	You must wear a costume to the Star Wars party.
experience	My trip to Madrid was an experience.
extravagant	My aunt is very extravagant with presents.
fan	She loves sci-fi and is a big fan of Star Wars.
fantasy	I read a fantasy book about a magic land.
gadget	It's a useful little gadget for opening bottles.
geek	The geeks spend every lunch break on the internet.
horror	Horror movies are awful – I don't like being scared.
replica	You can buy a replica of the famous costume.
sci-fi	*Dr Who* is my favourite sci-fi programme.

Pages 26-27

Electronic goods

CD	I got an Elvis CD for my birthday.
computer game	Do you want to play a computer game?
DVD	Let's watch a DVD.
video	I've got over fifty videos and about 100 DVDs.
vinyl	My dad's music is on vinyl, not CD.

Arts and crafts

ceramics	I'm looking for ceramics – I need a plate and a cup.
leather goods	That shop sells leather goods like wallets and belts.
textiles	We can look at textiles in the afternoon.

Clothes

designer	Don't buy expensive designer clothes.
men's	That shop only sells men's clothes.
second-hand	My jacket is second-hand - it used to be my mum's.
women's	Women's clothes are cheaper than men's.

Accessories

footwear	I need to buy footwear for walking in the snow.
handbag	I keep my wallet and keys in my handbag.
jewellery	Bracelets are my favourite pieces of jewellery.
scarf	The scarf is very pretty and cheap.

Food and drink

fish	I eat fish and seafood at the beach.
fruit	Mum wants me to eat more fruit and vegetables.
herb	This dish has lots of herbs and spices in it.
meat	Vegetarians don't eat any meat.
poultry	Shall we buy some poultry? How about chicken?
seafood	Lots of people don't like fish and seafood.
spice	I put some herbs and spices in the lunch.
vegetable	I try to be healthy so I eat lots of fruit and vegetables.

Size

large	I think the shirt is too large.
medium	I need a medium shirt.
small	The dress is too small.

alternative	She likes to wear alternative fashions.
antique furniture	My grandma's got lots of antique furniture in her house.
canal	We went for a long walk along the canal.
change	The scarf is £7 so here's £3 change.
changing room	I tried on the shirt in the changing room.
gold	I like your gold ring.
shopkeeper	The shopkeeper put my shopping into a paper bag.
silver	These are silver earrings, not gold.
stall	This market stall sells great clothes.
street performer	We spent a while watching the street performers.
try on	I want to try the dress on to see if it fits.
wrap	I haven't wrapped your birthday present yet.

Module 4: Stories

Page 29

Stories

adventure story	Kidnapped is an exciting adventure story.
classic	You must know that book, it's a classic.
comedy	I like comedies because they make me laugh.
cowboy story	Brokeback Mountain is a modern cowboy story.
crime story	My favourite books are crime stories.
detective story	The Sherlock Holmes stories are detective stories.
fairy tale	The children love reading fairy tales.
fantasy story	It's one of the fantasy stories by Terry Pratchett.
folk story	I'm reading a collection of Welsh folk stories.
ghost story	I don't get scared by ghost stories.
historical story	That historical story takes place in 1875.
horror story	I can't read horror stories at night.
love story	It's a love story about two young people.
romance	Her book is a romance about two lovers in Italy.
romantic comedy	My boyfriend didn't want to read a romantic comedy.
science fiction story	It's a science fiction story about a strange planet.
short story	It's a book of twelve short stories.
thriller	His latest book is a thriller about a murder.

Opinion adjectives

boring	I thought the film was really boring.
brilliant	Declan thought the book was brilliant.
depressing	I find sad stories depressing.
exciting	It's an exciting story about a detective called Bosch.
funny	I laughed because the story was really funny.
imaginative	The book is really imaginative and original.
interesting	The programme about birds was interesting.
romantic	Do you think it's a romantic story?
sad	The ending was very sad and we all cried.
scary	It's a really scary horror movie.
violent	The fighting in the film was very violent.

be about	The story is about three best friends.
bestseller	In 1939, the book was a bestseller.
favourite	What is your favourite book?
in my opinion	In my opinion, it's too long.
take place	The story takes place in a desert in Africa.

Pages 30–31

escape	They escaped out of the window.
ghost	I saw a ghost in the house.
hike	We went hiking in the Lake District.
massacre	300 people were killed in the massacre.
soldier	He was a soldier in the British army.
spirit	His spirit lives in the house even though he is dead.
valley	There is a green valley between the mountains.

Pages 32–33

Adjectives and prepositions

afraid of	Don't be afraid of him, he won't hurt you.
bad at	I'm very bad at geography.
good at	I wish I was good at cooking.
interested in	We are interested in art.
relaxed about	My parents are relaxed about homework.
worried about	I'm worried about the exam next week.

Multi-part verbs

come back to	They come back to the village every summer.
get to	I had to get to the shop before it closed.
go away	We decided to go away for the weekend.
go back to	I want to go back to Hawaii one day.
go straight to	When he got home, he went straight to bed.
pick (someone) up	Bill promised to pick Lisa up from the station.
sail back to	We sailed back to the island before dark.

arrest	The police arrested the thief later that night.
body	A man walking his dog discovered the body.
castle	The castle was old and scary.
cave	There were many paintings in the cave.
cell	He lived in a cell for five years.
emperor	He was the emperor of a large country.
exile	He lived in exile in the mountains.
guard	A guard was sitting by the door.
judge	The judge sentenced him to one year in prison.
knife	This knife is very sharp – don't cut yourself.
priest	The priest was in the church all day on Sunday.
prisoner	The king was a prisoner in the castle.
royal	The king is head of the royal family.
sailor	The sailors travelled from Cape Town to London.
ship	We travelled across the sea on a ship.
silver	He found a lot of silver in the bag.
treasure	The map shows that the treasure is buried here.
wave	The sea was cold and there were a lot of waves.
wise	The wise old man gave me good advice.

Page 34

Relationships

ask somebody out	Martin asked Carol out for a meal.
couple	Sally and Dave have been a couple for a while now.
date	They went on a date to the cinema.
fall in love	They have fallen in love.
get engaged	They got engaged six months later.
get married	They're getting married in July.
get on well	The couple got on well together.
go out with	I went out with Simon for six months.
honeymoon	After the wedding, we went to Italy on honeymoon.
love at first sight	He knew immediately – it was love at first sight.
meet	Where did you meet for the first time?
romance	Their story is a wonderful romance.

airline	That airline has cheap flights to Australia.
flight	The flight from Santiago to Paris was very long.
flight attendant	The flight attendant brought us drinks on the plane.
passenger	There were 400 passengers on the boat to Calais.
seat	My seat was next to the window.

Page 35

Time expressions

after that	After that, I rang my sister.
at first	At first, I thought there was a problem with the bus.
immediately	When he saw us, he immediately stopped the car.
in the end	In the end, everyone was okay.
later	It was sunny at 12 p.m. Later, it rained.
luckily	It was raining but luckily I had an umbrella.
quickly	The teacher quickly opened the window.
suddenly	I suddenly realised that I was alone.

adventure	I had a real adventure after school yesterday.
ambulance	The ambulance took my grandma to the hospital.
bee	My bees produce a lot of delicious honey.
breathe	The room was so crowded I could hardly breathe.
quad bike	I rode on a quad bike and it was great fun.
serious	He stopped just in time to avoid a serious accident.
sting	A bee stung me on the leg.
swollen	My hand got really swollen and it hurt a lot.

Page 36

Telling stories

and then	And then we went to see my grandma at her house.
anyway	Anyway, the man was really angry with us.
but then	But then we said that we were from Hungary.
well	Well, there were no taxis or buses nearby.
you know	You know, I was really quite scared.

Module 5: Families

Page 37

Relatives

aunt	My aunt Sally lives in Finland.
brother	I don't get on with my brother.
cousin	Flynn is one of my seven cousins.
father/mother-in-law	My father-in-law is a policeman.
grandparent	We visited my grandparents at the weekend.
half-brother/sister	My half-brother is thirty years older than me!
nephew	I have six nephews and two nieces.
niece	My brother-in-law has three nieces.
parent	My parents don't like the same kinds of music as me.
stepfather/mother	I've got a father and a stepfather.
uncle	My parents visit my uncle every summer.

Fashion

baggy	Baggy jeans are very comfortable to wear.
dress	My dad gets angry about the way I dress.
dyed hair	I haven't got dyed hair.
hairstyle	My parents can't stand weird and colourful hairstyles.
hood	I don't like young people wearing jackets with hoods.
jacket	How cold is it – do I need to wear a jacket?
jeans	People often wear jeans at weekends.
leggings	Grandma says leggings are very comfortable.
piercing	Dayana has a piercing in her nose.
skirt	Girls can wear skirts to school.
slogan	Gran didn't like the slogan on my T-shirt.
tattoo	I can't stand men with tattoos all over their bodies.
tight	I don't like tight jeans – they make my legs look fat.
T-shirt	This T-shirt is a nice colour and it's quite cheap.

angry	I get angry when my brother wears my clothes.
argue	I often argue with my sister about music.
come home late	My parents get angry when I come home late.
computer	I want to use the computer to send an email.
get on okay with	Terri gets on okay with my sister.
get on well with	I get on well with my sister.
homework	I have to do two hours homework every evening.

stand	I can't stand short skirts or tight jeans.
taste	Mum doesn't have the same taste in clothes as me.
tidy my room	It drives my mum crazy when I don't tidy my room.

Pages 38–39
Technology

chat	Pete and I were having an online chat.
connected	Can I chat? Are you connected to the Net?
digital	You don't need film for a digital camera.
disconnected	My internet is broken. I'm disconnected from the web.
download	You can't download videos from the internet for free.
homepage	I have a photo of my cat on my homepage.
interactive	I bought my daughter some interactive maths CDs.
laptop	I can use my laptop anywhere in the house.
mobile	Ring me on my mobile when you arrive!
multitask	He can multitask with a laptop, mobile and the TV.
Net	Linda surfed the Net to find cheap holidays.
offline	You can download books and read them offline.
online	We do most of our work online now.
post	I posted a message on my cousin's website.
real-time	My son has real-time chats online with his friends.
surf	How much time do you spend surfing the Net?
upload	She uploaded the picture to her webpage.
virtual	Many people play games in virtual worlds.
webpage	Go to the 'Contact us' webpage for more information.
website	For more information, visit our website.

Pages 40–41

communist	This used to be a communist country.
democracy	I believe in freedom and democracy.
democratic	Poland has been a democratic country since 1989.
generation gap	There is a big generation gap between my parents and me.
government	The new government promised not to increase taxes.
politics	She always wanted a career in politics.
prison	There is a big prison not far from my town.
revolution	We are in the middle of a technological revolution.
war	Everyone was relieved when the war ended.
youth	I lived in London in my youth.

Pages 42–43
Arguments

argue	We argue about who is the best singer.
disagree	I'm sorry, but I totally disagree.
get angry	He gets angry when I listen to loud music.
interrupt	I tried to explain but people kept interrupting me.
loudly	'Stop!' she shouted loudly.
offer	He came over and offered me a drink.
opinion	In my opinion, the teacher was very good.
patient	My teacher was patient when I didn't understand.
personally	Personally, I think that's a bad idea.
positive	I can think of three positive things about the idea.
reason	Give me a reason why you should win the prize.
right	You're right that the homework is very difficult.
shout	Don't shout at me, you need to calm down.
suggestion	I don't like your suggestion about the garden.
unfair	It's unfair to make him do all the work.

appearance	A person's appearance is very important.
come back	I have to come back home before 11 p.m.
forget	I think she forgot to tell me about the party.
go out	We went out on Saturday but not on Sunday.
lay	My brother laid the table for dinner.
mark	If I get good marks, my parents will be happy.
mess	The house was in a mess.
noise	If you make too much noise, you'll wake the baby.
party	He's going to have a party when his parents are away.
pocket money	My best friend gets £10 pocket money a week.
punishment	I got a punishment because I came home late.
round	I want to have friends round but my parents say no.
shopping	I helped with the shopping at the weekend.
spend	My sister always spends too long in the bathroom.
take out	Please take the rubbish out before you go to bed.
tidy	Please tidy your room – it's very messy.
watch	You can't watch TV before dinner.

Module 6: Music
Page 45
Styles of music

blues	I love listening to Etta James singing the blues.
classical	My dad loves listening to classical music.
country and western	My sister is a fan of country and western.
dance	I don't really like dance music.
folk	I used to like folk music when I was young.
heavy metal	Jake loves heavy metal like Black Sabbath.
hip hop	I truly can't stand hip hop.
indie	I'm not crazy about indie music either.

jazz	Armstrong had a great voice for jazz.
new age	She's really into new age music.
pop	Julie loves listening to pop music.
punk	I never did like punk.
rap	I can't listen to rap when I read.
rock	I love rock when it is loud.
soul	I love listening to a big choir singing soul.
world	Do you like to listen to world music?

Instruments

bagpipes	Jimmy has been playing the bagpipes in Scotland.
cello	Ann is learning to play the cello.
clarinet	Sadie is learning to play the clarinet.
drums	He plays the drums in a band.
flute	I wish I could play the flute.
guitar	Is there anybody here who can play the guitar?
harp	Mary O'Hara can play the harp beautifully.
piano	I'd like to be able play the piano really well.
saxophone	Jed's learning to play the saxophone.
trumpet	Richard plays the trumpet and teaches it as well.
violin	Sally would like to learn to play the violin.

dance	My friends like to dance at the club in town.
sing	I only sing when I feel very happy.
voice	I haven't got a good singing voice.

Pages 46–47

allow	My parents won't allow me to go to the concert.
audition	I have an audition tomorrow for a part in *Annie*.
autograph	Can I ask the star for his autograph?
band	He plays the drums in a band.
can	Girls can wear dresses to the concert.
competition	I really want to win the band competition.
group	The group have a drummer, singer and guitarist.
have to	We have to practice three times a week.
musician	The musicians played three songs.
necessary	It's not necessary to wear sun cream in winter.
perform	The band performed four songs at the concert.
possible	It's possible to learn quickly if you practise a lot.
practise	I have to practise playing the trumpet every day.

Pages 48–49
Festivals

arena	The concert was in a huge arena.
atmosphere	The town has a nice, friendly atmosphere.
audience	The audience stood up and cheered.
crowded	The beaches can get very crowded in the summer.
stage	I stood at the front of the stage and sang.
tent	There are four tents for different types of music.
theme	The theme this year is African music.
volume	Turn up the volume – I really like this song.

Verbs and adjectives

feel	The town feels very quiet in the evenings.
look	That hairstyle looks amazing.
sound	The music sounds like punk or rock.

Multi-part verbs

switch off	I don't switch off my mobile at night.
switch on	He switched on the TV to watch the news.
turn down	Please turn down your music! It's too loud.
turn off	We can turn off the computer when we go out.
turn on	Can you turn on the light? It's a bit dark!
turn up	This song is great, let's turn it up.

Pages 50

attend	You must attend every class.
choir	Sue sings in the school choir.
compulsory	Some countries have compulsory military service.
concert	The concert starts at 6 p.m.
may	You may bring your own lunch to eat.
must	Students must wear uniform to school.
orchestra	She plays the violin in the school orchestra.
regulation	You must obey the strict regulations.
rehearsal	There is one more rehearsal before the show.
rule	We have several rules about uniform.

Page 51
Adjectives describing music

catchy	I can't get that catchy tune out of my head.
disappointing	The new CD is very disappointing.
imaginative	The song is okay and the lyrics are imaginative.
interesting	This record is quite interesting.
original	What an original record!
poor	His song was good but hers was poor.
repetitive	I don't like the song because it's repetitive.
terrible	This band is terrible, don't buy their CD.

album	My favourite album is by Arctic Monkeys.
record	My dad has a big record collection.

review	The newspaper gave the CD a good review.
singer	That singer has a great voice.
song	Which song do you like best?
track	I really like the third track on his latest CD.

Page 52

book	I'll ring them up and book two tickets for tomorrow.
box office	Ring the box office and buy a ticket.
express	The express boat takes fifteen minutes.
stop	There is a tube stop opposite the arena.
ticket	I haven't got a ticket for the concert.
transport	Please tell me about the transport.
underground	Is it fastest to travel on the underground?

Module 7: Health

Page 53

Illnesses

allergy	Do you have any allergies?
cold	I haven't had a cold all winter.
cough	If you have a bad cough, stay at home.
diarrhoea	Do you ever have diarrhoea when you go abroad?
earache	Charlie has really bad earache and it's very painful.
flu	I had flu so I stayed in bed.
hayfever	Do you sometimes have hayfever in the summer?
headache	I had a really bad headache so I went to bed.
sick	I couldn't eat lunch because I felt sick.
sore throat	I can't sing when I have a sore throat.
stomachache	After that meal I had a bad stomachache.
temperature	Her little boy has a temperature of 39°C.
toothache	I've got a terrible toothache.

Health

accident	Oh no, sorry to hear about your accident!
depressed	She felt very depressed after losing her job.
exercise	I do a lot of exercise like cycling and swimming.
faint	It was very hot in the club and I began to feel faint.
fit	My best friend is quite fit and loves swimming.
healthy	I think I am quite healthy.
hospital	My granddad went to hospital when he was ill.
illness	Have you ever had a serious physical or mental illness?
smoke	Stop smoking if you want to live longer.
tired	The students are all tired on Mondays.
unhealthy	It's unhealthy to eat too much junk food.
weak	He felt weak so he had to lie down.

Pages 54–55

actually	Actually, that's my house, not Ellie's.
damage	Maybe you have damaged your computer.
dandruff	I used to get a lot of dandruff when I was in my teens.
diet	There is too much sugar in your diet.
hormone	Teenagers produce a lot of hormones.
hurt	Ouch, that hurt! Don't do that again!
laser	Tattoos can be removed with lasers.
meal	Lunch is the most important meal of the day.
organ	This disease affects the internal organs.
protect	Wear a hat to protect your head from the sun.
remedy	What's a good remedy for headaches?
risk	There is a risk you might get skin cancer.
shade	You should stay in the shade at midday.

Skin

dry	I have dry skin so I use a cream.
fair	Fair skin can get burnt easily.
oily	This cream is for people with oily skin.
pale	People with pale skin must be careful in the sun.

high factor	The sun cream is high factor, it will protect you.
microbe	Microbes are invisible because they are so small.
moisturising cream	Grace puts moisturising cream on her face at night.
skin cancer	Wear sun cream or you might get skin cancer.
soap	I always wash my hands with soap.
spot	I had spots on my face when I was younger.
sun cream	Use sun cream and wear a hat on the beach.
sunburn	Use sun cream to avoid sunburn.
tattoo	I want to get a tattoo on my leg.

Pages 56–57

Health threats

AIDS	AIDS has killed millions of people.
asthma	Both sisters suffer from asthma.
bacteria	Antibiotics kill bacteria.
Bird Flu	Bird Flu can be dangerous to humans.
bug	Bugs spread quickly in warm countries.
diabetes	He found out he had diabetes when he was ten.
disease	Deaths from heart disease are increasing.
epidemic	There might be an epidemic next year.
germ	This cleaner kills all household germs.
malaria	My dad caught malaria when he travelled to Asia.

obesity	Eating too much junk food can lead to obesity.
pollution	Plants and fish are dying because of pollution.
Swine Flu	Swine Flu affected only pigs in the past.
tuberculosis	Tuberculosis is an illness that is increasing.
virus	A virus causes the common cold.

Medicine

antibiotic	Antibiotics should stop your spots.
drug	You can treat the disease with drugs.
vaccine	All children need the measles vaccine.

evidence	There is a lot of evidence that he is wrong.
infectious	He gave the infectious disease to his wife.
resistant	Is this drug resistant to antibiotics?

Pages 58–59

Emergencies

Accident and Emergency	I went to Accident and Emergency when I hurt my leg.
ambulance	Someone called an ambulance for me.
amputate	His leg was amputated after a car crash.
bleed	The cut on his arm has started bleeding again.
bone	She broke a bone in her leg.
break	Someone threw a stone and broke a window.
breathing problems	Granddad had breathing problems, it was scary.
emergency call	I used my mobile to make an emergency call.
first aid	Peter is trained in first aid.
get over	It took me three weeks to get over the infection.
hurt	Injections don't usually hurt.
infection	This infection is very serious.
injection	The nurse gave me an injection against tetanus.
medicine	You must take medicine twice a day.
operation	Doug's got to have an operation on his back.
pain	I was in a lot of pain and I cried.
painkiller	I took two painkillers for my headache.
patient	There were no other patients at the doctor's.
pill	I need to take my pills at the same time every day.
sick	Bart felt sick after he ate too many sweets.
tablet	She took a tablet for her headache.
treatment	I was sent to hospital for immediate treatment.
unconscious	She was still unconscious after the accident.
vomit	I vomited because I ate a bad egg.
X-ray	The doctor sent him to hospital for an X-ray.

Module 8: Environment

Page 61

Places

garden	The flowers in this garden are beautiful.
green space	There are wonderful green spaces all over the city.
lake	Can people swim in this lake?
nature reserve	Many animals live in this nature reserve.
park	This is the biggest park in the town.
river	Many fish live in that river.
wood	The trees in that wood are very old.

Animals

bat	At night, you can hear bats flying in the sky.
bear	The black bear is common in North America.
bee	Brian keeps bees and sells the honey they make.
bird	The birds sing every morning.
deer	This large country estate has its own herd of deer.
fox	I can often hear the foxes in my garden after dark.
insect	A mosquito is a small flying insect.
monkey	Monkeys sometimes steal tourists' cameras.
rat	I am very scared of rats.
shark	Sharks aren't often dangerous to humans.
snake	The zoo has a great variety of snakes.
spider	Lynne has a huge fear of spiders.
toad	Each year, toads cross the road near here.
wolf	The Arctic wolf is a beautiful animal.
worm	I saw a bird eating worms in the garden.

Environmental problems

air pollution	Air pollution is a big problem in cities like Paris.
climate change	Climate change means that summers are hotter.
habitat loss	Pandas are at risk from habitat loss.
noise	There is a lot of noise near the main road.
over-fishing	Many species are disappearing due to over-fishing.
over-hunting	I'm worried about the over-hunting of deer.
traffic	The journey was slow because of the traffic.
water pollution	The water pollution in that river is very bad.

climate	The climate in the Maldives is hot and sunny.
endangered	The Siberian tiger is an endangered species.
mammal	The whale is a mammal, not a fish.
nature	Storms remind us of the power of nature.
reptile	Snakes and lizards are both reptiles.
species	Fifteen different species of fish live here.

WORD LIST

Pages 62–63

cautious	Scientists are being cautious about the drug.
chemical	This chemical could be very dangerous.
destroy	The forest will be destroyed in ten years.
ecologist	Ben loves nature and wants to be an ecologist.
eliminate	We are trying to eliminate air-pollution.
lizard	There's a lizard running up the wall of my room.
poisonous	These poisonous chemicals can harm wildlife.
research	We are doing research into the causes of cancer.
sugar cane	Sugar cane grows in hot countries.
whale	Whales are larger than sharks.
zoo	You can see lions and tigers at the zoo.

Pages 64–65
Animals

alligator	There are dangerous alligators in that river.
hippo	We saw hippos cooling themselves in the river.
lion	Lions have very sharp teeth.
mosquito	She put a net over her bed because of the mosquitoes.
puma	You don't often see pumas in the wild.
scorpion	There was a scorpion in his shoe and it bit him.
tiger	Tigers have beautiful, stripy fur.

Multi-part verbs (3)

come across	I came across a fox in my garden.
fight back	It's dangerous to fight back against a bear.
get away	She got away from the wolves by climbing a tree.
run away from	Diana ran away from the big dog.
stay away from	I try to stay away from dark, scary places.

bedding	The hotel provides bedding but not towels.
bite	Sophie was bitten on the leg by a dog.
blanket	It's cold so you need a blanket.
climb	Bears can climb trees very well.
creepy crawly	I hate creepy crawlies like spiders!
cute	He kissed his baby daughter on her cute little nose.
deadly	Snake bites can be deadly to humans.
hind leg	The bear stood on its hind legs.
killer	There's a killer shark in this area.
laid-back	She seems very laid-back about her exams.
long-sleeved	It's best to wear long-sleeved clothes in the jungle.
predator	Birds are predators of mice and snails.
react	You must react quickly if you are attacked.
sheet	There was a blue sheet on the bed.
tiny	Some birds are very small but mosquitoes are tiny.
venom	The venom from that snake is poisonous.

Page 66

agriculture	That area is known for agriculture.
butterfly	This plant attracts lots of butterflies in the summer.
food chain	Grass is the plant at the bottom of the food chain.
honey	My bees produce a lot of delicious honey.
pollen	Pollen levels are high and can cause hayfever.
pollinate	Bees are needed to pollinate lots of plants.
wasp	I've just been stung by a wasp!

Page 67

catch	Let's catch some fish to cook for dinner.
countryside	The countryside is more beautiful than the city.
craft	Students can take lessons in several crafts.
fire	A fire will keep us warm at night.
shelter	They built themselves a shelter out of branches.
wild	Be careful when you eat wild mushrooms.
wood	Our table and chairs are made of wood.

Module 9: Flight
Page 69
Transport

aeroplane	She is scared of travelling by aeroplane.
bike	It's quick and cheap to travel by bike.
boat	We crossed the Channel by boat.
bus	Where can I get a bus to the city centre?
canoe	They travelled down part of the river by canoe.
car	It's too far to walk, let's go by car.
helicopter	He travelled to the island by helicopter.
horseback	They completed the journey on horseback.
kayak	We travelled down that river by kayak.
micro-light	It would be great to try flying in a micro-light.
moped	Many Thais travel everywhere by moped.
motorbike	Ian comes to work by motorbike.
plane	The plane was half an hour late.
roller skate	Dana often goes to the shops on her roller skates.
train	I would prefer to get the train to Manchester.
tram	Travelling by tram is quicker than by bus in the city.
underground	Many people in London travel on the underground.

cheap	Bus tickets are very cheap – only 1 euro.
convenient	The train is a convenient way to get to London.
crash	Her car was involved in a crash with a large truck.
crowd	I don't like big parties because of the crowds.
delay	There were delays on the roads due to traffic.
exciting	Plane journeys can be quite exciting.
queue	There are queues every morning at the bus stop.
quick	Walking isn't a very quick way to travel.
uncomfortable	Planes have uncomfortable seats.

Pages 70–71
Opposites

impossible	It's impossible to find a cheap flat in the city centre.
inexperienced	The inexperienced teacher didn't know the answer.
unaccompanied	He travelled unaccompanied to the North Pole.
unconventional	The headmaster was rather unconventional.
unhappy	Barbara had a very unhappy childhood.
unknown	The name of the victim is unknown.
unlucky	You were very unlucky to lose your keys.
unreliable	Leeds has an unreliable bus service.
unusual	It's unusual to have snow in March.

aviator	There were several famous aviators in the 1920s.
flight	The first flight was made by the Wright brothers.
pilot	Bob is a pilot for British Airways.
pioneer	The bank was one of the pioneers of online banking.

Pages 72–73
Space

astronaut	The astronauts will spend two weeks in space.
Earth	Earth is the third planet from the sun.
launch	The rocket launch took place at 1 a.m.
Mars	Mars is also known as 'the red planet'.
Moon	Do you want to go to the Moon?
Moon landing	Thousands of people watched the Moon landing.
orbit	The satellite is now in orbit around Earth.
planet	Mercury is the planet nearest to the sun.
satellite	The TV signal is transmitted by satellite.
solar system	Jupiter is the biggest planet in our solar system.
space junk	There's quite a bit of space junk around the Earth.
Space Shuttle	There will be no more Space Shuttle flights this year.
spacecraft	The spacecraft took off from Cape Canaveral.
spacewalk	They will do a spacewalk outside the spacecraft.
telescope	Have you looked at the Moon through a telescope?
Venus	Venus is easy to see in the night sky.

Pages 74–75
Air travel

airline	Which airline are you flying with?
airport	The airport is thirty minutes from the city centre.
aisle seat	I prefer an aisle seat.
arrival gate	Your taxi driver will meet you at the arrival gate.
baggage	My baggage was left in Germany.
board	We boarded the plane at 14.10.
boarding gate	Go to boarding gate 26.
case/suitcase	Your case is too big to take on the plane.
catch	I'm worried I might not catch my flight!
check-in desk	Please report to Atlantic Airlines check-in desk.
collect	You must collect your baggage before 2.30.
departure lounge	The departure lounge was full of passengers.
duty-free shop	That camera will be cheaper in the duty-free shop.
excess baggage	Fred had to pay excess baggage charges.
information desk	You can find out about hotels at the information desk.
land	We were all glad when the plane finally landed.
on time	The plane landed on time.
pack	Did you remember to pack your swimming costume?
passenger	There are 250 passengers on this flight.
passport	You probably need a passport to travel abroad.
passport control	We have to go through passport control.
security control	We had to take off our shoes in security control.
souvenir shop	Presents are quite expensive in the souvenir shop.
take off	How long is it till we take off?
terminal	Our plane leaves from Terminal 4.
ticket	I bought a ticket for the flight at 8.40.
ticket office	Go to the ticket office and ask for a day pass.
weight limit	The weight limit for each of your suitcases is 20 kilos.

Module 10: Holidays
Page 77
Holiday activities

bird-watching	The area is very good for bird-watching.
cycling	I want to go cycling round the island.
diving	I saw a lot of fish when I went diving.
hiking	I did a lot of hiking in the mountains.
kayaking	We found a fast river and went kayaking.
sailing	Jen's dad took us sailing on the lake.

sightseeing	We all went sightseeing round the town.
snorkelling	You will see some fish if you go snorkelling.
sunbathing	Sunbathing can damage your skin.
surfing	We went surfing every day in Australia.
windsurfing	I go windsurfing when there is enough wind.

Natural features
beach	Hawaii has beaches with black sand.
coral reef	Australia's coral reefs are now in danger.
forest	The north of Scotland has some beautiful forests.
hot spring	I want to bathe in the hot spring.
lagoon	The beach is sheltered by the lagoon.
mountain	The mountains are good for hiking.
river	A lot of fish live in that river.
sea	Swimming in the sea can be dangerous.
stream	There's a little stream at the bottom of the garden.

Climate
cool	England has a cool climate.
sunny	Spain is good because of the sunny climate.
tropical	The climate in the Caribbean is tropical.

abroad	I spent six weeks on holiday abroad.
apartment	The apartment is on the third floor.
campsite	We stayed at a campsite near the river.
castle	The castle was built on top of a hill.
church	I like taking photos of the windows in old churches.
coast	We can go to the coast if the weather's good.
country	A holiday in the country is very relaxing.
hotel	Which hotel are you staying in?
stay	I'm staying in a beautiful hotel.
village	It would be nice to live in a quiet old village.

Pages 78–79
boy scout	My brother used to be a boy scout.
fire	We cooked some fish on the fire.
fresh water	We can get fresh water from mountain streams.
matches	The matches have got wet and I can't light them.
reality show	I was watching a reality show on TV.

Pages 80–81
Holidays
beach volleyball	You can watch beach volleyball on TV.
canoeing	We could go canoeing in the lake.
chill out	I enjoyed chilling out on the beach.
discotheque	The discotheque was too noisy for me.
dive site	This area has some famous dive sites.
dolphin watching	On Wednesday, we went dolphin watching.
health spa	You can relax at the health spa.
luxury	I want to stay in a luxury hotel with a spa.
palm tree	Palm trees grow in hot countries.
paradise	It's a paradise of tropical fruit trees.
resort	Playa de las Americas is a popular tourist resort.
sandy	There's a lovely, sandy beach near the hotel.
speedboat	A small speedboat took us to the island.
storm	Stay in the hotel because there will be a storm.
tropical	I went on holiday to a tropical island.
turquoise	The water is a beautiful turquoise colour.
uninhabited	This island is mainly uninhabited.
wave	If the waves are big, we can go surfing.

Multi-part verbs
go back	I want to go back to the place where I was born.
go down	The price of oil has gone down lately.
go on	What is going on in the city centre?
go on	Whatever happens, life will go on!
go out	I usually go out on Friday and Saturday evenings.
go up	Prices will go up a lot after the election.

rise	The amount of crime in our cities is rising.
sea level	Sea level around the islands is rising.
tsunami	The tsunami affected all the villages along the coast.

Pages 82–83
Activity holidays
climbing	John went climbing in the mountains.
exploring	They spent the afternoon exploring the town.
horse riding	I went horse riding along the coast.
whale watching	On Saturday, we are going whale watching.

Geographical places
continent	Is Asia the biggest continent?
country	France is a bigger country than Italy.
geyser	Old Faithful is a geyser in Yellowstone National Park.
lake	The water in the lake is very cold.
mountain	We climbed a very high mountain!
mountain range	The Sangre de Cristo is a mountain range in the USA.
ocean	Hawaii is a group of islands in the Pacific Ocean.
river	The river is 200 km long.
sea	The sea is too cold for swimming.

volcano	Ash from the volcano stopped all the flights.
waterfall	We'll cross the river above the waterfall.

Page 84
Tourist information
discount	Are there any discounts for students?
hostel	You can stay in this hostel for $10 a night.
information	I need some information about art galleries.
international student card	I've lost my international student card.
visa	We don't need a visa for this country.

Module 11: Friends
Page 85
Appearance
attractive	His new girlfriend is very attractive.
dark-skinned	The man was dark-skinned and had dark hair.
fair-skinned	Many Swedish people are fair-skinned.
good-looking	Your dad's a very good-looking man, you know.
handsome	He was tall and handsome.
overweight	I've been overweight for years. I'm going on a diet.
pale	Pale-skinned people must be careful in the sun.
pretty	She's been very pretty ever since she was a baby.
skinny	Your brother used to be skinny, but now he's fat!
slim	My friend Katie is very slim.
tall	That man must be 1.8 metres tall!
well-built	The man is well-built, I think he must be very strong.
young	I think he's quite young.

Hair
blond	Liam's hair is very blond, especially in the summer.
curly	My hair is dark and curly.
dark	I love her beautiful dark hair.
dyed	She had dyed hair and wore very large earrings.
fair	I've got fair hair and fair skin.
long	She's tall and slim, with long hair and legs.
red	I would like to have red hair.
short	I had short hair when I was younger.
straight	My mum's got straight, shiny hair.
wavy	Gran had wavy grey hair and wore glasses.

Personality
confident	Jenny is always very confident about doing exams.
easy-going	Harry's a very easy-going kind of guy.
friendly	Everyone said hello and was very friendly.
funny	Marie is very funny – she always makes me laugh.
hard-working	Most of my students are very hard-working.
helpful	The teacher was helpful when I didn't understand.
honest	My father was honest about breaking the glass.
impatient	I get impatient when I have to wait for anything.
kind	Tom was very kind to me when I had no money.
lazy	Don't be so lazy – come and help me wash up.
moody	A lot of people are moody in the morning.
outgoing	Sally is very outgoing and cheerful.
quiet	Matthew is a very quiet boy.
romantic	My boyfriend isn't romantic. He never gives me flowers.
sensible	You can trust Julia. She's very sensible.
sensitive	He is very sensitive to other people's needs.
shy	Bill is quite shy when there are a lot of people around.
sociable	Our neighbour is very sociable and often eats with us.
talkative	Kay becomes talkative when she is in a group.
tidy	I'm very tidy and I hate mess.
unhappy	I feel unhappy when I'm away from home.
untidy	Helen is very untidy – she never puts anything away.

Pages 86–87
get
get bored	Do you get bored in English classes?
get good marks	I usually get good marks at school.
get on with	I always get on well with my wife's mother.
get rid of	The company got rid of some old computers.

achieve	You can achieve a lot if you work hard.
as	Marek is as tall as his older brother.
autocracy	This country doesn't have an autocracy.
dictator	The dictator was a very cruel man.
experiment	We did an experiment to test his idea.
salute	We invented a salute to show our respect.
sporty	I hate playing football, I'm not very sporty.
tragedy	It was a tragedy that the girl died.
uniform	Workers at that factory wear a uniform.

Pages 88–89
arrange	We arranged to meet outside the train station.
fix	Shall we fix a time to play tennis?
intention	It's my intention to buy her a nice present.
offended	The girl was offended by the joke.
potato salad	This potato salad is very tasty.

WORD LIST

see off	My friends came to see me off at the station.
spaghetti bolognese	Eating spaghetti bolognese can be very messy!
surprise	It will be a surprise for him on his birthday.

Pages 90-91
Social networking

comment	I left a comment about the photo.
cyber-bullying	Cyber-bullying is a growing problem amongst children.
delete	I deleted a file by mistake.
homepage	I have a picture of myself on my homepage.
internet	The internet has changed the way we communicate.
keep in touch with	I keep in touch with friends via email.
online	We can chat online about the maths homework.
password	I've forgotten my password so I can't log on.
personal information	I don't put personal information on the Net.
personalise	You can personalise your webpage with photos.
post	He posted a video and a photo on my blog.
profile	His profile on the website says he's tall.
reply	I replied to the post about the photo.
safety	Think about internet safety. Don't chat to strangers.
socialise	I socialise with people from my school and area.
stranger	It's not nice when strangers try to talk to you.
text message	I sent him a text message when I arrived.
view	You can view more information on the internet.

Telephoning

available	Sorry, he's not available.
hang on	Can you hang on for a minute?
hold on	Hold on, I'll just see if he's in.
message	He's not here – do you want to leave a message?
moment	After a moment, Lou returned.
out	I'm afraid Mr Roberts is out today – can I help you?
put through	Mr Smith is on the phone – shall I put him through?
ring	Give me a ring before you leave your house.
sec	I'll be there in a sec.
aggressive	She sent an aggressive reply to my message.
nasty	She was really nasty to my sister.

Module 12: Emotions
Page 93
Emotions

angry	My father was angry about the broken window.
annoyed	She gets annoyed with me for being untidy.
bored	Sadie soon got bored with the game.
confused	I got confused about all the rules.
down	I felt very down for a few weeks after he died.
enthusiastic	Her parents were very enthusiastic about the idea.
excited	Emma was so excited that she couldn't sleep.
happy	I was so happy to see my sister.
interested	The students are interested in modern art.
irritated	I got irritated by the mess in the kitchen.
lonely	I felt really lonely while my parents were away.
nervous	Julie looked nervous before the test.
relaxed	She looked happy and relaxed on her wedding day.
sad	I felt sad when I said goodbye to my family.
scared	I get scared when a big dog comes near me.
shocked	I was deeply shocked by her death.
stressed out	I get stressed out before exams.
surprised	He was surprised that I spoke French.
terrified	I'm terrified of flying.
upset	I know David was very upset about losing his job.
worried	Lucy was worried other girls would laugh at her.

Adjectives

annoying	It was annoying that the shop was closed.
boring	The programme was so boring she fell asleep.
confusing	I find some of the maths a bit confusing.
depressing	The winter weather can be really depressing.
exciting	The most exciting game is also very difficult.
interesting	For me, the film wasn't very interesting.
relaxing	I find that painting pictures is very relaxing.
scary	Going abroad on my own will be really scary.
shocking	It's shocking that so many people are homeless.
stressful	Flying an aeroplane can be very stressful.
surprising	This is a very surprising result.
terrifying	Friday the Thirteenth was a terrifying film.
upsetting	Going to his funeral was an upsetting experience.
worrying	Climate change is a very worrying problem.

Pages 94-95

acceptable	It's not acceptable to arrive ten minutes late.
attitude	She had a bad attitude towards her homework.
burst	The little girl was scared and burst into tears.
control	It's hard to control your emotions.
cry	I cried when I said goodbye to my mum.
express	It's okay to express your emotions.
feeling	She doesn't care about anybody else's feelings.

honest	I try to be honest about how I'm feeling.
sentimental	Jack gets very sentimental about his grandparents.
tear	A tear rolled down her cheek.
unemotional	George was strangely unemotional at the funeral.
weakness	My weakness is that I am very impatient.

Pages 96-97
make and *do*

do better	I think you can do better in the next exam.
do exercise	Try to go to the gym to do exercise every week.
do things (for other people)	I don't often do things for other people.
do well	I want to do well in the Spanish exam.
make a difference	I want to make a difference to people's lives.
make an effort	Please make an effort with your homework.
make decisions	I need to make a decision about where to go.
make money	The company made a lot of money this year.
make people happy	I like to try to make people happy.
belong	I belong to the drama club.
blessing	It's a blessing to be good at languages.
body	Sport and exercise is good for the body.
count	Try to be positive and count your blessings.
deal with	It's not always easy to deal with stress.
enough	The weather is not warm enough to go swimming.
grateful	I lent him the money but he wasn't grateful.
headmaster	Our headmaster is a very clever man.
meditation	Meditation can help people to relax.
mind	You're imagining things – it's all in your mind.
nerves	Most people suffer from nerves before an exam.
physical exercise	Running is very good physical exercise.
relationship	She's in a relationship with her neighbour.
steady	His hand was very steady as he signed his name.
stress	I suffered from stress in the week before the exam.
successful	The way of coping with stress was successful.
technique	He thought of a new technique to reduce stress.
too	The exam was too difficult for the new students.
well-being	My health and general well-being has improved.

Page 98

advice	I need some advice about revision.
advise	Can you advise me about this problem?
ask	The teacher asked the girls to come to her office.
break	I'll work for two more hours and then have a break.
breath	Take deep breaths and try to relax.
deep	You will feel better if you take deep breaths.
panic	Don't panic, you still have one week left to revise.
revision	Have you done enough revision for the maths exam?
tell	The doctor told me that I had the flu.
want	I want you to stop eating junk food.

Page 99

chat	We had a chat about how she felt.
note	Amparo wrote me a note to say sorry.

Page 100

congratulations	Congratulations on passing your exams!
imitate	We imitate their music and their style.
tribute band	Jimmy sings in an Abba tribute band.

Language Choice

Contents

MODULE 1: LANGUAGE CHOICE 1-6

PRACTICE

1 Time prepositions **Complete the description.**

¹ _In_ the morning, I usually feel very tired. I get up ²____ seven thirty and my bus leaves ³____ a quarter to eight. ⁴____ the afternoon, I get home ⁵____ four o'clock and go to the sports centre. ⁶____ the evening, I have dinner and do my homework on my computer and I always go to bed late ⁷____ night. ⁸____ the weekend, I spend time with my friends. ⁹____ Saturday afternoon, we play football and ¹⁰____ Sunday we go to the sports centre.

2 Collocations: Routines **Complete the sentences.**

1 I don't usually _have_ breakfast.
2 I often ____ tired and sleepy in the morning.
3 I always ____ to school by bus.
4 I ____ my homework on the bus.
5 I ____ to extra classes after school.
6 Then I ____ time with my friends.
7 We ____ computer games.
8 Sometimes we ____ to the cinema.
9 I go to ____ at 11 p.m.
10 I ____ nine hours a night.

3 Making adjectives **Complete the description with the correct forms of the words in brackets.**

Molly Sutcliffe comes from a ¹ _famous_ (fame), ² ____ (aristocrat) family. She lives in a ³ ____ (beauty) but ⁴ ____ (wind) part of Wales with thirty-six cats, ten dogs and three donkeys. Molly is a ⁵ ____ (success) travel writer and visits lots of ⁶ ____ (history) monuments. She is very ⁷ ____ (adventure). Molly also has a ⁸ ____ (wonder) garden. She is not a ⁹ ____ (profession) gardener but she talks to her plants ¹⁰ ____ (day), like Prince Charles!

4 Present Simple and Continuous **Complete the dialogues with the verbs in brackets in the Present Simple (dialogue 1) and the Present Continuous (dialogue 2).**

1 A: ¹ _Do_ you _often cycle_ (often / cycle) to school?
   B: No, I ²____ (not cycle). But my brother ³____ (cycle) a lot. He only ⁴____ (go) by bus when it ⁵____ (rain).
   A: I ⁶____ (not like) cycling. I always ⁷____ (walk) to school.
2 A: What ⁸____ (you / do)?
   B: I ⁹____ (answer) emails. Why?
   A: I'd like to use the computer. We ¹⁰____ (do) this project on Australian animals. I need to go on the internet.
   B: Use Dad's computer! He ¹¹____ (not work).

5 Present Simple and Continuous
Complete the sentences with the verbs in brackets in the Present Simple or the Present Continuous.

1 We _don't_ usually _spend_ (not spend) our holidays at the seaside: I ____ (go) hiking in the mountains and my brothers ____ (look for) holiday jobs abroad.
2 Heather ____ (wear) a lovely dress today. Where ____ (she / buy) her clothes?
3 My mum ____ (be) a doctor but she ____ (not work) in a hospital.
4 My dad ____ (live) in London at the moment – he's got a job there.
5 Tim can't talk to you now – he ____ (have) a shower.
6 I usually ____ (eat) muesli for breakfast but this morning I ____ (have) eggs.

6 Collocations: Races **Complete the sentences.**

1 The Tour de France is the most famous _cycling_ race in the world.
2 The best time for the 100____ sprint is 9.58 seconds.
3 The New York Marathon is a famous ____ race.
4 For freestyle swimming events, you can swim crawl or back____ .
5 ____ races have three parts: swimming, cycling and running.
6 You need to wear a helmet for mountain ____ events.

REFERENCE

Time prepositions

at + times of day:
*I usually get up **at** seven o'clock.*

at + **night:**
*I feel tired **at** night.*

at + **the weekend:**
*I play football **at** the weekend.*

in + **morning/evening/afternoon:**
*I feel tired **in** the morning.*

on + days of the week:
***On** Tuesday, I go to piano class.*

Collocations: Routines

feel *tired/sleepy/relaxed/stressed*
have *breakfast/lunch/dinner/a shower*
do *my homework/jobs in the house/sport*
play *football/basketball/computer games*
get *home*
go *swimming/jogging*
go on *Messenger*
go to *bed/school/extra classes/the cinema/ the park/parties*
sleep *eight hours a night*
spend *time with my friends/family/at home*

Making adjectives

beautiful/successful/wonderful
famous/adventurous
aristocratic/historic
daily/windy/friendly/funny
national/personal/professional

Present Simple and Continuous

We use the Present Simple to talk about:
- **habits and activities we do regularly.**
  I go to yoga classes twice a week.
  ***Do** you **meet** your friends regularly?*
  *He **doesn't** work hard.*
- **present states, feelings and opinions.**
  *He **wants** to become vegetarian.*
  ***Does** she **know** that fast food is unhealthy?*
  *We **don't have** a garden.*

Time expressions: *always, often, usually, regularly, sometimes, never*

Present Simple	
Affirmative	
I/You/We/They love fruit. *He/She often goes to restaurants.*	
Negative	
I/You/We/They don't eat fast food. *He/She doesn't do much exercise.*	
Questions	**Short answers**
Do I/you/we/they cook every day? *Does he/she live in London?* *Where do you buy food?*	*Yes, I/you/we/they do. / No, I/ you/we/they don't.* *Yes, he/she does. / No, he/she doesn't.*

We use the Present Continuous to talk about:
- **activities happening right now, at the time of speaking.**
  *I can't help you now, I'm **watching** the news.*
  *Why **are** you **laughing**? It isn't funny.*

- **activities happening around now, not exactly at the moment of speaking.**
  *Mary **is learning** to play the guitar.*
  *I'm in London now, I'm **staying** at my aunt's home.*

- **changes and processes.**
  *Be careful, you**'re getting** fat.*
  *The number of students **is growing**.*

Time expressions: *(right) now, at the moment*

Present Continuous	
Affirmative	
I am living in London. *You/We/They are cooking lunch.* *He/She is practising yoga.*	
Negative	
I'm not laughing. *You/We/They are not learning to dance.* *He/She is not working now.*	
Questions	**Short answers**
Are you having dinner? *Is he/she having a good time?* *Where are you going?*	*Yes, I am. / No, I am not.* *Yes, he/she is. / No, he/she isn't.*

Collocations: Races

*cycling/running/swimming/triathlon, road/track **race***
*mountain bike/swimming **event***
*100 metres/200 metres **sprint** (athletics)*
breaststroke/backstroke/crawl/freestyle (swimming)
*mountain/road **bike**, **cycling** helmet*
***swimming** cap/goggles*
***running** shoes/shorts*

MODULE 2: LANGUAGE CHOICE 7-12

PRACTICE

7 Preferences (1) **Complete the description.**

I'm a very active person and I really like ¹ _doing_
sport. I enjoy ² _____ football and tennis and I'm
really ³ _____ doing gymnastics. I'm also creative
and I like ⁴ _____ the piano and singing. I also like
⁵ _____ coins and stamps but I'm ⁶ _____ into playing
board games like chess. They're really boring!
I enjoy ⁷ _____ computer games and I do it ⁸ _____
night after dinner. I'd like to ⁹ _____ yoga and also
try ¹⁰ _____ model aeroplanes.

8 Present Perfect (1): Irregular verbs **Complete
the sentences with the 3ʳᵈ forms of the verbs in
brackets.**

1 Gary is happy. Arsenal have _won_ (win)
   the game.
2 Mark is here. I've _____ (see) him.
3 The laptop is broken. It has _____ (fall) off the
   desk.
4 You look sad. What has _____ (happen)?
5 The classroom is empty. The students have
   _____ (go out).
6 I feel sick. I've _____ (eat) too much.
7 The jacket is clean. I've _____ (wash) it.
8 Look! I've _____ (buy) a new bike.

9 Present Perfect (1) **Complete the sentences
with correct forms of the verbs in brackets.**

1 I'm not hungry. I _have had_ (have) lunch.
2 Her shoes are dirty. She _____ (not clean)
   them.
3 My laptop is not here. _____ (you / take) it?
4 We don't have your address. We _____ (lose) it.
5 It's cold in here. Who _____ (open) the
   window?
6 I can't discuss the film with you. I _____ (not
   see) it.
7 Mark is not here. He _____ (leave).
8 I can't go out. I _____ (not write) the essay for
   tomorrow.

10 Opinions: *think that* **Use the cues in brackets to
complete the sentences.**

1 I think that _chess is boring_ (chess / boring).
2 I don't think _____ (board games /
   very interesting).
3 I think _____ (photography / fantastic).
4 I don't think that _____ (yoga /
   very exciting).
5 I think that _____ (free running /
   challenging).
6 I don't think _____ (making model
   aeroplanes / interesting).

11 Modifiers **Choose the correct modifiers to
complete the computer game review.**

The story is ¹*very/really* amazing but the
game play is ²*a bit/absolutely* slow. The characters
are ³*very/absolutely* interesting and the graphics
are ⁴*a bit/really* creative. The locations are
⁵*absolutely/very* fantastic, too but the sound is
⁶*absolutely/a bit* bad and the music is ⁷*really/a bit*
terrible. In conclusion, I like the game but some
things in it are not ⁸*very/a bit* good.

12 *some, any, no, a lot of, a few, a little* **Choose the
correct words to complete the text.**

I love watching films. When I have ¹*a few/a little*
money, I buy a DVD. I have ²*any/a lot of* famous
Hollywood films, ³*a little/a few* old films and
⁴*any/some* comedies. I don't buy ⁵*some/any* horror
films – I hate them. On weekdays, I have ⁶*any/no*
time to watch films. But on Saturday, I invite
⁷*some/a little* friends over and we usually watch
⁸*a few/any* films. If there are ⁹*some/no* new films,
we watch the old classics. And we always have
¹⁰*no/a lot of* fun.

REFERENCE

Preferences (1)

Verb + noun
I'm into chess.
I'm not into board games.
I like sport.
I don't like yoga.
I enjoy computer games.
I don't enjoy gymnastics.

Verb + -ing
I'm really into acting.
I'm not into collecting stamps.
I like playing chess.
I don't like singing.
I enjoy playing computer games.
I don't enjoy making things.

would like + to try + -ing/noun
I'd like to try making jewellery.
I'd like to try yoga.

every
I play chess every weekend.
I do it every Saturday.

Present Perfect (1)

We use the Present Perfect to talk about past actions when we can see their consequences now:
I've had lunch. (so now I'm not hungry)
She hasn't come. (so now we are worried about her)
We've lost the key. (so now I can't open the door)

Form: Subject + have/has + 3rd form of the verb (see Irregular Verb List p.115)
I have had lunch.
He hasn't had lunch.
Have they had lunch?

Opinions: *think that*

It is very boring.
I **think (that)** it is very boring.
It's not very interesting.
I don't **think (that)** it's very interesting.

Modifiers

Modifiers come before adjectives or adverbs:
*That game is **very** good.*
*I play it **very** well.*

General adjectives
*It is **quite** interesting.*
*It is **very** good.*
*It is **really** nice.*

Negative adjectives
*It is **quite** difficult.*
*It is **very** boring.*
*It is **a bit** long.*
*It is **really** bad.*

Strong adjectives
*It is **really** fantastic.*
*It is **absolutely** terrible.*

some, any, no, a lot of, a few, a little

We use:
- **some** with uncountable and countable plural nouns, usually in affirmative sentences.
  *There are **some** good museums in Barcelona.*
  *I've got **some** new CDs.*
  *We still have **some** time.*

- **any** with uncountable and countable plural nouns, usually in questions and negative sentences.
  *Do you have **any** biscuits?*
  *I don't eat **any** meat.*
  *Are there **any** foreign students in your class?*
  *I don't need **any** help.*

- **no** with uncountable and countable plural nouns.
  *There are **no** girls here.*
  *I have **no** money.*

- **a lot of** with uncountable and countable plural nouns.
  *We know **a lot of** people.*
  *He eats **a lot of** fatty food.*

- **a few** with countable plural nouns.
  *I'd like **a few** apples.*
  *I've got **a few** good friends.*

- **a little** with uncountable nouns.
  *Give me **a little** time!*
  *We've got **a little** money.*

MODULE 3: LANGUAGE CHOICE 13-17

PRACTICE

13 Collocations: Money **Complete the description.**

I'm very good ¹ _with_ money. I ² _____ £10 pocket ³ _____ a week. I do a part-time ⁴ _____ , too at the weekends and I ⁵ _____ £30 a week. I'm quite careful and I ⁶ _____ about £50 a month and always put it in my bank ⁷ _____ . I usually ⁸ _____ money on cosmetics but I don't spend a lot of money ⁹ _____ clothes. I enjoy shopping ¹⁰ _____ shopping centres because there is a lot of choice.

14 Quantities **Complete the sentences.**

1 I bought a really cool _pair_ of sunglasses and a new _____ of shoes yesterday.
2 I always get my mum a _____ of chocolates and a _____ of flowers on her birthday.
3 I had a _____ of money last month so I bought a _____ of aftershave for my boyfriend.
4 I was really hungry and thirsty so I bought a _____ of peanuts and a _____ of water.
5 At the weekend, we bought lots of food and some _____ of cola and had a _____ of fun at a friend's house.

15 Present Perfect (2) **Complete the sentences with the correct forms of the verbs in brackets.**

1 _Have you bought_ (you / buy) a birthday present for Eva?
2 I _____ (not earn) any money in my life.
3 My parents _____ (not see) *The Lord of the Rings*.
4 _____ (your dad / sell) his car?
5 My sister _____ (give) her wedding dress to a charity shop.
6 The rain _____ (stop). We can go out.
7 I know Mary. We _____ (meet) a few times.
8 Don't worry. The exam _____ (not start) yet.
9 _____ (you / be) to Italy? What are Italians like?
10 I _____ (read) this magazine. You can take it.

16 Present Perfect (2): *ever, never, already, yet* **Choose the correct adverbs to complete the dialogue.**

A: Have you found a holiday job ¹*already/yet*?
B: No, I haven't. I have ²*ever/never* looked for a holiday job before. It's not easy.
A: I have ³*already/yet* found a job at a restaurant. I can ask them. Maybe they need more people.
B: I have ⁴*ever/never* worked in a restaurant.
A: Well I haven't done any cooking ⁵*never/yet*, either! But I'm sure it's easy. Have you ⁶*ever/already* helped your mother in the kitchen? It's the same.

17 Collocations: Products **Complete the sentences.**

1 Maybe they're very healthy but I don't like fruit and _____ . I love meat!
2 I never buy _____ clothes, like Calvin Klein jeans, because they're expensive.
3 My sister has just had her ears pierced so I bought her some silver _____ at an _____ and crafts shop in town.
4 La Boqueria market in Barcelona has got a fantastic selection of _____ and seafood but the Grand Bazaar in Istanbul has got more herbs and _____ .
5 I bought a second-hand _____ jacket in the market. It was quite expensive but it goes with my black boots.
6 I bought some _____ clothes at a charity shop at the weekend. I got a _____ scarf for £2 and a _____ blouse for £5. They are nearly new and are in very good condition.

REFERENCE

Collocations: Money

I'm quite **good with money**.
I'm very **bad with money**.
I **get** ten pounds a week **pocket money**.
I **earn** thirty pounds a week **from a part-time job**.
I **do a part-time job**.
I **save** fifteen pounds a month.
I **don't save** any money.
I **put** fifteen pounds **into my bank account**.
I **spend money on** clothes.
I **don't spend money on** food.
I **enjoy shopping** at street markets.
I **buy** second-hand clothes and books.

Quantities

a bit of advice/information/fun/luck/money
(any uncountable noun)
a bottle of perfume/aftershave/water/orange juice/
milk/cola (liquid)
a box of chocolates/matches
a bouquet of roses/flowers
a can of cola/lemonade/beans (also- 'a tin of beans'
etc.)
a packet of crisps/biscuits/sweets/chewing gum/
peanuts
a pair of jeans/socks/sunglasses/glasses/trousers/
shoes

Present Perfect (2)

**We use the Present Perfect to talk about past
actions and experiences if we do not know or are not
interested in exactly when they happened:**
I**'ve visited** Prague a few times.
Have you **seen** The Birds by Hitchcock?
She **hasn't been** abroad.
We**'ve finished** the project.
My mother **has travelled** all over the world.
Have you **worked** in a shop before?
Have you **had** lunch?
I **haven't seen** Tom for a long time.
He **hasn't read** today's papers.

ever, never, already, yet

**We often use the Present Perfect with these
time expressions:**
They've **already** bought the tickets for tonight.
(affirmative sentences)
Have you heard the news **yet**? She hasn't come back
yet. (questions and negative sentences)
Have you **ever** slept on the beach? (questions)
He has **never** travelled by plane. (negative sentences)

Collocations: Products

Words that go together + and
There are good places to buy **food and drink** at
the Boqueria Market in Barcelona and the **fruit and
vegetables** are fantastic.
We bought our Christmas turkey at the **meat and
poultry** section of our local market.
The **fish and seafood** in Spain is fantastic.
Indian food uses a lot of **herbs and spices**.
There is a new arts and crafts shop in town with lovely
silver and gold earrings.

Other collocations
Designer clothes are too expensive and I buy **second-
hand clothes** in charity shops.
You can buy **men's and women's clothes** in that shop.
That shop sells cheap **electronic goods** and I bought
my MP3 player there.
You can buy **antique books and furniture** at
Portobello Market in London.

Materials
With money from Christmas, I bought a second-hand
leather jacket, a **silk scarf**, a **cotton blouse** and some
nice **silver earrings**.

MODULE 4: LANGUAGE CHOICE 18-22

PRACTICE

18 Talking about books and films **Complete the book review.**

One of my [1] _favourite_ novels is *The Blind Assassin*. It is [2]_____ Margaret Atwood, one of my favourite writers. It is long but it is never [3]_____ and I could not stop reading it. The story [4]_____ place in a town in Canada. It is [5] _____ two sisters, Iris and Laura. Laura meets a young man, falls in love with him and [6]_____ dies mysteriously.

19 Past Simple and Continuous **Complete the text with the correct forms of the verbs in brackets.**

We [1] _were driving_ (drive) home after a party in December when we [2]_____ (see) a young woman near the local school. It [3]_____ (rain) but she [4]_____ (not have) a coat. She [5]_____ (wear) a white dress. She [6]_____ (look) lost so I [7]_____ (stop) and [8]_____ (offer) her a lift. She [9]_____ (not say) anything but she [10]_____ (get) into the car. A few minutes later, when we [11]_____ (pass) the cemetery, she suddenly [12]_____ (disappear). Fifty years ago, a lorry [13]_____ (kill) a girl in front of that school when she [14]_____ (walk) to a dance. Now her body is in the cemetery. I think she [15]_____ (go) home that night.

20 Adjectives and prepositions **Complete the sentence with the same meaning as the one above.**

1 I love thrillers and crime movies. I've got a big collection of DVDs.
I'm interested _in thrillers and crime movies_ .
2 I came last in the swimming competition.
I am not very good _____ .
3 I've got a maths exam and I really don't want to fail it.
I'm worried _____ .
4 I really hate seeing rats in the streets. They're absolutely horrible!
I'm afraid _____ .
5 We sometimes have to give presentations in class but I don't get worried.
I'm relaxed _____ .

21 Multi-part verbs (1) **Complete the multi-part verbs in the description.**

Last year, we went on holiday to Cornwall. The bus [1] _picked_ us up from outside our house and we [2]_____ to the hotel that afternoon. The next day, we went on an excursion to King Arthur's castle and came [3]_____ to the hotel late. On Thursday, we went on a boat trip to watch dolphins and [4]_____ to the port when it was getting dark. Suddenly, we saw a very large whale and took photos of it before it went [5]_____ . It was the best moment of the holiday. We [6]_____ back home two days later.

22 Present Perfect and Past Simple **Complete the sentences with the correct forms of the verbs in brackets.**

1 I _met_ (meet) my first boyfriend on a summer camp.
2 I'm worried about Gina. She _____ (never / be) so late before.
3 Your granddad and I _____ (go) on our first date to the zoo.
4 Oh, no, I _____ (lose) Lena's phone number. I can't call her!
5 Where _____ (parents / go) on their honeymoon?
6 You're so unhealthy! How many cakes_____ (you / eat) today?
7 My boyfriend and me _____ (not get on) well at first.
8 She's so romantic. She _____ (fall) in love hundreds of times.
9 We can't start the wedding ceremony. The bride _____ (not arrive).
10 I _____ (watch) a programme about love in literature last night.

REFERENCE

Describing stories

My favourite film is Avatar.
It's a science-fiction film and it is (directed) by James Cameron.
My favourite book is Little Dorrit.
It is (written) by Charles Dickens.
It was a **bestseller** and now it's a **classic** of English literature.
Some people think Dickens is very boring but I think this book is really interesting.
It takes place in a prison in London.
It's about a young girl called Amy. She is born in prison and then gets a job with an old lady.

Past Simple and Continuous

We use the Past Simple to talk about completed past actions, habits and states:
Michael Jackson **died** in 2009.
I **didn't like** hamburgers when I was a child.
I **went** to school in London.

We use the Past Continuous to talk about:
- activities that continued for some time in the past, around a particular moment.
  At six o'clock I **was cooking** dinner.

- activities that form background for a story or were interrupted by an event.
  It **was raining** when I arrived in Cracow.
  We **were watching** a concert on TV when the lights went off.

We often use *when* **with these tenses:**
When we got home, I found a note from my sister. (*when* = after)
When I was walking home, I saw an accident. (*when* = at the same time)

Adjective and prepositions

I'm **good at** maths.
I'm **bad at** playing football.
I'm **interested in** art.
I'm **not interested in** collecting things.
I'm **afraid of** rats.
I'm **not afraid of** flying.
I'm **worried about** exams.
I'm **relaxed about** marks at school.

Multi-part verbs (1)

My mum **picked** me **up** from the sports centre at three o'clock.
I **got to** school ten minutes late this morning.
I **came back to** the hotel after dinner.
We **went straight to** the hotel after lunch.
I **went back to** my old school last week.
We **sailed back to** the port after two days at sea.
My friend **went away** at the end of term.

Present Perfect and Past Simple

We use the Present Perfect for past activities when we do not know or it does not matter exactly when they happened:
I think we**'ve met** before.
We**'ve been** to London many times.
I**'ve lost** the car keys.
Spielberg **has made** a lot of films.

Time expressions: *before, just, already, yet, ever, never*

We use the Past Simple to talk about past activities if it is clear when they happened:
I **spent** my summer holidays last year working.
Dickens **wrote** Oliver Twist in 1838.
We **didn't meet** at John's wedding.
I **went** to primary school in Hungary.

!!! **We never use the Present Perfect with a time expression, e.g.** *last week, in 1999, three days ago.*

9

MODULE 5: LANGUAGE CHOICE 23-27

PRACTICE

23 Talking about family **Complete the description.**

I've [1] _got_ one brother and one sister. My grandparents, two uncles, one aunt and twelve [2]_____ live in Norway. I get [3]_____ well with my cousin, Alice – she comes here in the summer. I sometimes argue [4]_____ my little brother, Edward. My mum and I [5]_____ different tastes in clothes and hairstyles. She can't [6]_____ some of my clothes! My parents [7]_____ angry when I come home late or wear 'different' clothes.

24 Compounds: Technology **Complete the words in the description.**

In the evenings, I usually have a chat [1]on_line_ with my friends and then do my homework. I use my computer for projects – I keep a list of good [2]web_____ like encyclopaedias and dictionaries. I often [3]down_____ things to read later when I am working [4]off_____ . When I have finished my homework, I usually go to the [5]home_____ of my Facebook account. I [6]up_____ photos, music and jokes.

25 Present Perfect (3): *always/never* **Complete the sentences with the correct forms of the verbs in brackets and *always* or *never*.**

1 I _have never enjoyed_ (never / enjoy) big parties.
2 My sister _____ (always / have) a lot of friends.
3 My parents _____ (never / be) young!
4 There _____ (always / be) a lot of bright students in this school.
5 My granny _____ (never / like) big cities.
6 My grandfather_____ (always / love) animals.
7 My friends _____ (never / be) interested in politics.
8 I _____ (always / be) good at maths.

26 Present Perfect (3): *for/since* **Complete the sentences with *for* or *since*.**

1 My family has lived in a big city _for_ years.
2 My granny has had grey hair _____ the war.
3 My granddad has been a football fan _____ our team won the World Cup.
4 My mum has worked as a computer expert _____ fifteen years.
5 We have had a dog _____ I was a child.
6 I've known my girlfriend _____ a few months.
7 My dad has been be in love with my mum _____ twenty-five years.
8 My brother has liked computer games _____ primary school.

27 Collocations: At home **Complete the dialogue.**

A: What do you and your brother do to help at home?
B: Well, I usually [1]_ lay _ the table for dinner and we [2]_____ the rubbish out every night. My sister and I sometimes [3]_____ the shopping with my parents, too.
A: Do you ever argue with them?
B: Sometimes! My parents get angry when I [4]_____ the bathroom in a [5]_____ or when I spend too [6]_____ there. And they don't like it when I [7]_____ bad marks at school.
A: Do you ever argue with your brother?
B: A bit. He makes too much [8]_____ when he [9]_____ friends round and I'm trying to [10]_____ my homework.
A: And how often do you go out?
B: I'm very busy in the week but I always go [11]_____ with my friends on Saturdays and Sundays.
A: Do you ever come [12]_____ home late?
B: I've been a bit late once or twice.

REFERENCE

Talking about family

*I **'ve got** one brother, two sisters and ten cousins.*
*I **get on well with** my grandmother.*
*I **get on okay with** my uncle.*
*I **sometimes argue with** my sister.*
*My parents and I **have different tastes in** music.*
*My parents **get angry** when I spend hours on the computer.*
*They **can't stand** baggy jeans.*

Collocations: Adjectives and nouns
***tight/baggy** jeans/trousers*
***long/short** skirts/dresses*
***short/long/dyed/brown/black/fair** hair*

Compounds: Technology

Nouns
*I read that review on a fantastic **website**.*
*I've got some new photos on my **webpage**.*
*You can find the information on the **home page**.*
*I bought a new **laptop** (computer) last week.*

Adjectives/adverbs
*I often do **online** shopping./I go **online** about two hours a day.*
*I get information for projects from websites and then work **offline**.*
*In **real-time** chats you get replies from the other person immediately.*

Verbs
*I sometimes **download** films to watch because they are cheaper than buying DVDs.*
*I **uploaded** lots of photos to my web page.*
*I am very good at **multitasking** - I can listen to music, chat online and do my homework at the same time.*

Present Perfect (3)

We use the Present Perfect to talk about situations that started in the past and are still true, when we look at them from the present point of view:
*I**'ve always loved** chocolate.*
*She**'s lived here** all her life.*
*She**'s always had** a lot of friends.*
*We**'ve never been** good at sports.*

Present Perfect (3): *for/since*

We use time expressions with *for* and *since* with the Present Perfect:
* ***for** + a period of time*
  *I've known her **for** two years.*
  *She's been my friend **for** a long time.*
* ***since** + point in time*
  *He's been in love **since** Wednesday.*
  *They've lived in this house **since** they got married.*

!!! We do not use the Present Simple for these situations:
~~I live here all my life.~~
~~I am here since morning.~~

Collocations: At home

*I usually **take the rubbish out** at night.*
*I always **tidy my room** on Saturdays.*
*We **do the shopping** on Friday night.*
*My sister usually **lays the table.***
*I sometimes **leave** my bedroom **in a mess**.*
*My little brother often **makes too much noise**.*
*I sometimes **spend too long** on the computer.*
*My parents get angry with me when I **get bad marks** or **get a punishment** at school.*
*On Saturdays I **go out with my friends** but I never **come back home late**.*
*I'd like to **have more pocket money**.*
*We **had a party** last week - I **had all my friends round**.*

MODULE 6: LANGUAGE CHOICE 28–33

PRACTICE

28 Talking about music **Complete the description.**

I'm really ¹ _into_ music and listen to it all the time. I like various different ² _____ but I ³ _____ love listening to rock and heavy metal. I'm crazy ⁴ _____ groups like Dimmu Borgir and Slipknot. I can't ⁵ _____ pop and dance music and I'm not ⁶ _____ about soul and jazz either. They're really boring! I haven't got a very good singing ⁷ _____ but I can ⁸ _____ the drums a bit. I'd like ⁹ _____ start a rock group with my friends and I'd also ¹⁰ _____ to learn to play the guitar.

29 *have to/not have to, can/can't* **Choose the correct verbs to complete the text .**

I go to a music school. I'm learning to play the guitar so I ¹*have to*/*don't have to* practise every day. I ²*have to/can* be very careful with my fingers: I ³*don't have to/can't* play basketball or volleyball but I ⁴*can/have to* swim. The good thing is that I ⁵*have to/don't have to* bring my own guitar – the school has a lot of instruments. At weekends our school band often gives concerts and I ⁶*have to/can't* play too.

30 *have to/not have to, can/can't* **Complete the sentences with *can, can't, have to* or *not have to.***

1 In the library you _have to_ be quiet and you _____ eat or drink.
2 When you go to the theatre, you _____ arrive on time but you _____ wear casual clothes.
3 If you are a musician, you _____ practise every day and usually you _____ sleep until noon.
4 In the museum, you _____ touch the paintings but you _____ buy souvenirs in the museum shop.
5 When you are at a concert, you _____ have a ticket but you _____ sing along and dance.
6 On a plane you _____ walk around. You _____ wear a seatbelt.

31 Verbs and adjectives **Complete the sentences with the correct forms of *look, feel* or *sound.***

1 That new song by Snow Patrol _sounds_ really amazing. I just love the guitar.
2 I'm not crazy about those new shoes. They _____ absolutely horrible!
3 I _____ really tired because the concert finished at one o'clock.
4 I _____ relaxed when I listen to classical music.
5 The poster for that concert _____ great. I love the design.
6 My dad's old rock CDs _____ terrible but he loves listening to them.
7 Are you okay? You _____ very sad.
8 I always _____ very happy on Friday afternoons.
9 That listening test _____ very difficult because they speak very fast.
10 It _____ very cold in here. Can you close the window, please?

32 Multi-part verbs (2) **Complete the verbs.**

1 'Can you turn that music _up_ ? It's great!'
2 'Switch _____ the TV and go to bed! It's after midnight.'
3 'Can you turn _____ the radio? I want to know the football results.'
4 'Please turn _____ your mobile phones during the concert.'
5 'Turn that music _____ , please. It's really loud.'

33 *may, must* and *must not* **Choose the correct modals to complete the school rules.**

1 Students *must/mustn't* smoke in the school building.
2 Students *may/mustn't* borrow up to five books from the school library.
3 Students *may/must* come to lessons prepared.
4 Students *may/mustn't* fight or use bad language.
5 Students *may/mustn't* take part in after school activities.
6 Students *mustn't/must* damage school equipment.
7 Students *must/mustn't* wear shorts or miniskirts.
8 Students *must/may* arrive at their classrooms on time.

REFERENCE

Talking about music

*I'm **really into** music.*
*I'm **not really into** hip hop and rap.*
*I **like** various different styles.*
*I **just love** listening to soul and dance music.*
*I **can't stand** country and western.*
*I'm **crazy about** world music and folk.*
*I'm **not crazy about** heavy metal.*
I haven't got a very good singing voice.
*I **can play** the violin.*
*I'**d like to play** the flute.*
*I'**d like to** start a rock group.*

can/can't, have to/not have to

We use:

*   **can** to talk about permission or possibility (*can* + infinitive without *to*).
    *You **can** go home now.*
    *We **can** meet in the library after school.*
    *They **can** write it in pencil.*

*   **can't** to say that something is not possible or not allowed (*can't* + infinitive without *to*).
    *I **can't** go out after 10 p.m.*
    *We **can't** buy the tickets now - the office is closed.*
    *The kids **can't** watch TV after 10 p.m.*

*   **have to** to talk about necessity and obligations (*have to* + infinitive).
    *I **have to** write this essay for tomorrow.*
    *She **has to** practise playing the piano every day.*
    *We **have to** buy her a nice present.*

*   **not have to** to say that there is no necessity or obligation to do something (*not have to* + infinitive).
    *You **don't have to** buy a ticket - the concert is free.*
    *We **don't have to** wear uniforms at my school.*
    *He **doesn't have to** bring a girlfriend to the party.*

Verbs and adjectives

We use verbs + adjectives to describe how something is:

look
*These clothes **look great** - I love the colours!*
*The singer of that group **looks very attractive**.*
*Are you okay? You **look tired**.*

sound
*That guitar **sounds amazing** but it's very expensive.*
*I don't like heavy metal. It **sounds horrible**.*
*I've spoken to Luke on the phone. He **sounds very unhappy**.*

feel
*The concert was great but it **felt very crowded**.*
*I **feel tired** today after last night's concert.*
*Do you **feel all right**? You look sad.*

Multi-part verbs (2)

*I **turn on** the radio when I wake up in the morning.*
*I **turned off** my MP3 player and went to sleep.*
*I always **switch on** the CD player when I get into the car.*
*I forgot to **switch off** my computer yesterday.*
*That song is great. Why don't you **turn** the volume **up**?*
*Can you **turn** the music **down**, please? I'm trying to study.*

may, must and must not

We use *may*, *must* and *must not* in formal situations, often in public notices, written regulations, instructions, etc. We use:

*   **may** to give permission (*may* + infinitive without *to*)
    *Students **may** borrow up to five books from the library.*
    *Visitors **may** use the kitchen.*

*   **must** to impose obligation (*must* + infinitive without *to*)
    *Students **must** wear school uniforms.*
    *Visitors **must** follow the sightseeing route.*

*   **must not** to forbid (*must not/mustn't* + infinitive without *to*)
    *Passengers **mustn't** keep their feet on the seats.*
    *Students **must not** use their mobile phones in the school building.*

PRACTICE

34 Talking about health **Complete the description.**

My aunt is not very old but she has been ¹ _in_ hospital lots of times. In the winter, she often ²_____ colds and flu and in the summer she gets bad ³_____ fever. In the spring and autumn, she often ⁴_____ a bit depressed and tired. She's also got bad teeth and often has ⁵_____ . She needs to ⁶_____ more sport, eat ⁷_____ junk food and ⁸_____ smoking.

35 Confusing words **Correct the underlined words in the sentences when necessary.**

1 Tattoos are <u>actually</u> fashionable *nowadays* but they are <u>actually</u> terrible for your skin.
2 Tattoos <u>damage</u> your skin and cause infections. They also <u>damage</u> you a lot!
3 Spanish <u>meal</u> is healthy but people eat their evening <u>meal</u> at 10 p.m.!
4 We had a <u>great</u> time skateboarding but afterwards I noticed a <u>great</u> cut on my leg.
5 I <u>use</u> creams for my skin but I never <u>use</u> a hat.

36 *will* and *won't* **Complete the sentences with *will* or *won't*.**

1 Don't worry! It's just a cold. I'm sure you _will_ be fine in a few days.
2 Epidemics _____ probably kill a lot of people this century.
3 You've got flu. I'm afraid antibiotics _____ help you.
4 Take an aspirin and your temperature _____ definitely go down.
5 Wash your hands with antibacterial soap! It _____ kill the germs.
6 The doctor is very punctual. I'm sure he _____ be late.
7 Don't go out in a T-shirt! You _____ catch a cold!
8 I've put on sunscreen so I _____ get sunburn.

37 *will, may* and *be going to* **Complete the sentences with the verbs below and the correct forms of the words in brackets.**

fail   work   ~~rain~~   miss   help   be   catch   win

1 The sky is very dark. It _is going to rain_ . (*be going to*)
2 Lisa is at the doctor's. She _____ a little late. (*may*)
3 Where is your coat? You _____ a cold. (*will*)
4 My dad is a doctor. He _____ us with this project on obesity. (*may*)
5 Oh no! It's eight o'clock! I _____ the first lesson. (*be going to*)
6 You're good at running. I'm sure you _____ the race. (*will*)
7 The test is difficult. They _____ . (*may*)
8 He's got two dogs, a snake and three budgies. He _____ with animals in the future. (*be going to*)

38 Collocations: Accidents **Complete the story.**

Last year, I ¹ _had_ quite a bad accident. I was riding my bike to school when a car crashed into me. I was ²_____ for a few minutes and when I woke up in the ambulance, my leg ³_____ a lot. I also had a ⁴_____ in my left arm and it was ⁵_____ a bit, but not badly. In the ambulance, I ⁶_____ an injection and when I got to the hospital, a doctor gave me an ⁷_____ to check my leg. I had a broken leg but my arm wasn't ⁸_____ . Luckily, I didn't need to ⁹_____ an operation. I was in hospital for twenty-four hours but it took me three months to get ¹⁰_____ my broken leg.

REFERENCE

Talking about health

I've only **been in hospital** once.
I've never **had** a **bad accident**.
I often **have colds and coughs** in the winter.
I **had** a bad **stomachache** last week.
My friend **had flu** in December and **had a high temperature**.
My sister **has** a lot of allergies like **hayfever**.
I've got good teeth and have never **had toothache** but I sometimes get bad **earache**.
I often **feel tired** in the evenings after school.
I've never **felt depressed** but I feel unhappy sometimes.
After the accident, I **felt faint** and very **weak**.
I **felt sick** on the boat to France.
I **need to do** more sport, eat more fruit and sleep more.
I **need to eat** less pizza and spend less time on my computer.
I need to **stop eating** sweets and biscuits.

Confusing words

Sunbathing is **actually** very dangerous. (in fact)
~~Actually~~ **Now**, I am studying English.

You need to **wear** trousers and **use** sun cream.
You need to ~~use~~ **wear** a hat.

Italian **food** is great and my best **meal** ever was in Rome.
I like Spanish ~~meal~~ **food**.

Dandruff can **damage** your hair but it doesn't **hurt**.
Tattoos ~~damage~~ **hurt** you a lot and ~~hurt~~ **damage** your skin.

That cream is **great** and gets rid of **big** spots.
I've got a ~~great~~ **big** spot on my face.

will, may and be going to

We use:
* **will** and **won't** to express our opinions and beliefs about the future (often with words like *I think, I'm sure, maybe/perhaps/probably/definitely*).
  I'm sure he'll be a good doctor.
  They **will definitely** want to visit the castle.
  I know him, he **won't** stay in bed because of a cold.

* **may** and **may not** to make uncertain predictions or to guess.
  You **may** catch a tropical disease if you go there.
  This drug **may not** help him.

* **be going to** to make predictions based on evidence in the present situation.
  This test is too difficult for me. I**'m going to** fail.
  She's eaten three bags of sweets. She**'s going to** be sick.

Collocations: Accidents

My dad **had an accident** last year at work and **was unconscious** for ten minutes.
I've never **broken a bone** but my sister **broke her arm** when she was skiing last month.
My mum cut her finger when she was cooking and **it was bleeding badly**.
When I cut my foot I **had an injection** and **it hurt a lot**.
My grandfather **had an operation** last week because he has cancer.
She **had a pain in** her foot so she went to the hospital and **had an X-ray**.
After the accident, I **was vomiting** and **felt terrible**.
It took him six months to **get over** his broken leg.
I **took** a lot of **painkillers** because of my **broken foot**.
I don't like **taking pills or tablets**, or any **medicine** really.

MODULE 8: LANGUAGE CHOICE 39-44

PRACTICE

39 Compounds: Environment **Complete the words in the description.**

In my city, Buenos Aires, there are lots of green ¹_spaces_ like Lezama Park. There is also La Costanera, a very big nature ²_____ next to the Plata River; it has got lots of wildlife with many wild ³_____ like birds and reptiles. There are also quite a few environmental problems in my city. There are a lot of cars and buses and they cause ninety percent of the air ⁴_____ in the centre. Water ⁵_____ is a problem, too and the Plata River and other smaller rivers are badly polluted. There is definitely climate ⁶_____ in Buenos Aires – my grandma says that the winters were colder forty years ago.

40 Future Conditional **Use the cues to write sentences with the Future Conditional.**

1 you / not feed the dog → it / get angry.
If _you don't feed the dog, it'll get angry_ .
2 there / be too much rain in summer → bees / not produce a lot of honey
If _____ .
3 we / put the cat and the dog in one room → they / fight
If _____ .
4 I / go sailing → I / catch some fish
If _____ .
5 the cat / be sick → we / take him to the vet
If _____ .
6 I / see a toad → I / take a photo
If _____ .

41 Multi-part verbs (3) **Complete the sentences.**

1 I _came across_ a snake in my garden but it wasn't poisonous.
2 You should _____ from the forest at night because of the bears and other dangerous animals.
3 If a bear attacks you, you should not _____ because it is very strong and can kill you.
4 I was taking my dog out in the park when he saw a rabbit and _____ from me.
5 I swam very fast to _____ from the shark.
6 The bees were behind us but we ran through the forest and the trees _____ them _____ .

42 Pronoun: it **Add it to the story when necessary.**

It Is difficult to remember when happened. I think was in November or the start of December. Was about five o'clock in the evening. Was snowing a lot, was very cold and was getting dark. My mobile phone was broken and I wanted to take to town to the shop. Is about two miles from my house to the local town of Banff, Alberta. Anyway, I went outside to get my car and then I saw the bear. Was outside the garage looking in the rubbish bins. Was very frightening to see because was very large and I screamed. Saw me and ran towards me very fast. Luckily, my wife heard me and opened the door. I went in and closed quickly before the bear could catch me.

43 all, most, many, some, no/none **Complete the sentences with the correct animals.**

sharks ~~elephants~~ kangaroos bears birds

1 Some _elephants_ live in India.
2 Most _____ are dangerous for swimmers.
3 Many _____ migrate to warmer places in winter.
4 No _____ live in tropical climates.
5 All _____ can jump.

44 all, most, many, some, no/none **Choose the correct words to complete the text.**

¹(Most)/No people like animals and ²many/all of us keep pets. ³Some/Most people keep exotic animals, like snakes or spiders but ⁴most/no pets are cats and dogs. ⁵Most/All dogs are very friendly and love to play. However, ⁶some/no dogs can be dangerous. ⁷Many/All experts say that everything depends on training. ⁸Most/Some dog owners teach their dogs to attack people and animals. We read about ⁹many/no accidents where children are seriously injured by aggressive dogs. So remember to be careful when you go jogging in the park – ¹⁰all/no dogs are completely safe.

REFERENCE

Compounds: Environment

Two words: *air pollution, water pollution, green spaces, nature reserves, wild animals, climate change, habitat loss*
Hyphens: *over-fishing*
One word: *wildlife*

Future Conditional

We use the Future Conditional to talk about possible future events, when they depend on other future events:
*If it **rains**, we**'ll stay** at home.*
*They **may leave** without us if we**'re** late.*

Form

if + present simple, (condition)	***will/may*** + infinitive (consequence)
will/may + infinitive (consequence)	***if*** + present simple (condition)

We use the Present Simple (not *will*) after *when*, *before* and *as soon as* to talk about the future:
*I'll help you **when I come** home.*
***Before they start** cooking, they'll clean the kitchen.*

Multi-part verbs (3)

*You should **run away** from alligators because they can't go very far.*
*When a wild turkey attacks you, **fight back** with your umbrella.*
*You should **stay away** from bears because they are very dangerous.*
*If you **come across** a mother bear with cubs you are in trouble.*
*Don't try to **get away** from bears because they can run fast and climb trees.*
*When killer bees are chasing you, you should run through some bushes to try to **slow** them **down**.*

Pronoun: *it*

We use *it*:
to refer to something mentioned before:
*The elephant can be very dangerous because **it** is so large and strong.*

with common expressions about the weather/date/ distance etc.:
***It** is six o'clock and **it** is raining outside.*
***It** is Friday 10 June and **it's** very cold.*
***It's** October and **it's** getting dark earlier.*
***It** is five kilometres from here to the town.*

it + infinitive + ***to*:**
***It** is dangerous to go swimming.*
***It** is difficult to learn a language.*

all, most, many, some, no/none

We use *all, most, many, some, no* and *none of the* with plural countable and uncountable nouns.
We use *many* with plural nouns only.

- ***all*** **= every thing or person of a particular type, the whole amount**
  ***All** my friends like dancing.*
  *They've eaten **all** the meat.*

- ***most*** **= almost everyone or everything**
  ***Most** birds eat insects.*
  ***Most** water in this town comes from the river.*

- ***many*** **= a lot of people or things**
  *There are **many** wild birds in this area.*

- ***some*** **= a number of people, things or a certain amount**
  ***Some** snakes are dangerous.*
  ***Some** luggage disappeared from the train.*

- ***no/none*** **= not any**
  *There is **no** time left.*
  *We've got **no** animals at home.*
  ***None** of the trees is healthy.*

MODULE 9: LANGUAGE CHOICE 45-50

PRACTICE

45 Prepositions **Complete the description with the correct prepositions.**

I go to school ¹ _by_ car with my dad. After school, I go to the sports centre ² ____ foot and from there I go back home ³ ____ the underground. On Saturday afternoon, I go into the town centre ⁴ ____ bus to go to a film or do some shopping.
We go ⁵ ____ holiday ⁶ ____ plane and we always go ⁷ ____ Greece. We always go ⁸ ____ boat from Athens to one of the small islands. It's a great place and I go around the island ⁹ ____ bike. Once, we rented horses and went around the island ¹⁰ ____ horseback.

46 Opposites **Choose the correct adjective to complete the sentences.**

1 We were *lucky/(unlucky)* to lose the game because the other side scored a/an *lucky/unlucky* goal in the last minute.
2 I went to school at the *usual/unusual* time and saw a/an *usual/unusual* car from the 1920s in the street.
3 *Accompanied/Unaccompanied* children can't go into that shop – they have to be *accompanied/unaccompanied* by an adult.
4 Now she's very *reliable/unreliable* and always arrives on time but before, she was *reliable/unreliable* and was always late.
5 It is *known/unknown* that Bessie Coleman had a terrible accident but the cause of it is *known/unknown*.
6 Now it is *possible/impossible* to be a space tourist but it is *possible/impossible* to visit the Moon.

47 The Passive **Complete the sentences with Passive forms of the verbs in brackets. Use correct tenses.**

1 Aeroplane crews _are prepared_ (prepare) for various accidents.
2 A lot of spacecraft _____ (send) over the years to explore Venus.
3 A water tank _____ (damage) last night on the International Space Station.
4 New stars _____ (discover) all the time.
5 A lot of objects _____ (lose) in space so far.
6 Water _____ (just / find) on the Moon.
7 Satellites _____ (use) for weather forecasts and communication.
8 The telescope _____ (invent) in the Netherlands in the early seventeenth century.

48 The Passive: *by* phrases **Use the cues in brackets to answer the questions. Use the Passive and *by* phrases.**

1 Who discovered the hole in the ozone layer? _The hole in the ozone layer was discovered by a satellite_ . (a satellite)
2 What destroys the windows in the International Space Station? _____ . (pieces of space junk)
3 Who saw the last solar eclipse? _____ . (millions of people in Asia)
4 Who played the captain in the 1995 film *Apollo 13*? _____ . (Tom Hanks)
5 Who has explored Venus and Mars? _____ . (space robots)
6 What observes the sky twenty-four hours a day? _____ . (the Hubble telescope)

49 Compounds: Airports **Complete the description.**

When I got to the airport, I went to the ¹ _check-in desk_ and got my boarding card. There were big queues at ² _____ and I had problems because I was carrying a bottle of shampoo. I only had ten minutes to do some shopping and buy a present for my girlfriend in the ³ _____ . Then I had to go to the ⁴ _____ because my flight was leaving. When we got to Heathrow, there were long queues at ⁵ _____ but I was in the European Union queue. I waited half an hour at ⁶ _____ and was going to go to ⁷ _____ but then my suitcase arrived. My girlfriend was waiting for me at the ⁸ _____ and it was great to see her!

50 Compounds: Airports **What are these places in an airport?**

1 You can buy or change tickets here. _ticket office_
2 You can get information about hotels and transport here. _____
3 You collect your baggage here. _____
4 You go here if your luggage does not arrive. _____
5 You can leave your car here. _____
6 Here people check you and your hand baggage before you get on the plane. _____
7 You get on the plane here. _____
8 People check your passport here when you arrive in a foreign country. _____
9 You go here to get your boarding card and leave your luggage. _____
10 You can buy cheap products here (e.g. electronic goods). _____

REFERENCE

Prepositions

*I go **to** school **by** bus.*
*I'd like to go **to** school **by** bike.*
*We go **on** holiday **by** plane.*
*I'd like to go **on** holiday **by** train.*
*I come back **from** school **on** foot.*
*I'd like to come **back** from school **on** roller skates.*
*I go **on** the underground when I go **to** London.*
*I've never been **on** horseback.*
*I've never been **in/on** an aeroplane.*
*I've never been **on** a big boat.*
*I'd like to go **in** a canoe or kayak.*

Opposites

*experienced/**in**experienced   possible/**im**possible*
*conventional/**un**conventional   reliable/**un**reliable*
*lucky/**un**lucky   usual/**un**usual   happy/**un**happy*
*accompanied/**un**accompanied   known/**un**known*

The Passive

Form
Present Simple: *am/is/are* + 3rd form of the verb
*The internet **is used** all over the world.*
*I **am lost** in the middle of a forest.*

Present Perfect: *has been/have been* + 3rd form of the verb.
*The computer **has been** badly **damaged**.*
*They astronauts **have been informed** about the danger.*

Past Simple: *was/were* + 3rd form of the verb
*Some planets in our solar system **were not known** in ancient times.*
*Copernicus **was born** in Torun, Poland.*

We often use the Passive when we do not know who the 'doer' of the action is or the action itself is more important than the 'doer':
*The computer **was stolen** last night.* (we don't know who stole it)
*New galaxies **are discovered** every day.* (the discovery is more important than who made it)

The Passive: *by* phrases

We sometimes use the *by* phrase at the end of the Passive sentence to say who did it:
*The Moon was explored **by American spaceships**.*

Compounds: Airports

Arrivals
*When we got to New York we had to wait hours in **passport control**.*
*My suitcase didn't arrive at the baggage reclaim and I had to go to **lost luggage**.*
*After we went through the **arrival gate** I phoned my parents.*
*We found a good hotel at the **tourist information** office and then picked up a car at the **car rental** office.*

Departures
*We left our car at the **car park** and went to the **ticket office** to buy a ticket.*
*We got our boarding cards at the **check-in desk** and checked in our luggage.*
*I had to leave a bottle of water at the **security control**.*
*I bought a new camera at the **duty-free shop** in the **departure lounge**.*
*The airport was very crowded but we went to the **VIP lounge** because my dad is a frequent business traveller.*
*It took half an hour to get to the **boarding gate** from the security control.*

MODULE 10: LANGUAGE CHOICE 51-55

PRACTICE

51 Talking about holidays **Complete the description.**

I usually go ¹ _abroad_ on holiday and don't stay in Britain. I often go ²_____ my family to the coast in Bulgaria because it's got good weather and lovely beaches. We usually stay ³_____ a hotel because they are not too expensive. I often ⁴_____ sailing in the Black Sea and sometimes we go walking in the forests near the coast. Once, we went to the coast in Turkey and ⁵_____ at an apartment. I ⁶_____ windsurfing every day and we went ⁷_____ to some amazing ancient ruins. My ⁸_____ is to go to the USA because it's got fantastic cities like New York and beautiful places like the Grand Canyon.

52 Unreal Conditional **Complete the sentences with the correct forms of the verbs in brackets.**

1 If I _had_ (have) a lot of money, I _would buy_ _____ (buy) a desert island.
2 If reality shows _____ (not be) interesting, people _____ (not watch) them.
3 I _____ (take part) in a desert island reality show if I _____ (not have to) go to school.
4 If I _____ (appear) in a reality show, my friends _____ (laugh) at me.
5 If there _____ (be) no fresh water on an island, people _____ (can collect) rainwater.
6 We _____ (die) if we _____ (drink) only seawater.
7 TV channels _____ (not produce) reality shows if people _____ (not want) to watch them.
8 I _____ (not survive) if I _____ (be) on a desert island alone.

53 -ing forms **Complete the description with the correct forms of the words in brackets.**

Slovenia is a great country for all kinds of adventure sports. On the coast you can go ¹ _sailing_ (sail) or go ²_____ (waterski) and there are also some good places if you enjoy ³_____ (dive). ⁴_____ (kayak) and ⁵_____ (canoe) are also popular, especially on the Soca River. In the mountains, you can go ⁶_____ (ski) in resorts in the Slovenian Alps and in the summer there are some great places if you like ⁷_____ (hike) and ⁸_____ (cycle).

54 Multi-part verbs (4) **Complete the sentences.**

1 Something is _going on_ in the centre of town – I can hear police cars and ambulances.
2 My family comes from a small town in the mountains and I _____ there every summer in the holidays to stay with my grandparents.
3 The number of tourists has _____ in the last few years and there are a lot of new hotels in the town.
4 I usually _____ with my girlfriend on Saturday night to a club in the centre of town.
5 I didn't enjoy the film – it _____ for over three hours!
6 It hasn't rained for weeks and the level of the rivers has _____ a lot.

55 the in geographical names **Use the cues to write sentences about these locations.**

1 Lake Titicaca / the largest lake / South America
   Lake Titicaca is the largest lake in South America.
2 Prague / capital / Czech Republic
   _____
   _____ .
3 Hvar and Korcula / beautiful islands / Adriatic / Croatia
   _____
   _____ .
4 Nile / the longest river / Africa
   _____
   _____ .
5 America / situated between / Pacific / Atlantic
   _____
   _____ .
6 Aconcagua / highest mountain / Andes
   _____
   _____ .
7 Ganges / begins / Himalayas / flows into / Indian Ocean
   _____
   _____ .
8 United Kingdom / consists of / England, Wales, Scotland and Northern Ireland
   _____
   _____ .

REFERENCE

Talking about holidays

*I usually **go abroad on holiday, to** the Spanish coast.*
*I sometimes **go to** the country in the south-west of England.*
*I always **go with** my family and sometimes a friend comes with me.*
*We usually **stay at** a campsite or **in** a hotel in Spain or **with** my grandparents in England.*
*I **often go** cycling and sailing and sometimes we **go** sightseeing.*
***My dream is to go to** Tahiti because it's got beautiful coral reefs and mountains.*

Unreal Conditional

Form
if + past simple, *would/could* + infinitive

We use the unreal conditional to talk about:
*   **impossible situations in the present.**
    ***If** my family was rich, we **wouldn't** live in a small flat.* (we are not rich)
    ***If** I had a job, I **wouldn't** have time to watch TV.* (I don't have a job)

*   **imaginary, unlikely situations in the future.**
    ***If** I won Millionaires, I **would** be famous.* (I don't think I'll win Millionaires)
    ***If** I landed on a desert island, I **would** look for fresh water first.* (it is unlikely that I will land on a desert island)

-ing forms

-*ing* forms can be the subject of sentences:
***Canoeing, windsurfing** and **sailing** are available at most resorts.*
***Diving** and **surfing** are my favourite hobbies.*
***Waiting** for planes at airports is really boring.*

-*ing* forms come after certain verbs (e.g. verbs of preference):
*You can enjoy **dancing** the night away at the discotheque.*
*I love **swimming** in the sea and surfing.*
*I really hate **going** on aeroplanes.*
*I can't stand **sightseeing** in crowded cities.*
*I often go **surfing** and **windsurfing** when I am on holiday.*

-*ing* forms come after expressions with prepositions:
*I'm **really into listening** to chill-out music.*
*I'm **crazy about hiking** in the mountains.*

Multi-part verbs (4)

*I love **going out** with my friends on Saturday evening.*
*You look worried. What's **going on**? Did you fail your exams?*
*The price of petrol has **gone up** three times in the last six months.*
*The population in my town has **gone down** because people have moved to the cities.*
*I'd like to **go back** to my old primary school and talk to my old teacher.*
*The party **went on** until three in the morning.*

the in geographical names

We use these names without articles:
continents: *Australia, Europe*
countries: *Bulgaria, Poland*
cities: *New York, London*
lakes: *Lake Victoria, Lake Ontario*
mountains: *Mont Blanc, Kilimanjaro*
islands: *Majorca, New Zealand*

We use *the* with these names:
countries: *the United Kingdom, the United States* (when they are plural or contain a common noun (republic, state, kingdom, etc.))
rivers: *the Amazon, the Nile*
seas/oceans: *the Pacific, the Mediterranean Sea*
mountain ranges: *the Alps, the Himalayas*

MODULE 11: LANGUAGE CHOICE 56-60

PRACTICE

56 Describing people **Complete the description.**

Sheila is a very good friend of ¹ _mine_ . We've known ² _____ other since we were very little. She's tall and good-looking but she's a bit ³ _____ – she just loves eating pizzas! She's ⁴ _____ long, curly blond hair. Sheila loves parties and is an outgoing person but sometimes she's a ⁵ _____ impatient and moody.

57 *get* **Match the words and expressions below with the uses of *get* in the description.**

bought   found   argued all the time   eliminate
became (x2)   have a good time together   ~~received~~

Last week, I ¹*got* received some money from my aunt for my birthday – she and I always ²*get on*. So I went shopping and ³*got* a new pair of jeans on Saturday with a friend. Unfortunately, we ⁴*got on badly* so I ⁵*got* a bit depressed and went home. I ⁶*got* an old DVD and sat down to watch it but there was a problem with the picture and I couldn't ⁷*get rid of* it. Then, when it ⁸*got* dark, I decided to go to bed.

58 Intentions and arrangements **What could these people say?**

1 Mark is at the airport. He has already checked in for his flight.
   'I'm flying to Budapest.'
   'I'm going to fly to Budapest.'
2 Sally is looking through the TV guide for the weekend.
   'I'm watching an old Hitchcock film on Saturday.'
   'I'm going to watch an old Hitchcock film on Saturday.'
3 Alex is waiting in front of the cinema with a bunch of beautiful flowers.
   'I'm taking Julia to the cinema.'
   'I'm going to take Julia to the cinema.'
4 Katie's friend asks her to walk the dog tonight.
   'I can't, I'm playing in a concert at the school club.'
   'I can't, I'm going to play in a concert at the school club.'

59 Intentions and arrangements **Complete the dialogue with the correct forms of the words in brackets.**

A: Hi, Charlotte. I've got two tickets for Arctic Monkeys. They ¹ _are playing_ (play) in Prague tomorrow. Would you like to go?
B: I can't, I ² _____ (go) away to Slovakia today. Actually, my train ³ _____ (leave) in two hours.
A: What ⁴ _____ (you / do) there?
B: We ⁵ _____ (do) some hiking in the Tatras. And my brother ⁶ _____ (try) paragliding, I think. He's into extreme sports.
A: When ⁷ _____ (you / come back)?
B: On Sunday. The train ⁸ _____ (arrive) at 6 a.m.

60 Collocations: Networking **Complete the dialogue.**

A: What advice have you got about social networking for teenagers?
B: Well, networking sites are great for teenagers. They can ¹ _keep_ in touch with their friends and ² _____ videos and music on their homepages. But there are dangers, too.
A: What are they?
B: First, people sometimes put a lot of ³ _____ information on their homepage. You should never ⁴ _____ away your name, address or telephone number if strangers can ⁵ _____ your homepage. And you should be careful when you ⁶ _____ personal photos online, too when everyone can see them.
A: What about cyber-bullying?
B: It's a problem and a lot of people ⁷ _____ from it and get aggressive and nasty ⁸ _____ on their homepage.
A: Should you talk to people online? For example when a stranger ⁹ _____ a comment on your homepage.
B: No. You don't know who the person is when they are trying to ¹⁰ _____ friendly with you. And NEVER arrange to meet a stranger you have met online!

REFERENCE

Describing people

*Tom is a **very good friend of mine**.*
***We've known each other** for a very long time.*
*He's **short** and a **bit skinny** but he's quite **good-looking**.*
*He's got **long, straight red hair**.*
*He's a bit **overweight**.*
*He's usually very **easy-going** but sometimes he's a **bit moody**.*

*His sister, Kelly, is **tall** and **well-built** – she's a very **pretty** woman.*
*She's slim and has got **short, curly blond hair**.*
*She's very **outgoing** and **friendly** but sometimes she's a bit too **talkative**.*

get

become
*I **got** angry when my computer didn't work yesterday.*
*It **gets** dark at about six o'clock these days.*

receive/achieve
*I **got** a great present from my uncle at Christmas.*
*I usually **get** quite good marks in maths.*

find/buy
*I **got** a book from the library for my science project.*
*I **got** a new mobile phone yesterday – it's amazing!*

have a good/bad relationship with
*I **get on** very well **with** my cousin and we go hiking together.*
*I don't **get on with** my younger sister – we're always arguing.*
*My younger sister and I don't **get on** – we're always arguing.*

eliminate
*That shampoo **got rid of** my dandruff.*

Intentions and arrangements

We use *be going to* to express an intention to do something in the future:
*I**'m going to** study music.*
*She **is going to** cook something.*

We use the Present Continuous to talk about future events that we have arranged:
*Maria **is flying** home on Saturday.* (she's booked her flight)
*I**'m going** to the theatre tonight.* (I've already got the ticket)

We use the Present Simple to talk about things that are certain to happen and we cannot change the time, e.g. timetables, official events:
*Our plane **takes off** at 7.30.*
*The school year **starts** on 1 September.*

Collocations: Networking

*Today, I **posted a comment** on my friend's homepage.*
*I use my social networking site to **keep in touch with** my friends.*
*I look at my homepage twice a day and **post photos** on it at the weekends.*
*I'm very careful and never **give away personal information**.*
*Strangers can't **view the information** on my homepage. Only my friends can.*
*I've never **suffered from cyber-bullying** but once a friend of mine received some **aggressive messages**.*
*I never **get friendly with strangers** online.*

PRACTICE

61 **Adjectives (-ed and -ing) Complete the sentence with the same meaning as the one above.**

1 Attacks by bears are absolutely terrifying.
   People are _terrified of attacks by bears_ .

2 I was really excited in the last quarter of that basketball game.
   The last quarter of that basketball game _____
   _____ .

3 I find arguing with my parents very upsetting.
   I get very _____
   _____ .

4 I get very confused when I read instructions for computers.
   I find instructions _____
   _____ .

5 That song on the radio is very annoying.
   I'm getting very _____ .

62 **Defining relative clauses Complete the sentences. Use the information in brackets.**

1 People often suffer from stress. (They work too much.)
   People _who work too much_ often suffer from stress.

2 I have a few books. (I have never read them.)
   I have a few books _____
   _____ read.

3 I don't remember the day. (I fell in love for the first time on that day.)
   I don't remember the day _____
   _____ for the first time.

4 I've read an article. (It describes different reactions to stress.)
   I've read an article _____
   _____ different reactions to stress.

5 We didn't find the cinema. (We had our first date there.)
   We didn't find the cinema _____
   _____ our first date.

6 Most people hide emotions. (The emotions are unpleasant for others.)
   Most people hide emotions _____
   _____ unpleasant for others.

63 **make and do Complete the sentences with the correct forms of make or do.**

1 I _made_ a big effort in English last year.
2 Money doesn't _____ you happy, in my opinion.
3 I have _____ well at school this year.
4 My brother is very kind and always _____ things for other people.
5 I'd like to _____ more exercise but I haven't got time.
6 I always _____ lists of things to _____ every week.

64 **not enough/too Complete the sentences with the same meaning as the one above. Use not enough and too.**

1 I'm too young to drive a car.
   I'm not _old enough to drive a car_ .
2 We're not rich enough to stay in that hotel.
   We're too _____ .
3 It's not warm enough to go swimming.
   It's too_____ .
4 I'm too shy to meet people at parties.
   I'm not _____ .
5 He's not tall enough to be in the basketball team.
   He's too _____ .

65 **Reporting advice, orders and requests Complete the sentences to report advice about the first date.**

1 'Put on nice smart clothes.'
   A friend told _me to put on nice smart clothes_ .
2 'Choose a quiet casual place for the date.'
   My brother advised _____ .
3 'Don't be late.'
   My mother told _____ .
4 'Plan some interesting topics to talk about with your date.'
   My father advised _____ .
5 'Don't talk all the time.'
   My sister told _____ .
6 'Be a good listener.'
   A friend advised _____ .